A Guide to the Insurance of Professional Negligence Risks

Digby Charles Jess B Sc
of Gray's Inn and the Northern Circuit, Barrister

London
Butterworths
1982

England	Butterworth & Co (Publishers) Ltd 88 Kingsway, London WC2B 6AB
Australia	Butterworths Pty Ltd 271–273 Lane Cove Road, North Ryde, NSW 2113 Also at Melbourne, Brisbane, Adelaide and Perth
Canada	Butterworth & Co (Canada) Ltd 2265 Midland Avenue, Scarborough, Ont M1P 451
	Butterworth & Co (Western Canada) Ltd 409 Granville Street, Ste 856, Vancouver, BC V6V 1T2
New Zealand	Butterworths of New Zealand Ltd 33–35 Cumberland Place, Wellington
South Africa	Butterworth & Co (South Africa) (Pty) Ltd 152–154 Gale Street, Durban 4001
United States of America	Mason Publishing Company Finch Bldg, 366 Wacouta Street, St Paul, Minn 55101
	Butterworth (Legal Publishers) Inc 160 Roy Street, Ste 300, Seattle, Wash 98109
	Butterworth (Legal Publishers) Inc 381 Elliot Street, Newton, Upper Falls, Mass 02164

© Digby Charles Jess 1982

ISBN 0 406 25710 8 ✓

Typeset by Colset Pte Ltd, Singapore
Printed and bound in Great Britain by
Biddles Ltd; Guildford & Kings Lynn

A Guide to the Insurance of
Professional Negligence Risks

Preface

The two areas of law that are embraced in the ambit of this book, namely, professional negligence and insurance, are generally approached with much trepidation by professional people of all descriptions. Such a cautious awareness of the difficulties encountered in both these legal topics is a credit to one's learning, and there is a paucity of published material on each. Increasingly important to every practising professional person, however, is the adequate insurance of the apparently ever-growing exposure to claims for breach of professional duty, or professional negligence.

The aim of this book is to provide a work that serves the needs of professional people of all descriptions, and some ten professions are specifically considered in detail throughout the book, who wish to have a guide through the expanding field of professional negligence law, and the maze of the law of insurance relevant to professional indemnity insurance. This is the first work written for the very people who, each year, pay considerable sums for professional indemnity insurance to protect their practices and professional activities, and yet may be able to find little authority concerning such policies. It is hoped that their many questions will be answered within the following pages.

In addition to the law of professional negligence and of insurance, the 'basic' policy of professional negligence insurance and common extensions of cover are considered in chapters 3 and 4. Thereafter, relevant underwriting principles of the professions are explained in chapter 5, and chapter 6 deals with forms of professional indemnity policies popularly provided for the professions in 'special schemes'. The practice and procedure of claims is an area of concern, and the many features are considered in chapter 7. The final chapter, chapter 8, provides an outline of the duties owed by an insurance broker to his client, and the regulation of insurance brokers, being pertinent aspects of any discussion on the insurance of a specialised risk in the insurance market.

I am indebted to the facilities provided by the Manchester Incorporated Law Library, and the John Rylands University Library of Manchester, without which my task would have appeared insurmountable within any sensible period of time. My deepest thanks, however, are reserved for my wife, Bridie, whose understanding and encouragement were a continual source of rejuvenation during the long months of research devoted to this work, and it is to her that this book is dedicated.

Finally, but far from least, I acknowledge the assistance of the publishers in the preparation of the tables and the index, and the publication of this book.

D C J
December 1981
Manchester

Contents

Table of statutes

References in this Table to *Statutes* are to Halsbury's Statutes of England (Third Edition) showing the volume and page at which the annotated text of the Act will be found.

List of cases

Chapter 1

Professional negligence

Introduction

As a term, 'professional negligence' can be defined as such a neglect of professional duty of care as to render the professional person committing the act, error or omission of neglect liable in law to a client or some other third party who occasions loss by reason of that neglect. This is the sense in which the term is used in this book, and therefore embraces not only tortious negligence committed in the course of a professional practice or business, but also breach of the contractual duty of care that arises between a professional person and his client.

In this chapter, the liability of the members of the various professions that seek insurance of their professional negligence risks in the commercial market, will be considered in some detail, so that the nature and extent of respective liabilities may be appreciated. Prior to such discussion, there are various matters that need to be mentioned, being pertinent to an appraisal of professional negligence liability and its insurance. The relationship between partners in a professional practice is relevant, both as regards their relationship 'inter se', and also in their joint and several liability to others for partnership liabilities. Also of concern is the liability of an employer for the negligent acts, errors or omissions of his employees, and of the principal for the negligence of his agents.

What is the general nature of the professional's duty of care? Is it owed in both contract and tort? To what extent does the Limitation Act 1980 provide a time bar to actions? And what is the general standard of care that the law expects from those professing skills? Is a higher standard of care to be expected from those who hold out to be 'experts'? These are all questions that need to be answered before the professional negligence liabilities of the various professions can be dealt with, for the answers provide the legal backcloth to their respective responsibilities.

1

Partnership liabilities

The root of modern partnership law is the Partnership Act 1890, and this Act defines a partnership as the relation which subsists between persons carrying on a business in common with a view to profit.[1] The term 'business' needs clarification, and the Act defines it as including every trade, occupation or profession,[2] and so embraces most commercial activities except that of the barrister, who is forbidden by his professional rules from carrying on his profession in partnership with anyone. The Act refers to 'persons', and it is clearly a requirement that two or more 'persons',[3] not one, must be carrying on the business with a view to the sharing of the profits, i.e. the net gain resulting after payment of the outgoings.[4] The division of those profits need not be equal as between the partners, and it is possible to have partners who shall receive a fixed salary rather than a proportionate share of any profits, if all partners will contribute to any losses.[5] Overall, although not expressly stated in the Act, it may be inferred from the Act's provisions, and from the state of the law prior to 1890, that the partnership relationship arises by contractual agreement, be it express or implied, between the participating partners.[6]

Once there is a legally recognisable partnership in existence, it will fall to be considered to what extent partners, acting in the course of the partnership business, may bind that partnership by their actions. Section 5 of the Partnership Act 1890 states:

> Every partner is an agent of the firm and his other partners for the purpose of the business of the partnership; and the acts of every partner who does any act for carrying on in the usual way business of the kind carried on by the firm of which he is a member bind the firm and his partners, unless the partner so acting has in fact no authority to act for the firm in the particular matter, and the person with whom he is dealing either knows that he has no authority, or does not know or believe him to be a partner.

The general law of agency is therefore applicable to dealings of the partners within the scope of their partnership and in the ordinary business of the firm ('firm' being the collective term for the partnership).[7] It is to be noted that the section is in two parts, the first stating the general law of agency, the second appears to cater for any

---

1 Partnership Act 1890 s. 1(1).
2 Ibid, s. 45.
3 This term includes a registered company, Interpretation Act 1978.
4 *Re Spanish Prospecting Co Ltd* [1911] 1 Ch 92.
5 *Watson v Haggitt* [1928] AC 127; *Stekel v Ellice* [1973] 1 All ER 465, [1973] 1 WLR 191.
6 *Davis v Davis* [1894] 1 Ch 393.
7 Partnership Act 1890, s. 4(1).

variation of each partner's powers to act on behalf of the firm[8] agreed by the partners, thus binding the firm unless any of the circumstances last mentioned is applicable. It also follows that the firm is not liable for acts of a partner that, although performed on behalf of the partnership, were not done in the course of the firm's activities in the usual way, unless authorised by the firm, or ratified by the other partners.[9] No general propositions may be stated for the determination of the issue of whether a particular partner's act is within the usual course of the firm's business, for this will depend upon the nature of the business, and the normal practices of those who carry it on – all will turn on the particular facts and circumstances.[10]

Several other statutory provisions affect the binding of the firm by acts of partners, the first being under section 6 of the 1890 Act, which provides that:

> An act or instrument relating to the business of the firm and done or executed in the firm-name, or in any other manner showing an intention to bind the firm, by any person thereto authorised, whether a partner or not, is binding on the firm and all the partners.

Thus, any authorised person, be he a partner or not, may enter into a written or oral contract with a third party that is within the normal scope of partnership business (e.g. to perform certain professional services), and this contract will bind the partnership, whether or not the fact that he was contracting on behalf of the firm was disclosed to the third party.[11] Such is not the case, however, when a contract is made under seal (i.e. a deed). Only the party executing the deed will be liable upon it, even if it is declared that he is acting as agent for the firm,[12] therefore, deeds should be signed by all the partners if the firm is to be bound. Nor will the firm be liable upon contracts entered into by a partner for his own benefit and on the basis that he acted in his own right, and not as agent of the firm.[13]

Other acts of partners which affect the firm are admissions or representations made concerning partnership affairs, in the ordinary course of business of the firm,[14] but they do not bind the firm conclusively, but may be used as evidence against the firm. Further, any notice of a matter that is given to a partner who habitually acts in the partnership business, relating to partnership affairs, operates as

---

8 Under ss. 19 and 46, Partnership Act 1890.
9 *Dickinson v Valpy* (1829) 10 B & C 128; *Crellin v Brook* (1845) 14 M & W 11.
10 See *Hogarth v Latham & Co* (1878) 3 QBD 643; *Taunton v Royal Insurance Co* (1864) 33 LJ Ch 406.
11 *Beckham v Drake* (1841) 9 M & W 79, affd (1843) 11 M & W 315; *City of London Gas Light and Coke Co v Nicholls* (1862) 2 C & P 365.
12 *Appleton v Binks* (1804) 5 East 148.
13 *Barton v Hanson* (1809) 2 Taunt 49.
14 Partnership Act 1890, s. 15.

effective notice to the firm of that matter, except in the case of a fraud committed by or with the consent of that partner.[15]

Further, in relation to the contractual liability of partners upon contracts made on behalf of the firm, the 1890 Act declares that the contracting partner shall not alone be liable for defaults upon such contracts, but that all partners shall be liable jointly.[16] Thus, all partners will be jointly liable to a third party who suffers damage by reason of a breach of a contractual duty of care on the part of the firm. The effect of joint liability, rather than joint and several liability, until recently had ramifications regarding legal proceedings, in that recovery of a judgment against some partners for a contractual partnership liability, prevented the plaintiff pursuing the remaining partners if a full recovery of loss was not made.[17] Statute has now intervened and removed this procedural bar[18] against other living partners, which, in any event, did not operate in favour of a deceased partner's estate.[19]

And what of the liability of the partners for the negligent act, error or omission, or other tortious wrong, committed by one or more of the partners in the firm? Section 10 of the 1890 Act provides the answer:

> Where, by any wrongful act or omission of any partner acting in the ordinary course of the business of the firm, or with the authority of his co-partners, loss or injury is caused to any person not being a partner in the firm, or any penalty is incurred, the firm is liable therefor to the same extent as the partner so acting or omitting to act.

Accordingly, where one partner of a professional firm gives negligent advice to a client of the firm in the ordinary course of business, all the members are liable, jointly and severally,[20] to that client for the damage he suffers by reason of that negligent advice.[1] The liability being joint and several, the plaintiff may sue one partner for the whole sum, or sue several partners in succession until a full recovery for the legal damage is made from them. The firm is not generally liable for the *wilful* tort (e.g. intentional omission to carry out a professional duty) of one partner, unless all members knew that the act or omission would be committed,[2] or that wilful tort was committed by a partner in the course of, and for the benefit of, the

---

15 Partnership Act 1890, s. 16.
16 Ibid, s. 9.
17 *Kendall v Hamilton* (1879) 4 App Cas 504, HL.
18 Civil Liability (Contribution) Act 1978, s. 3.
19 Partnership Act 1890, s. 9.
20 Ibid, s. 12.
 1 *Midland Bank Trust Co Ltd v Hett, Stubbs and Kemp* [1979] Ch 384, [1978] 3 All ER 571; *Blyth v Fladgate* [1891] 1 Ch 337.
 2 *Arbuckle v Taylor* (1815) 3 Dow 160.

business of the firm.[3] Likewise, with regard to frauds committed by a partner,[4] or false misrepresentations.[5]

As all professional men know, the common law of England renders every member of an ordinary firm liable to the last vestige of his property upon the debts and other liabilities of the partnership, for no seperate legal 'person' is created by a partnership – all debts and liabilities are those of its constituent members. Under the Limited Partnerships Act 1907, it is possible to limit the liability of some of the partners in the limited partnership, to the extent of their contributions to the partnership, but there must always, even here, be at least one partner who is liable for all the liabilities of the firm.

It has been explained that the liability of the firm for acts committed in the ordinary course of partnership business, arises naturally from the law of agency, each partner being agent of his fellow partners. It is a corollary of this reasoning, that the firm is not liable for acts or omissions committed by a person prior to his becoming a partner (apart from normal agency or employment relationships).[6] Equally, a person who is admitted as a partner into an existing firm does not thereby become liable to the creditors of the firm for anything done before he became a partner,[7] unless he agrees to be so liable. If the agreement is only between the partners, the new partner would still not be liable to be sued by a third party on such past liabilities, but would be liable to make contribution to his fellow partners in respect of any judgment.[8] On the other hand, an agreement to be liable for past debts, made by the new partner with those creditors, will bind him in this respect[9] (sometimes called a 'novation' agreement).

It will depend upon the facts in each case, but a new partner does not always become liable for new obligations of the firm after he has become a partner. For instance, even though notified of the new partnership, an existing client may continue to deal with only one partner, and always address the firm in its old style. A court may construe these facts as amounting to a non-acceptance of the new firm by the client, and, therefore, the client would be dealing with the partner concerned rather than the new firm, and so no liability would fall upon the new partner in this regard.[10] Although not

3 *Hamlyn v John Houston & Co* [1903] 1 KB 81; *Janvier v Sweeney* [1919] 2 KB 316, CA.
4 *Ludgater v Love* (1881) 44 LT 694; *Lovell v Hicks* (1837) 2 Y & C Ex 472.
5 *Arkwright v Newbold* (1880) 17 Ch D 301; *Redgrave v Hurd* (1881) 20 Ch D 1; and the Misrepresentation Act 1967, s. 2(1).
6 *Heap v Dobson* (1863) 15 CBNS 460.
7 Partnership Act 1890, s. 17(1).
8 *Ex p Peele* (1802) 6 Ves 602; *Ex p Williams* (1817) Buck 13.
9 *Ex p Whitmore* (1838) 3 Deac 365; *Rolfe and Bailey and Bank of Australasia v Flower, Solting & Co* (1865) LR 11 PC 27.
10 *British Home Assurance Corpn Ltd v Paterson* [1902] 2 Ch 404.

normally liable for past debts, a new partner may, in fact, find himself liable for them where the firm maintains a running account with a creditor, even though payments have been made since he became a partner which more than cover his share of the account.[11]

Next, the position of old partners of the firm must be considered. With regard to future liabilities of the firm, incurred after the old partner has left the partnership, the general rule is that the old partner will be liable upon all matters up to the date of receipt of notice by clients and creditors of his leaving the firm.[12] The agency authority can only be revoked by notice to those who deal with the firm, except in the case of a partner who dies, or becomes bankrupt, or retires when he was not known to be a partner,[13] but on dissolution of the partnership, or upon retirement, any partner may take it upon himself to notify the fact, and is entitled to insist on the other partners concurring in all necessary and proper acts.[14] Until due notice is given to creditors or clients of the firm, therefore, the old partner will continue to be liable for future liabilities, incurred subsequent to his departure, in both contract[15] and tort,[16] unless he falls into one of the three exceptional categories mentioned.

As regards existing or past liabilities incurred whilst a person was a partner, the 1890 Act provides that the mere retirement from that firm, does not discharge the retiring partner from those liabilities,[17] for which he will remain liable until the action is time-barred (see below), or the creditor agrees by novation to only treat the firm, as newly constituted, as liable.[18] This liability will follow a retiring partner into his grave, in that a claim may be enforced against the deceased partner's estate to the full extent of his partnership liability for that act or omission, be it based in contract,[19] or tort (e.g. negligence).[20] A claimant may sue both the surviving partners and the executors of the deceased partner, and obtain judgment against them all; but any judgment against the executors will be limited to administration of the estate in due course, unless sufficient assets are admitted.[1]

The above outlines the nature and extent of the partner's liability in respect of business conducted by himself or his fellow partners in

11 *Beale v Caddick and Hartland* (1857) 2 H & N 326; *Scott v Beale and Bishop* (1859) 6 Jur NS 559.
12 Partnership Act 1890, s. 36(1) and (2).
13 Ibid, s. 36(3).
14 Ibid, s. 37.
15 *Parkin v Carruthers* (1800) 3 Esp 248.
16 *Stables v Eley* (1825) 1 C & P 614.
17 Partnership Act 1890, s. 17(2).
18 Ibid, s. 17(3).
19 E.g. *Beresford v Browning* (1875) 1 Ch D 30.
20 *Smith v Blyth* [1891] 1 Ch 337.
1 *Hill v MacRae* (1851) 20 LJ Ch 533; Judicature Act 1873.

the ordinary course of the firm's trade or profession. A partner may also find himself responsible, together with his partners, for the acts, errors, omissions, or negligence of employees and agents of the firm. These are considered, in turn, below.

Employers' liability

The Partnership Act 1890 provides that the partnership will be bound by contracts entered into by employees in their ordinary, authorised course of the business or profession, and, in this way, it is clear that the firm will be responsible for breaches of such contracts entered into by employees.[2] Such liability can also be considered as arising from the agency relationship, when the employee is carrying out his duly authorised functions on behalf of his employer (the firm).

A firm, or individual, may also be vicariously liable to compensate third parties who suffer loss or damage by reason of a wrongful (tortious) act or omission committed by an employee. The type of tort committed is irrelevant – it may be negligence, libel, slander, conversion, or any other recognised tort – but it must be either, an expressly authorised[3] or ratified[4] act or omission, or, arise from the wrongful mode of discharging duties that are within the scope of the employee's employment.[5] It has been said that the relation of employer and employee amounts to a representation by the employer that the employee has authority (implied if not express) to perform the duties which he is employed to perform, and to do such acts as are incidental to their performance.[6] Whether or not the employer accepts the benefit of any wrongful act is irrelevant, provided the employee is acting within the scope of his employment.

An example of an employer being found liable for the wrongful act of his employee relevant to a discussion of professional persons, is *Lloyd v Grace, Smith & Co*.[7] In this case, a client of the defendant firm of solicitors had gone to the firm's office to seek advice about selling two cottages she owned, and the realisation of a mortgage bequeathed to her by her late husband. The solicitors' managing clerk interviewed Mrs Lloyd concerning these matters, for he was employed to carry out (inter alia) conveyancing transactions. On this occasion, however, the clerk fraudulently induced Mrs Lloyd to transfer the mortgage and the two properties to him, by dishonestly

2 Partnership Act 1890, s. 6.
3 *Gregory v Piper* (1829) 9 B & C 591.
4 *Wilson v Tumman* (1843) 6 Man & G 236; *Carter v Vestry of St Mary Abbotts Kensington* (1900) 64 JP 548, CA.
5 *Dyer v Munday* [1895] 1 QB 742, CA.
6 *Smith v General Motor Cab Co Ltd* [1911] AC 188, HL.
7 [1912] AC 716, HL.

misrepresenting the nature of the deeds of assignment. The case went all the way to the House of Lords, and it was there held that the firm was liable to their client, Mrs Lloyd, even though the fraud was committed solely for the benefit of the dishonest clerk. The managing clerk was performing the duties that he was employed to carry out, and therefore the employing firm were liable for any wrongful performance of the duties within the scope of employment of their employee. The fact that the clerk was acting for his own benefit was irrelevant so long as he acted within that scope of employment. These principles will apply in all similar cases, to place a vicarious liability on the shoulders of the employer — be he an individual, a firm, or a corporation.

The above case was concerned with a wrongful act perpetrated upon a client of the employer, do the same principles apply when the tort causes loss or damage to a third party unknown to the employing firm? This fell to be decided in *Uxbridge Permanent Benefit Building Society v Pickard*,[8] where, again, a solicitor's managing clerk had full authority to conduct the business of a solicitor's office on behalf of and in the name of his employing solicitor. The clerk had written to the plaintiffs enclosing an application for an advance of £500 on the security of freehold property. This application purported to be signed by a Mr Cox of Dover Street, London, and represented that he was proposing to purchase a particular property in Slough, and that it was on the security of this property that the loan was sought. The plaintiffs assented to the application, subject to the execution of a mortgage, and passed the matter to their own solicitors. In the course of the ordinary investigations of title, the defendant solicitor's clerk represented to the plaintiffs' solicitors that Mr Cox was a civil servant and was a contemplated purchaser of the house in Slough from one Mr Littlestone, who had acquired it from a retired naval officer of Feckenham, Worcestershire, some thirty years earlier. He also produced to the plaintiffs' solicitors title deeds purporting to show this devolution of title together with a conveyance from Littlestone to Cox. The mortgage was accordingly prepared and executed by 'Mr Cox', and the sum of £500 was advanced by the plaintiffs.

In fact, Mr Cox was not a civil servant, he was unknown at any address in Dover Street, London, and Littlestone and the retired naval officer were fictitious persons. The deeds that had been produced were forgeries. The Court of Appeal held that the defendant solicitor was liable to the plaintiffs for their loss arising from the fraudulent acts of his managing clerk, who, as far as the plaintiffs were concerned, was engaged in a transaction which was within his actual and ostensible authority by virtue of his position. In

8 [1939] 2 KB 248, CA.

considering a defence argument that the plaintiffs were not clients of the defendant solicitor, and therefore could not seek a remedy from him, Sir Wilfrid Greene MR had this to say:[9]

> I am unable to understand on what principle that can be so. The managing clerk put in charge of that office, as he was, was unquestionably given in fact full authority to conduct the business of a solicitor's office on behalf of and in the name of his principal. That authority would cover not merely acting for clients, but the carrying through of all transactions which would normally be carried through by a solicitor — namely, completion of conveyancing business with third parties having dealings with clients and the obtaining from such third parties upon completion of the transaction sums of money and giving receipts therefor. With regard to that part of the office activities, there is no question of the relationship of solicitor and client between the solicitor and the third party. Nevertheless the authority of a clerk occupying the position of the principal to deal with third parties in circumstances where the third parties are going to change their position as the result of the transaction in progress, or which appears to be in progress, cannot be denied. Accordingly I cannot see how the principle of *Lloyd v Grace, Smith & Co* can be confined to the narrow case where the authority which the clerk is purporting to exercise is an authority to treat with a client. It seems to me it must extend to cases where the authority which the clerk purports to exercise, and which upon the face of it he has got, is one which involves leading third parties to change their position on the faith that the business which brings them into contact with the firm is genuine business.

The intertwining of the principles of the vicarious liability of employers and those of the law of principal and agent can be seen to be present in cases that concern the actions of employees. The essential requirement is that the wrongful act must have been committed within the scope of the employee's employment, which can also be expressed as within the authority to act on his employer's (i.e. his principal's) behalf. Not every act by an employee will be within the scope of his employment so as to render his employer vicariously liable for its consequences, which can be illustrated by the case of *Kooragang Investments Pty Ltd v Richardson and Wrench Ltd*[10] which recently came before the Judicial Committee of the Privy Council on appeal from Australia.

The facts of this case were that the defendants were a company of estate agents which employed a Mr Rathborne as a valuer. During 1972, Mr Rathborne on their behalf had carried out a number of valuations for a particular group of companies, but in November of that year the defendants instructed their valuers that no further work was to be done for that group, due to the non-payment of fees for completed valuations. That same month, Mr Rathborne became a

---

9 Ibid at 253.
10 (1981) Times 28 July, PC.

director of one of the group's companies, and, fully knowing the prohibition of his employers, carried out thirty more valuations for the group. He wrote these valuations on the defendants' writing paper, signing them with the defendants' corporate name, but this was unknown to the defendants and no fees were charged. Two of the valuations had been used by the group to obtain advances of money from the plaintiff money-lenders, made against the valuations as security. Subsequently it was found that the valuations had been negligently made by Mr Rathborne, the properties were less valuable and the plaintiffs had lost money.

The question before the court was whether the defendants were vicariously liable for Mr Rathborne's negligent valuations by virtue of their being his employers. Valuations were acts of a class which Mr Rathborne could perform on the defendants' behalf, and the mere fact the defendants would not benefit from the valuations was not sufficient to avoid vicarious liability (*Lloyd v Grace, Smith & Co*).[11] The Privy Council was of the opinion that this was not a case concerning an employee's authority of a type which in the ordinary course of an everyday transaction would lead third parties to change their position on the faith of it, as in *Uxbridge Permanent Benefit Building Society v Pickard*,[12] but one where the issue was one of actual authority or total absence of authority. It did not follow from the fact that valuations were acts of a class performed by Mr Rathborne for his employers, that any valuation undertaken by Mr Rathborne without his employers' authority, and without any connexion with their business, was a valuation for which his employers were vicariously responsible. The Privy Council held that, on the facts, the defendants had had no part in the negligent valuations, for the group were no longer clients and Mr Rathborne had had no authority to make the valuations due to the prohibition. This was a clear case of departure from the course or scope of an employee's employment, and the defendants were not liable.

Professional negligence policies are obviously designed to include the employing professional's vicarious liabilities for the negligent acts, errors, or omissions of his employees engaged in the provision of professional services on behalf of the professional. As will be seen later, many professional indemnity policies will provide an indemnity to employees when sued for matters concerning professional duties to clients or third parties, if the action could have been brought against the insured professional (their employer). This is inserted because it is the employee in such cases who is the prime tortfeasor liable to the plaintiff who suffers loss or damage, it being no defence available to the employee that he committed the act or

11 [1912] AC 716, HL, and above.
12 [1939] 2 KB 248, CA, and above.

omission solely in his capacity as employee of another, and that, were it not for the contract of employment, he would not have done what he did.[13] Often, the plaintiff will sue the employer, relying on vicarious liability, rather than the negligent employee, who will, in the great majority of cases, be quite unable to meet any substantial judgment unless covered by insurance.[14]

But can an employer who has been held to be responsible vicariously for his employee's tortious act or omission seek an indemnity from the employee? The employee is under a common law duty to his employer not to carry out his duties in a negligent fashion,[15] and may therefore be liable to indemnify his employer against the damages which his employer must pay because of his vicarious liability for the employee's act or omission. The House of Lords has twice held this to be the law,[16] but, more recently, the Court of Appeal made certain pronouncements regarding liabilities covered by the employer's insurances. In *Morris v Ford Motor Co Ltd*,[17] Lord Denning MR expressed the view (obiter) that where the risk of an employee's negligence is covered by insurance, his employer should not seek to make that employee liable for it. If the matter did not extend that far, then at any rate, the courts should not compel the employer to allow his name to be used in subrogation proceedings to make the employee liable, the right being founded in equity. The position of insurance was not directly before the court in this case, however, and for this reason Stamp LJ expressly refused to express any opinion upon that issue without having further argument presented to the court. The remaining member of that Court of Appeal, James LJ, looked at the problem of subrogation by an indemnifier against employees, as one which must be considered by seeing if the contract either expressly or impliedly excluded subrogation by the indemnifier (often an insurer). There were circumstances that gave rise to an implied exclusion of subrogation by virtue of remedies against employees being unacceptable and unrealistic.

It therefore seems that a court would, as a matter of public policy, not permit an insurer to seek a remedy from the negligent employee of his insured, nor permit the employer to pursue an indemnification from his employee where the risk was covered by an insurance policy. This being said, many insurers will give an express waiver of

13 *Mill v Hawker* (1874) LR 9 Exch 309; affd (1875) LR 10 Exch 92.
14 *Cullen v Thomson's Trustees and Kerr* (1862) 6 LT 870, HL.
15 *Century Insurance Co Ltd v Northern Ireland Road Transport Board* [1942] AC 509, [1942] 1 All ER 491, HL.
16 *Digby v General Accident, Fire and Life Insurance Corpn Ltd* [1943] AC 121, [1942] 2 All ER 319, HL; *Lister v Romford Ice and Cold Storage Co Ltd* [1957] AC 555, [1957] 1 All ER 125, HL.
17 [1973] 1 QB 792, CA.

subrogation against employees in professional indemnity policies, either automatically, or upon request by the insured professional.[18]

The nature of professional responsibility in law

The normal relationship of professional person and client will arise in contract, i.e. that which has been agreed between the parties shall be done, and a method of determining the fee to be charged for these services. The agreement may be made in writing, orally, or by a combination of the two, and such contracts will be valid if the normal legal rules governing certainty, consideration, and the like are satisfied. The advantage of written contracts is that they provide evidence of the terms of the contract rather more readily than one made by word of mouth – disputes as to what was actually said tend to be very common. Many cases have upheld the liability of a professional person to his client for failure to render the agreed services, or, in other words, for breach of a contractual duty to perform the services in a satisfactory manner. Such claims arise out of the general law of contract, that where one party to a contract is in breach of the contract, and this breach causes the other party loss or damage, the party shall be liable to the injured party for such loss or damage to the extent that it either flowed naturally from the breach, or, due to special reasons known to the parties, could be expected to follow upon a breach. This has long been the law, and it was said in one case over one hundred and fifty years ago, that:

> Where two parties have made a contract which one of them has broken, the damages which the other party ought to receive in respect of such breach of contract should be such as fairly and reasonably be considered either arising naturally, i.e. according to the usual course of things, from such breach of contract itself, or such as may reasonably be supposed to have been in the contemplation of both parties, at the time they made the contract, as the probable result of the breach of it.[19]

Many of the cases referred to in the sections that follow in this chapter, dealing with the separate professions, will have been founded in contract. It may be stressed that exactly what is agreed between the parties is very important, and in this respect it is relevant to mention that the professional person will, impliedly, even if not expressly, agree as a term of the contract to provide his services that he will perform those services to the normal standard to be expected from a member of his profession. More will be said about the standard of care to be exercised, in the section following this. A professional person will not go so far as to guarantee that the services

18 See ch 4, below.
19 *Hadley v Baxendale* (1854) 9 Exch 341 at 354, per Alderson B.

will be one hundred per cent satisfactory, nor warrant their fitness for their intended purpose, in the general course of everyday business. It can be said to be in the nature of the contract that competent skill and care is to be expected from the professional, and that few seeking professional assistance of any description, be it financial advice, legal advice, architectural advice, or whatever, will expect such advice to be 'guaranteed' absolutely correct – but that is not to say that those seeking the advice will not expect the advice to be given carefully, and in accordance with the particular skill or knowledge that the professional holds himself out as possessing.

Sometimes, though, professionals do agree to terms of the contract whereby they accept a higher degree of contractual responsibility, and in these instances, the liability of the professional will rest upon a breach of the actual terms of the contract, and not some lesser responsibility that is 'the normal' standard of care to be expected. The House of Lords have recently shown the full extent of liability that can rest on a professional who, by a term of the contract to provide services, warrants the perfection of the services provided under the contract. This decision was the outcome of *Independent Broadcasting Authority v EMI Electronics and BICC Construction Ltd*,[20] where EMI had agreed in their contract with the IBA to accept responsibility for the design of a television mast that they were to provide and erect, even though EMI were to take no part in the design of the mast. The design of the mast was sub-contracted to BICC, but when the mast failed, EMI were held liable under the contract, for they had become contractually responsible to the IBA for their sub-contractor's negligent design. It is interesting to note that in his speech, Lord Scarman said that he felt there was a valid distinction to be made between cases of someone going to a professional and requesting an object to be made for a particular purpose, and the case where some professional service is to be performed which does not have as its purpose the provision of some thing or object to be used by the client (e.g. financial advice). In the former case, his Lordship believed that it would be an implied term of the contract that the design professional would design the article so that it was fit for the purpose made known to him.[1]

A professional person may thus be sued in contract by a client who suffers loss or damage from the failure of the professional to provide the agreed degree of skill and care to the services performed. It may also be that there will be an implied term of fitness for purpose when the professional is to provide an article or physical object. Moreover, the professional's liability to a client may be heightened by stringent terms imposed by the client, or voluntarily made by the

20 (1980) 14 BLR 1, HL.
 1 See also *Samuels v Davis* [1943] KB 526, [1943] 2 All ER 3, CA.

professional, or, which has not yet been mentioned, by contractually
agreeing to provide an extraordinary degree of skill and care, e.g. by
holding himself out to be an 'expert' or the 'leading specialist'. But
more may be said about this in the next section.

The doctrine of privity of contract, that runs throughout English
contract law, forbids any party not in a contractual relationship with
the professional, from suing him even if that party has suffered loss
or damage by reason of professional advice or services performed to
a contractual client. Until quite recently, it was considered that the
duty between a professional and his client was of purely a contractual nature, and this stultified the development of tortious liability of professionals to those not in a contractual relationship with
them. Inroads were made to situations where the professional owed
a particular position of trust, i.e. a fiduciary relationship as it is
called, to another person where responsibility for advice was
imposed on the professional, even in the absence of a contractual
relationship. If such advice were given without an appropriate
degree of care, the professional giving the advice would be liable.[2]
The decision of the House of Lords in *Hedley Byrne & Co Ltd v
Heller & Partners Ltd*[3] dramatically changed the legal position
existing at that time. Liability of professionals for negligent acts or
omissions was already recognised by the law, as a natural result of
the concept of the common duty of care that rests on everyone not to
cause injury or damage to those likely to be affected by an act or
omission,[4] but liability for negligent misstatements was not accepted
in the absence of a fiduciary position between the professional and
the injured party. In *Hedley Byrne*, the House of Lords accepted
that in some circumstances an action would lie in tort for negligent
misstatements made by a professional to persons who need not be his
clients, or, indeed, with whom he need necessarily be in direct
contact. Most professionals deal in words rather than deeds or
actions, and the implications of this decision were enormous. Their
Lordships did not, however, state with any precision the circumstances when liability would arise. They did state that there had to be
a 'special relationship' betwen the parties, and Lord Morris of
Borth-y-Guest explained the principle as follows:

> . . . I consider . . . that it should now be regarded as settled that if some-
> one possessed of a special skill undertakes, quite irrespective of contract,
> to apply that skill for the assistance of another person who relies upon
> such skill, a duty of care will arise. The fact that the service is to be given
> by means of or by the instrumentality of words can make no difference.

Furthermore, if in the sphere in which a person is so placed that others could reasonably rely upon his judgment or his skill or upon his ability to make careful inquiry, a person takes it upon himself to give information or advice to, or allows his information or advice to be passed on to, another person who, as he knows or should know, will place reliance upon it, then a duty of care will arise.[5]

The two essential ingredients to be gathered from his Lordship's speech are that the professional man must know that the other is relying on his skill, and the other must in fact rely upon it.[6] Moreover, since the decision of the House of Lords in *Hedley Byrne*, it is clear that, quite apart from any contractual obligation, a professional person owes a duty of care in tort to those who rely upon his skill or judgment, and it is immaterial that no fee was charged for the advice.[7] Gratuitous advice thus renders the professional person liable if the ingredients of reliance are present, to the same extent as advice for which a fee is charged. And, the duty being irrespective of contract, the class of party that may recover damages is not limited to clients of the professional, but includes any party who relies on the advice or judgment, and may reasonably be expected so to do by the professional.[8] To his clients, the professional now owes duties of care both in contract, as an implied term, and in tort, as a duty imposed by law.[9] This fact will thus have a bearing on the period of limitation applicable to the breach of duty, which will be considered later in this chapter, and may have an impact on the measure of damages that a claimant may recover, depending on whether the professional is sued in contract or in tort.

The standard of care required

The fact that a professional person owes both a contractual duty of care to his clients, and a tortious duty of care to clients and others that may be expected to rely, and do rely, on the skill and judgment he possesses, has been discussed above. Now what falls to be considered is the standard of care that the law requires to be exercised by the professional when giving advice, exercising his judgment, or making careful inquiries.

5 [1964] AC 465 at 502–503.
6 *Dutton v Bognor Regis UDC* [1972] 1 QB 373 at 395, per Lord Denning MR.
7 *Arenson v Casson, Beckman, Rutley & Co* [1977] AC 405 at 434, HL, per Lord Salmon.
8 *Ross v Caunters* [1980] Ch 297, [1979] 3 All ER 580.
9 *Esso Petroleum Co Ltd v Mardon* [1976] QB 801, [1976] 2 All ER 5, CA; *Midland Bank Trust Co Ltd v Hett, Stubbs and Kemp* [1979] Ch 384, [1978] 3 All ER 571; *Batty v Metropolitan Property Realisations Ltd* [1978] QB 554, [1978] 2 All ER 445; CA.

The starting points for such discussion are the judgments of Tindall CJ in two cases in 1833 and 1838. In *Lanphier v Phipos*[10] he said:

> Every person who enters into a learned profession undertakes to bring to the exercise of it a reasonable degree of care and skill. He does not undertake, if he is an attorney, that at all events you shall gain your case, nor does a surgeon undertake that he will perform a cure; nor does he undertake to use the highest possible degree of skill. There may be persons who have higher education and greater advantages than he has, but he undertakes to bring a fair, reasonable and competent degree of skill.

And in *Chapman v Walton*[11] he explained how the requisite standard of care may be evidenced to the court:

> The point, therefore, to be determined is, not whether the defendant arrived at a correct conclusion . . . but whether, upon the occasion in question, he did or did not exercise a reasonable and proper care, skill and judgment. This is a question of fact, the decision of which appears to us to rest upon this further inquiry, viz., whether other persons exercising the same profession or calling, and being men of experience and skill therein, would or would not have come to the same conclusion as the defendant. For the defendant did not contract that he would bring to the performance of his duty, on this occasion, an extraordinary degree of skill, but only a reasonable and ordinary proportion of it; and it appears to us, that it is not only an unobjectionable mode, but the most satisfactory mode of determining this question, to show by evidence whether a majority of skilful and experienced [persons in the same profession as the defendant] would have come to the same conclusion as the defendant. If nine [professionals] of experience out of ten would have done the same as the defendant under the same circumstances, or even if as many out of a given number would have been of his opinion as against it, he who only stipulates to bring a reasonable degree of skill to the performance of his duty would be entitled to a verdict in his favour.

Professional persons do not, therefore, have a special immunity from suit for errors of professional judgment. As Lord Fraser recently held in a medical negligence case:

> Merely to describe something as an error of judgment tells us nothing about whether it is negligent or not. The true position is that an error of judgment may, or may not, be negligent; it depends on the nature of the error. If it is one that would not have been made by a reasonably competent professional man professing to have the standard and type of skill that the defendant held himself out as having, and acting with ordinary care, then it is negligent. If, on the other hand, it is an error that such a man, acting with ordinary care, might have made, then it is not negligent.[12]

10 (1838) 8 C & P 475.
11 (1833) 10 Bing 57.
12 *Whitehouse v Jordan* [1981] 1 WLR 246 at 263, HL.

The duties are owed to clients in contract and in tort at the same time,[13] but in either case the professional is under one and the same duty to use reasonable care. For breach of that duty he is liable in damages; and those should be, and are, the same, whether he is sued in contract or in tort.[14]

The quoted passages emphasise, however, that an essential question for the court when considering allegations of breach of the professional's duty of care, is what degree of skill the professional held himself out as possessing. He is to be judged by the standards of those who possess the level and type of skill he professes he has, and, therefore, if a person leads those who rely on his advice to believe that he has a higher than normal degree of professional competence, then he is to adjudged by the standards of his fellow 'experts' or 'specialists'. Although this point was not decided in *Duchess of Argyll v Beuselinck*,[15] for the facts of the case turned on seeking advice from a solicitor in an area in which he did not hold himself out as being an expert, Megarry J (as he then was) had this to say:[16]

> No doubt the inexperienced solicitor is liable if he fails to attain the standard of a reasonably competent solicitor. But if the client employs a solicitor of high standing and great experience, will an action of negligence fail if it appears that the solicitor did not exercise the care and skill to be expected of him, though he did not fall below the standard of a reasonably competent solicitor? If the client engages an expert, and doubtless expects to pay commensurate fees, is he not entitled to expect something more than the standard of the reasonably competent? I am speaking not merely of those expert in a particular branch of the law, as contrasted with the general practitioner, but also of those of long experience and great skill as contrasted with those practising in the same field of the law but being of a more ordinary calibre and having less experience.

Limitation of actions

There have long been statutory provisions limiting the time during which a plaintiff must bring his action against the defendant, and the present periods are laid down in the Limitation Act 1980. In both contract and tort, the time bar operates six years from the date on

13 *Batty v Metropolitan Property Realisations Ltd* [1978] QB 554, [1978] 2 All ER 445, CA; *Midland Bank Trust Co Ltd v Hett, Stubbs and Kemp* [1979] Ch 384, [1978] 3 All ER 571.
14 *Esso Petroleum Co Ltd v Mardon* [1976] QB 801 at 820, CA, per Lord Denning MR.
15 [1972] 2 Lloyd's Rep 172.
16 Ibid at 183, per Megarry J; this case was not cited in *Greaves & Co (Contractors) Ltd v Baynham, Meikle & Partners* [1975] 3 All ER 99, [1975] 1 WLR 1095, when the Court of Appeal declined to decide this issue regarding an 'expert' standard of care, preferring, on the facts, to rely on an implied warranty of fitness for purpose.

which the cause of action accrued.[17] The date on which the cause of
action accrued will, however, be determined by different rules,
depending on whether the plaintiff is suing in contract or in tort (e.g.
negligence). In the discussion above it can be seen that a plaintiff will
generally now be able to choose whether to pursue his claim against
the defendant professional in contract or in tort, or, indeed, in
both,[18] and this has repercussions for professionals in that the period
in tort is likely to be longer than in contract.

In contract, the cause of action accrues on the date of the breach
of the contract,[19] and this is the base date from which the six years
will run. The date of breach, though, may be at a later date than one
assumes. In *Midland Bank Trust Co Ltd v Hett, Stubbs and Kemp*,[20]
W agreed to grant his son G an option to purchase from him his 300
acre farm, which at that time he was letting to G. In March 1961,
they went to the defendant firm of solicitors, and S, the senior
partner, drew up an option document which W signed. Unfortunately, S omitted to register the option as an estate contract under
the Land Charges Act 1925, which prevented the option being binding against G. In 1967, W discovered the option had not been
registered, and chose to sell the farm to his wife on 17 August. In
July 1972, G commenced proceedings against the defendant firm of
solicitors for breach of contract, to which the defendants pleaded
statutory limitation. Oliver J held that essentially the plaintiff's
claim sounded in nonfeasance, i.e. inaction, of the defendants,
rather than the giving of wrong and negligent advice which would be
referable to a fixed point in time, the action was not time-barred.
The duty of the defendant firm of solicitors to register the option
continued to bind them until it ceased to be effectively capable of
performance on 17 August 1967.

In actions based in tort, on the other hand, the cause of action
accrues, not on the date of the commission or omission complained
of, but at the time that damage occurs arising from the tort.[1] This is
not to say that this will be the same date as the plaintiff discovers his
right of action against the defendant. The vital factor, then, is the
date of the occurrence of damage to the plaintiff, and this may be at
some time distant from the date the negligence was committed (e.g.

---

17 Limitation Act 1980, ss. 2 and 5.
18 *Batty v Metropolitan Property Realisation Ltd* [1978] QB 554 at 566–568, CA;
    Midland Bank Trust Co Ltd v Hett, Stubbs and Kemp [1979] Ch 384, [1978] 3 All
    ER 571.
19 *Gould v Johnson* (1702) 2 Salk 422.
20 [1979] Ch 384, [1978] 3 All ER 571.
 1 *Catledge v E Jopling & Sons Ltd* [1963] AC 758, [1963] 1 All ER 341, HL;
    Sparham-Souter v Town and Country Developments (Essex) Ltd [1976] 1 QB 858,
    [1976] 2 All ER 65, CA; *Anns v Merton London Borough Council* [1978] AC 728,
    [1977] 2 All ER 492, HL.

the negligent approval of inadequate building foundations that only results in structural damage to the building many years later), or at some time simultaneous to the tortious act or omission. Such was held to be the case in *Forster v Outred & Co*,[2] the facts of which were that in February 1973, the plaintiff had signed a mortgage deed in the defendant solicitors' office, the effect of which was to encumber her estate with a legal charge and subject her to liabilities completely outside her control, because the money raised was to be passed to her son for a hotel project. The scheme failed, and the mortgage was foreclosed, causing the plaintiff to pay nearly £70,000 to discharge the mortgage. The plaintiff issued a writ in March 1980 against the defendant firm of solicitors, who, in reply, pleaded the action to be statute barred. The court held that the plaintiff suffered actual damage through the defendants' negligence on signing the mortgage deed in February 1973, and therefore her writ of March 1980 must fail, being more than six years from the date the cause of action accrued. It has similarly been held that where solicitors negligently insert rights under a lease they are drawing up, contrary to their instructions, the cause of action accrues at that time, and not at some subsequent date when those rights are exercised against the solicitors' client.[3]

The above are the normal time limits for the bringing of an action, but where the right of action has been concealed by the 'fraud' of the defendant or his agent, the period of limitation does not begin to run until the plaintiff has discovered the fraud, or could, with reasonable diligence have discovered it.[4] 'Fraud' in this sense is not used in its normal legal meaning as Lord Denning MR has explained:[5]

> It has long been held that 'fraud' in this context does not necessarily involve any moral turpitude: see *Beaman v ARTS Ltd* [1949] 1 KB 550. It is sufficient if what was done was unconscionable: see *Kitchen v Royal Air Force Association* [1958] 1 WLR 563: a test which was applied in the case of a building contract in *Clark v Woor* [1965] 1 WLR 650. Those cases show that 'fraud' is not used in the common law sense. It is used in the equitable sense to denote conduct by the defendant or his agent such that it would be 'against conscience' for him to avail himself of the lapse of time. The section applies whenever the conduct of the defendant or his agent has been such as to hide from the plaintiff the existence of his right of action, in such circumstances that it would be inequitable to allow the defendant to rely on the lapse of time as a bar to the claim.

2 (1981) Times 18 March, see also *Howell v Young* (1826) 5 B & C 259; *Nocton v Lord Ashburton* [1914] AC 932, HL.
3 *Simple Simon Catering Ltd v J E Binstock, Miller & Co* (1973) 117 Sol Jo 529, CA; see also *Melton v Walker and Stanger* (1981) 131 NLJ 1238.
4 Limitation Act 1980, s. 32(1)(b).
5 *Applegate v Moss* [1971] 1 QB 406 at 413, CA.

Special time limits apply to the bringing of an action in any case where negligence, or breach of duty (contractual or otherwise) occasions damage to a plaintiff which includes personal injury or death.[6] The period is limited to three years from whichever is the later of the following:

(a) the date on which the cause of action accrued;
(b) the date of knowledge of the person injured;
(c) the date of death; or
(d) the date of the knowledge of the person for whose benefit the action is brought (which includes personal representatives).

Various criteria are specified to assist the court in determining the relevant date of knowledge in the above.[7]

Apart from those special rules, the court also has an unfettered discretion to exclude the time limit, if it is deemed equitable so to do, in actions involving personal injury or death.[8] The court will have regard to certain matters to determine the equity of the situation, which will include the prejudice that the plaintiff will suffer if the time limit is not excluded. The court will also consider the prejudice that will be suffered by the defendant if he is denied the time bar, and this prejudice may not be found solely in the death or disappearance of witnesses, or their fading memories, or in the destruction of records, but in the difficulty experienced in conducting his affairs with the prospect of an action hanging indefinitely over his head. Thus, where a defendant was fully aware of claims, he may not take advantage of minor slips of a plaintiff's solicitor which technically render the action time-barred.[9] The court's discretion, being unfettered, permits the court to look at all the circumstances of the case.[10]

These special rules and powers of the court in relation to claims for personal injury or death are relevant to the area of professional negligence, for it must not be forgotten that professional persons are often put in the position of directing other persons in the execution of their professional duties. A wrongful direction may lead to the personal injury or death of the person they are directing.[11] Personal injury or death may also result directly out of a professional's advice, e.g. an architect's advice that a wall is safe, but it soon collapses and injures someone.[12]

6 Limitation Act 1980, ss. 11, 12, and 13.
7 Ibid, s. 14.
8 Ibid, s. 33.
9 *Firman v Ellis* [1978] QB 886, [1978] 2 All ER 851, CA.
10 *McCafferty v Metropolitan Police District Receiver* [1977] 2 All ER 756, [1977] 1 WLR 1073, CA; *Simpson v Norwest Holst Southern Ltd* [1980] 2 All ER 471, [1980] 1 WLR 968, CA.
11 See *Clayton v Woodman & Son (Builders) Ltd* [1962] 2 QB 533, [1962] 2 All ER 33, CA.
12 *Clay v A J Crump & Sons Ltd* [1964] 1 QB 533, [1963] 3 All ER 687, CA.

Exclusion or limitation of liability

Pondering on his potential liabilities to clients and others relying upon his advice and skill, the professional person is bound to ask himself whether the law will permit him to exclude or limit his professional liabilities by notice to those likely to be affected. A reading of *Hedley Byrne & Co Ltd v Heller & Partners Ltd*[13] might lead one to believe that this can be done by an express exclusion of responsibility, as protected the defendant bankers in that case. Since that decision, however, statute has intervened in the shape of the Unfair Contract Terms Act 1977.

The 1977 Act applies to all contractual terms or notices that purport to exclude or restrict the liability of persons for 'negligence' arising from things done or to be done in the course of a business[14] (which term includes a profession).[15] 'Negligence' is defined in a very broad way under the Act, and means the breach of any obligation, arising from the express or implied terms of a contract, to take reasonable care or exercise reasonable skill in the performance of the contract, and the breach of any common law duty to take reasonable care or exercise reasonable skill.[16] Thus, breach of both contractual and tortious professional duty is embraced.

Any contractual term or any notice or communication, which purports to exclude or limit a professional's liability in respect of personal injury or death arising from a breach of professional duty will be of no effect at all.[17] In the case of other loss or damage, the defendant professional will only be able to rely on such term or notice to the extent that he[18] shows the court that it is 'reasonable'.[19] The test to be applied to a contractual term is that the term shall have been a fair and reasonable one to be included having regard to the circumstances which were, or ought reasonably to have been, known to or in the contemplation of the parties when the contract was made.[20] For non-contractual notices or communications, the test is that it should be fair and reasonable to allow reliance on it, having regard to all the circumstances obtaining when the liability arose or, but for the notice, would have arisen.[1]

When applying the reasonableness test to any contractual term, or a notice or communication, which seeks to restrict the professional's liability to a specified sum of money, particular regard will be had to

13 [1964] AC 465, [1963] 2 All ER 575, HL.
14 Unfair Contract Terms Act 1977, s. 1(3)(a).
15 Ibid, s. 14.
16 Ibid, s. 1(1).
17 Ibid, s. 2(1).
18 Ibid, s. 11(5).
19 Ibid, s. 2(2).
20 Ibid, s. 11(1).
 1 Ibid, s. 11(3).

the resources which the defendant professional could expect to be available to him for the purpose of meeting the liability should it arise, and how far it was open to him to cover himself by insurance.[2]

In conclusion in this regard, it is submitted that a professional person will be unlikely to be able to satisfy the requirements of the Unfair Contract Terms Act 1977, and thus rely on contractual terms or other notices which exclude or restrict his liability for professional negligence, in the current climate of judicial opinion, as evidenced by the much widened scope of professional liabilities developed by the courts during the past two decades.

Accountants

The liability of an accountant in the provision of normal accounting services will be determined from the scope of the terms of his engagement. In *Mead v Ball, Baker & Co*[3] the defendant accountants were engaged by a solicitor to investigate the accounts of a business so that the solicitor could decide whether or not to advance a sum of money to that business and convert it into a limited company. The defendants duly reported, and on the basis of their report, the solicitor advanced the money and became a director of the new limited company. Several years later it was discovered that the stock had been overvalued by 3 per cent in the stock sheets. The defendants had examined the stock sheets for the purposes of their report, but had not discovered the overvaluation. The solicitor sued the defendants for failing to report to him on this overvaluation of stock. It was held that the solicitor's claim failed. The defendants had not been engaged to take stock, but to make a reasonable and proper investigation of the accounts and stock sheets. This they had done and it had not revealed the overvaluation or that anything was wrong. Accordingly, the defendant accountants had not been negligent in the performance of the contracted services.

A more stringent standard of investigation is required, on the other hand, where an accountant is engaged to check the books of account, even though not instructed to make a full audit. Thus, in *Fox & Son v Morrish Grant & Co*,[4] where an accountant was so engaged, and had drawn up a balance sheet by taking the figures of cash at bank and cash in hand from the cash book, he was held liable for not spotting discrepancies in the figures which had been entered by a dishonest employee of their client. The court held that where an accountant is retained to check books of account, unless there is an arrangement to the contrary or he informs his client accordingly, the

2 Unfair Contract Terms Act 1977, s. 11(4).
3 (1911) 27 TLR 269, affd on other grounds (1911) 28 TLR 81, CA.
4 (1918) 35 TLR 126.

accountant commits a breach of duty if he checks the books without verifying the cash figures by looking at the bank statements or seeking confirmation from the bank.

Many cases against chartered and certified accountants arise out of their appointments as company auditors under the Companies Acts 1948–80. The law is clear that auditors have an obligation to be fully aware of their auditing duties under the companies legislation,[5] and the law considers that the duty of the auditor is:

> not to confine himself merely to the task of verifying the arithmetical accuracy of the balance sheet, but to inquire into its substantial accuracy, and to ascertain that it contained the particulars specified in the articles of association (and consequently a proper income and expenditure account), and was properly drawn up, so as to contain a true and accurate representation of the company's affairs.[6]

A further exposition of the auditor's duties has been given in the Court of Appeal in *Re London and General Bank* by Lindley LJ:[7]

> It is no part of an auditor's duty to give advice, either to directors or shareholders, as to what they ought to do . . . His business is to ascertain and state the true financial position of the company at the time of the audit, and his duty is confined to that. But then comes the question how is he to ascertain that position? The answer is by examining the books of the company . . . But he does not discharge his duty by doing this without inquiry and taking any trouble to see that the books themselves shew the company's true position . . . He must take reasonable care to ascertain that they do so. An auditor, however, is not bound to do more than exercise reasonable care and skill in making inquiries and investigations. He is not an insurer; he does not guarantee that the books do correctly show the true position of the company's affairs; he does not even guarantee that his balance sheet is accurate according to the books of the company. His obligation is not so onerous as this. Such I take to be the duty of the auditor: he must be honest – i.e. he must not certify what he does not believe to be true, and he must take reasonable care and skill before he believes that what he certifies is true.

One year after saying this, Lindley LJ reiterated the relevant legal duty of the auditor during another case, holding that an auditor is not 'bound to be suspicious as distinguished from reasonably careful'.[8] The facts of this case were that for some years before a company was wound up, balance sheets were published by the directors to the shareholders in which the value of the company's stock-in-trade at the end of each year was grossly overstated. The defendant accountants, as the company's auditors, had signed the company

5 *Thomas v Devonport Corpn* [1900] 1 QB 16, CA.
6 *Leeds Estate Building and Investment Co v Shepherd* (1887) 36 Ch D 787 at 802, per Stirling J.
7 [1895] 2 Ch 673 at 682–683, CA.
8 *Re Kingston Cotton Mill Co (No 2)* [1896] 2 Ch 279 at 284, CA.

balance sheets each year as presenting a true and accurate record of the company's affairs. They had relied on certificates of value of stock-in-trade given to them by X, the managing director of the company. On the footing of these balance sheets, dividends had been paid for some years, whereas, in truth, the company had no profits from which dividends could have been declared. If the auditors had compared the different books and added to the stock-in-trade at the beginning of the year, the amounts purchased during the year, and deducted the amounts sold, they would have seen that the statement of the stock-in-trade at the end of the year was so large as to call for explanation; but they did not do so. The Court of Appeal held that, it being no part of the duty of auditors to take stock, they were justified in relying on the certificates of the manager. He was a person of acknowledged competence and high reputation, and the auditors were not bound to check his certificates in the absence of anything to raise suspicion. Accordingly the auditors were not liable for the dividends wrongly paid; 'what in any particular case is a reasonable amount of care and skill depends on the circumstances of the case; that if there is nothing which ought to excite suspicion, less care may properly be considered reasonable than can be so considered if suspicion was or ought to have been aroused'.[9]

Two leading cases reflect judicial opinion on the extent of the auditor's duty to be reasonably careful. In *Re City Equitable Fire Insurance Co Ltd*[10] it was held that auditors were not liable for failing to discover that the company's managing director had misappropriated a large part of the company's funds. In three successive years, the managing director had bought a large amount of Treasury Bills just before the audit, so as to reduce the company's indebtedness, then sold the Bills immediately thereafter, restoring the true indebtedness. The court held that, although these transactions in isolation should have made the auditors suspicious, they formed only one item in a large annual audit, and the auditors did not fail in their duty of making a reasonable and proper investigation of the company's accounts.

The court came to a different conclusion upon *Re Thomas Gerrard & Son Ltd*.[11] In this case the managing director of a company falsified the company's books by three methods. He caused the half-yearly stock valuation to be inflated by the inclusion of non-existent stock; he caused the price payable on the purchase of stock made at the end of each half-yearly period to be included in the outgoings of the succeeding period by altering invoices in a manner immediately apparent to anyone looking at the invoices; and he

9   Ibid at 284.
10   [1925] Ch 407.
11   [1968] 1 Ch 455.

caused the price payable for sales made after the end of the relevant period to be included in the preceding period. In discharging the auditing functions under the Companies Act 1948, the auditors obtained most of their information from the managing director, whom they believed to be of the highest integrity. They did ask him about the altered invoices, and readily accepted his explanation.

Relying on these certified accounts, over a period of five years, tax was paid on inflated profits and enlarged dividends were distributed. The frauds were then discovered and the company went into liquidation, and the auditors were pursued for breach of their duty. Pennycuick J held that the auditors were liable for the amount of the dividends overpaid, the costs of recovering the excessive tax paid, and any tax not recovered.

> I find the conclusion inescapable alike on the expert evidence and as a matter of business common sense that (upon discovering the altered invoices) . . . he should have examined the suppliers' statements and where necessary have communicated with the suppliers. Having ascertained the precise facts so far as it was possible for him to do so, he should then have informed the board. It may be that the board would then have taken some action. But whatever the board did he should in each subsequent audit have made such checks and inquiries as would have ensured that any misattribution in the cut-off procedure was detected..He did not take any of these steps. I am bound to conclude that he failed in his duty. It is important in this connection to remember that this is not a case of some isolated failure in detection. The fraud was repeated half-yearly on a large scale for many years . . . Here suspicion ought emphatically to have been aroused and the auditors ought to have taken the steps which I have indicated.[12]

If acting in arbitration of a dispute, accountants will not be liable for a negligent valuation of shares, but it must clearly be shown that the accountants were acting in a judicial capacity. In *Arenson v Casson, Beckman, Rutley & Co*,[13] the plaintiff owned a number of shares in A Ltd. In 1970, he agreed to sell these shares to the first defendant, who was the chairman of the company, at 'the value as determined by the auditors for the time being of the company whose valuation acting as experts and not as arbitrators shall be final and binding on all parties'. In May 1970, the second defendants, who were the auditors of A Ltd, valued the shares at some £5,000, and in June the shares were sold to the first defendant at that valuation. In September, a holding company was formed to acquire the share capital of A Ltd, and in the prospectus a joint report by the second defendants and another firm of accountants valued the plaintiff's shares (pro rata to the whole) at £29,000. The plaintiff, inter alia,

12 Ibid at 476.
13 [1977] AC 405, [1975] 3 All ER 901, HL.

sued the auditors for his loss due to their negligent valuation. They applied to have the action struck out, pleading that there was no cause of action for they were acting as arbitrator.

The House of Lords held that the essential prerequisite for a valuer to claim immunity as an arbitrator was that at the time the matter was submitted to him for decision there should be a formulated dispute between at least two persons, which his decision was required to resolve. The auditors in this case could only show that parties who might be affected by the decision had opposing interests, and this was insufficient to obtain the immunity of suit of an arbitrator.[14]

Architects

There is a restriction on the use of the designation 'architect', in that only persons registered in the Register of Architects may practise or carry on any business under any name, style or title containing the word 'architect'. The designation 'naval architect' and 'landscape architect' may, however, be freely used.[15]

An architect may not delegate tasks entrusted to him by his client. Thus, in *Moresk Cleaners Ltd v Hicks*,[16] the plaintiffs had employed the defendant architect to draw up plans, specifications and contracts for the building of an extension to their laundry. Two years after the extension was built, defects became apparent, and the plaintiffs sued the defendant, claiming that he had negligently designed the extension, causing it to be defective. He denied liability on the ground that it was an implied term of his employment that he could delegate specialist design tasks to qualified sub-contractors, which he had done. Alternatively, he said that he had implied authority to act as the plaintiffs' agent and so employed the sub-contracts to design the extension. The Senior Official Referee held that the design of the building was defective and the defendant was negligent in approving the drawings, and, furthermore, the defendant had no implied authority to employ the sub-contractors to design the extension. Accordingly, the defendant architect was liable to the plaintiffs: '. . . if a building owner entrusts the task of designing a building to an architect he is entitled to look to that architect to see that the building is properly designed.'[17]

In common with other professionals, the architect is expected to be familiar with the law so far as it is relevant to the practise of his profession, but he is not expected to be a legal expert. Thus, where an

---

14 See further, *Leigh v English Property Corpn Ltd* [1976] 2 Lloyd's Rep 298.
15 Architects Registration Act 1938, ss. 1(1) and 4(1).
16 [1966] 2 Lloyd's Rep 338.
17 Ibid at 342, per Sir Walker Carter QC.

experienced architect, equipped with a practical working knowledge of planning law, notices that a local planning officer appears to be taking an unlawful attitude in granting planning permission to his client, but does not warn his client of his belief that the planning permission may be void, the architect is entitled to assume the local authority know their job as regards planning and the interpretation of planning circulars.[18]

Often, an architect will be asked by his client to undertake responsibility for supervision of the construction of a building. In such circumstances, an architect owes the building contractor a duty of care in his supervisory duties, but this does not extend to a duty to instruct the contractor as to the manner in which the work should be carried out. The architect is entitled to assume that the contractor is competent,[19] but such is not the case where an architect is instructing a worker whom he knows to be unfamiliar with the task to be supervised. In *Clayton v Woodman & Son (Builders) Ltd*[20] an architect was engaged to supervise the construction of a lift shaft in an existing wall. The building owner believed the gable wall to be unsafe, but, notwithstanding the owner's express wish to have the gable shored or supported by struts, the architect instructed a workman of the contractors, who was only a bricklayer by trade, to cut a chase in the gable wall. He gave no instruction as to shoring or strutting the wall. Whilst cutting the chase, the wall suddenly collapsed on top of the bricklayer. The architect was held liable to the injured bricklayer, for he owed him a duty of care to give him proper instructions so that the work might be carried out in safety, but the Court of Appeal reversed this decision on the ground that, in this case, the architect had not taken upon himself the responsibility of ordering the bricklayer to do dangerous work, or to do it in an unsafe manner.

An architect may be jointly liable with others for giving negligent advice upon which another party relies and consequently suffers loss or damage. Accordingly, where both an architect and a local authority building inspector are aware that a particular site is prone to dehydration, yet permit inadequate foundations for a block of flats to be laid, they are both liable to the building owner. The apportionment between them will determined by the court upon the particular facts.[1] Another illustration of the liability of the architect, with others, for negligent advice which results in loss or damage, is *Clay v A J Crump & Sons Ltd*.[2] The owner of a site on which there were some old buildings, appointed an architect to plan and supervise its

18 *B L Holdings v Robert J Wood & Partners* (1979) 12 BLR 3, CA.
19 *Oldschool v Gleeson (Construction) Ltd* (1976) 4 BLR 1053.
20 [1962] 2 QB 533, [1962] 2 All ER 33, CA.
 1 *Acrecrest v W S Hattrell & Partners* (1979) 252 Estates Gazette 1107.
 2 [1964] 1 QB 533, [1963] 3 All ER 687, CA.

redevelopment, and demolition contractors to clear the site according to the architect's plan. A particular wall was specified by the architect for demolition, but during a telephone conversation with the owner, the architect said the wall could remain if the demolition contractor's managing director thought it was 'safe to do so'. The architect, despite visiting the site on several occasions, did not inspect the wall and issued his certificate to the demolition contractors.

Several weeks later the building contractors moved onto the site, and erected a workmen's hut adjacent to the wall. Their managing director had only made a cursory inspection of the wall in question. Without warning, the wall subsequently collapsed, injuring a worker who was in the hut at the time.

The Court of Appeal found as a fact that the wall would have been discovered to be in a dangerous condition by anyone making a proper inspection. It was held that since both the architect and the demolition contractors knew that the building contractors would be working on the site after they had left, they should reasonably have foreseen that if they left a dangerous wall standing, it might fall and injure the building contractors' employees. Accordingly, both were under a duty to make a careful inspection of the wall, and this duty was not absolved by the fact that, subsequently, the building contractors had a reasonable opportunity for, and actually made, an examination of the wall, which was careless. Therefore, the architect was apportioned 42 per cent of the responsibility for the accident, the demolition contractors 38 per cent, and the building contractors 20 per cent.

Where an architect is engaged and instructed to adapt into his plans a new material or method of construction, failure of the experiment will not, per se, be evidence of negligence. This was the finding in *Turner v Garland and Christopher*,[3] where an architect was employed to design and supervise the erection of model lodging-houses, with the clear instruction to utilise a new patent concrete roofing costing only a fraction of traditional roofing methods. In the event, the patent concrete roofing proved to be a failure and let in water. The matter was tried before a jury, and the following direction was given by Erle J to the jury to assist them in their determination of whether the architect was negligent:

> You should bear in mind that if the building is of an ordinary description in which (the defendant architect) had had abundance of experience, and it proved a failure, this is evidence of want of skill or attention. But if out of ordinary course you employ him about a novel thing, about which he has had little experience, if it has not had the test of experience, failure may be consistent with skill. The history of all great improvements shows

3 (1853) 2 Hudson's BC (4th edn) 1.

failure of those who embark in them, this may account for the defect of the roof.

The jury returned a verdict that the defendant architect had not been negligent in his use of the new patent roof.

When an architect issues interim certificates, he does not, apart from specific agreement, act as an arbitrator between the building owner and the building contractor. Accordingly, the architect is under a duty to act fairly in making his valuation, and will be liable to either party who suffers by reason of their negligent under- or over-valuation. This was the conclusion of the House of Lords when the RIBA standard form contract was considered in *Sutcliffe v Thackrah*.[4] The facts were that the plaintiff had employed a building contractor to build him a house, and he engaged the defendant architects' firm as architect and quantity surveyor. The firm signed interim certificates regarding work done by the contractors, and upon which they received payment from the plaintiff. Before the work was completed, the plaintiff justifiably turned the contractors off the site and engaged others to complete the work, who discovered certain work had either not been done or improperly done by the first firm of building contractors. The plaintiff, as building owner, then sued the defendant architects' firm, alleging negligence and breach of duty as architects in supervising the building process and in certifying for work not done or improperly done by the contractor. In defence, the architects pleaded that they were acting in an arbitral capacity, and were thus accordingly absolved from liability for negligence. The House of Lords rejected this defence, and held the architects to have failed in their duty to act fairly in making their valuation for the interim certificates, and were liable in negligence to the plaintiff building owner.

Finally, an architect may be liable for breach of statutory duty in respect of a new dwelling which is not covered by a National House Builders' Council certificate. Under the Defective Premises Act 1972:[5]

A person taking on work for or in connection with the provision of a dwelling (whether the dwelling is provided by the erection or by the conversion or enlargement of a building) owes a duty –
(a) if the dwelling is provided to the order of any person, to that person; and
(b) without prejudice to paragraph (a) above, to every person who acquires an interest (whether legal or equitable) in the dwelling;
to see that the work he takes on is done in a workmanlike or, as the case may be, professional manner, with proper materials and so that as regards that work the dwelling will be fit for habitation when completed.

4 [1974] AC 727, [1974] 1 All ER 859, HL.
5 S. 1(1).

The Court of Appeal has held that the Act imposes a duty which normally arises when a person agrees to carry out work, and cannot arise later than the start of the work.[6] It was also considered that the Act imposes this duty upon all persons who took on such work, and it would not matter that the work was done voluntarily and in the absence of contract.[7]

As regards buildings that become defective due to negligence, the time period under the Limitation Act 1980 for common law negligence will begin to run only when the defective building becomes a danger to the health and safety of the occupiers.[8] The time period for limitation purposes in respect of a breach of the statutory duty under the Defective Premises Act 1972, however, begins to run at 'the time when the dwelling was completed, but if after that time a person who has done work for or in connection with the provision of the dwelling does further work to rectify the work he has already done, any such cause of action in respect of that further work shall be deemed for those purposes to have accrued at the time when the further work was finished'.[9]

Auctioneers

An auctioneer must exercise reasonable care and skill in carrying out his functions on behalf of his clients, and a number of cases illustrate the law relating to the negligence of auctioneers.

If an auctioneer improperly describes the property he has been entrusted to auction, whereby the vendor is obliged to make compensation for the misdescription to the purchaser, the auctioneer is liable to the vendor in that amount, if it represents the difference in likely purchasing price of the property accurately described. This was the finding in *Parker v Farebrother*,[10] where the plaintiff had engaged the defendant auctioneer to conduct the sale by auction of three houses, to prepare particulars of the said sale, and a description of the property to be sold. This was in the ordinary course of business of the defendant auctioneer. The houses were sold at auction, but upon negligently prepared and incorrect particulars and description. On discovery of the misdescription, the purchaser refused to complete the sale until he had received compensation from the vendor for the incorrect and improper description of the three houses. The vendor then sought to recover this sum of

6 *Alexander v Mercouris* [1979] 1 WLR 1270.
7 Ibid at 1273, per Buckley LJ.
8 *Anns v Merton London Borough Council* [1978] AC 728, [1977] 2 All ER 492, HL.
9 Defective Premises Act 1972, s. 1(5).
10 (1853) 21 LTOS 128.

compensation from the auctioneer, and it was held that the auctioneer was liable to the plaintiff vendor in that amount. The negligent
misdescription had caused loss to the client vendor, and the auctioneer was responsible.

Many cases which have come before the courts concern the duties
of the auctioneer once a bidder's offer has been accepted by the
auctioneer on behalf of the vendor. In *Hardial Singh v Hillyer and
Hillyer*,[11] the defendants, a well-known firm of auctioneers, offered
the plaintiff's house for sale at their auction. The house was knocked
down to a bidder for £9,800, and the auctioneers attempted to obtain
his name and address, but he would not give them and vanished. The
house therefore had to be resold, but this time only achieved a price
of £9,000, from a different purchaser. The plaintiff sued the defendants for the difference in sale price, i.e. £800, claiming it was a consequential loss of the defendants' negligence in failing to secure the
name and address of the first purchaser. Forbes J held that the claim
failed. The evidence was that a purchaser had never before vanished
in any of the defendants' auctions, thus proof of negligence was
absent. Moreover, in law, an auctioneer had no power to coerce a
purchaser into giving his name and address.

On the other hand, it may well be negligent for an auctioneer to
permit a purchaser to take away auctioned goods without paying. In
Brown v Staton[12] the defendant auctioneer had sold the plaintiff's
goods to a purchaser at his auction. The purchaser had told the
defendant that the plaintiff vendor owed him money, and that the
sale price of the goods should be set off against that debt. The auctioneer, without confirming this with the plaintiff, then permitted
the purchaser to take the goods away without payment. The plaintiff
sued the auctioneer for failing to account to him for the full value of
the goods sold, which was his duty as agent of the plaintiff. Upon
evidence that it was the custom of the trade of the auctioneer that
goods were not surrendered to a purchaser until paid for, the court
held the defendant to be liable to the plaintiff for the value of the
goods. Per Lord Ellenborough CJ:[13]

> The auctioneer was employed to sell the goods, and not to pay the debts;
> and it was meant that he should pay over the price of the goods to the
> plaintiff.

An auctioneer is under no general duty to a client to obtain a
deposit from a purchaser, even if their conditions of sale make it
clear to purchasers that a deposit will be required. This is clear from
Cyril Andrade, Ltd v Sotheby & Co,[14] where the plaintiffs entrusted

11 (1979) 251 Estates Gazette 951.
12 (1816) 2 Chit 353.
13 Ibid at 354.
14 (1931) 47 TLR 244.

the defendant auctioneers to sell a suit of armour at their auction. One of the conditions of sale was that the purchaser should pay 10s in the £ or more if required in part payment of the purchase money. One B, who had previously bought for an American millionaire, bid at the auction and the armour was knocked down to him, but the defendants did not ask B for a deposit as they assumed that he was acting for the millionaire. In fact, the millionaire repudiated B's authority, and B, when asked to take the armour away, could not pay for it. The sale was thus not carried out, and the plaintiff sued the defendants for a sum representing half of the sale price (i.e. 10s in the £) which they argued the defendants should have secured from B. It was held by the court that the defendants were not negligent or in breach of their duty to the plaintiff – their general duty as auctioneers was to sell, and due skill and care did not call for the rigorous enforcement of conditions of sale on every occasion. In this case it was clear that if the defendants had straightway asked B for the deposit, he would have replied that he could not pay it. Under the conditions of sale, that would have cancelled the sale, and the armour would have been put up for sale again, but the evidence here was that no purchaser would have been found. The plaintiff had therefore, in any event, suffered no loss by the defendants' failure to request a deposit from B.

The auctioneer is under a duty to obtain a deposit from a purchaser, if the terms of his engagement specify that the auctioneer's conditions of sale will be enforced by the auctioneer, and such conditions of sale specify that a purchaser shall pay a deposit. Moreover, an auctioneer is further liable for failure to comply with such conditions of sale that require the purchaser to immediately sign documents to complete the sale. These points were decided in *Hibbert v Bailey*[15] which concerned the sale by auction of a ship. It was sold to the first purchaser for £2,950, but the defendant auctioneer's clerk failed to procure his signature to the completion documents upon the purchaser saying that he would return in half an hour with the deposit. The sale was not completed, and when resold, the ship achieved a lesser sum of £2,600. The plaintiff, the ship owner, sued the defendant for the difference in price, namely £350. The court, however, held that whilst there had been a neglect of duty by the defendant, the plaintiff was only entitled to nominal damages for he could not prove that he suffered any real injury by the loss of sale, for the ship may have reached a price near £2,925 upon the resale.

Just as the auctioneer is only under a general duty to sell the goods or property entrusted to him for auction, and not, in the absence of a contrary agreement with the vendor, under a general duty to obtain a

15 (1860) 2 F & F 48.

deposit from a buyer, so also is he under no general duty to get in the purchase price for the vendor, from the buyer. It is true that an auctioneer has a right to sue in his own name for the whole of the purchase price,[16] but that entitlement does not impose an obligation to get in the purchase money. This was the decision in *Fordham v Christie Manson and Woods Ltd*,[17] where the plaintiff had the defendants include her painting in a sale in March 1973. The painting was knocked down to an Italian buyer for £3,675. In April, the buyer, who had neither removed the painting from the defendants' premises nor paid for it, gave notice that it may be a forgery. In accordance with a condition of their agreement with the plaintiff, the defendants told the plaintiff, this allegation gave rise to their obligation to suspend any payment on the painting. The plaintiff took this to mean that the defendants were in receipt of the purchase money. The plaintiff later sued the defendants, claiming breach of their duty to take steps in and about getting in the purchase price.

May J considered that auctioneers were under an obligation to use reasonable care and skill in and about their work: they must, for example, obtain the best price possible and ensure that contracts made were binding. Also, they must act in accordance with the terms of their contracts with clients. But, in general, auctioneers were under no duty to get in purchase money from buyers, notwithstanding that they had authority to receive it and account for it to the vendor. There was nothing in the instant contract with the plaintiff to lead to the conclusion that the defendants had undertaken to get in the purchase money, therefore, the defendants were not liable to the plaintiff.

Barristers

Barristers are persons who have passed the Bar exams, and have been 'called' to the Bar by one of the historic Inns of Court – Gray's Inn, Lincoln's Inn, Middle Temple, or Inner Temple. Practising barristers are forbidden by their professional rules from practising otherwise than solely by themselves (partnerships are not permitted), from a professional set of chambers, either within the Inns in London, or in suitable premises in the provincial centres. Only barristers may be advocates in the higher courts, both civil and criminal, and will also appear in cases before the lower courts – magistrates' courts and county courts. Barristers also undertake a great deal of legal advisory work in all aspects of non-criminal law, but in all areas are instructed, not by the lay client, but by the solicitor to whom the lay client has initially gone for advice.

16 *Chelmsford Auctions Ltd v Poole* [1973] 1 QB 542, [1973] 1 All ER 810, CA.
17 (1977) Times 24 June, (1977) 244 Estates Gazette 213.

34   *Professional negligence*

Until the decision of the House of Lords in the *Hedley Byrne* case,[18] it had appeared to be settled law that barristers could not be sued by their lay client for breach of duty. This immunity from suit evolved from the fact that a barrister could not sue for his fees, which were only an honorarium;[19] or that there was no contractual relationship formed upon receipt of a brief in the normal way;[20] or that acting honestly granted the barrister immunity;[1] or that the mere status of the barrister rendered suits against him 'improper and impertinent'.[2] As a result of that case, however, it could be seen that the special relationship created between barrister and lay client exposed a barrister to actions for negligence and breach of duty, and the question of a barrister's total immunity from suit would have to be reconsidered.

The first opportunity for an authoritative pronouncement to be made came in *Rondel v Worsley*[3] which was eventually heard by the House of Lords. This case, though, was concerned solely with the responsibility of a barrister for his professional negligence in respect of acts or omissions during the trial of criminal proceedings against his lay client, where the outcome was unfavourable to the lay client. The facts of the case were that Rondel was employed as a rent collector by a certain London landlord. At premises where he was also caretaker, some tenants were holding a party and Rondel wanted to enter the flat. A person at the door of the flat would not let him in and a fight took place, resulting in Rondel facing a charge of grievous bodily harm by reason of his tearing the door-keeper's hand and severing part of his ear. At court he selected the defendant barrister to defend him on the old 'dock brief' system. The outcome of the trial was that Rondel was convicted. Almost six years later, Rondel brought proceedings against that barrister alleging professional negligence in his handling of the evidence in his defence.

The barrister applied to have the action struck out as disclosing no reasonable cause of action. The House of Lords held that the barrister should have the action against him struck out, for the allegations concerned the barrister's conduct and management of a case in court, and, on the grounds of public policy alone, because of the barrister's overriding duty to the court, the administration of justice required that a barrister should be able to carry out this duty fearlessly and independently. If fearful of an action by his client, the barrister might be inhibited from performing this duty to

18 [1964] AC 465, [1963] 2 All ER 575, HL.
19 *Kennedy v Broun* (1863) 13 CBNS 677.
20 *Swinfen v Lord Chelmsford* (1860) 5 H & N 890.
 1 Ibid.
 2 *Fell v Brown* (1791) Peake 131.
 3 [1969] 1 AC 191, [1967] 3 All ER 993, HL.

the court. Moreover, the public interest would not be served by the relitigation, between the client and the barrister, of what was litigated between the client and his opponent. Thus, a barrister is immune from actions for professional negligence concerning his conduct and management of a criminal case in court.

This immunity of suit extends to all those who take part in a court trial:

> It is well settled that judges, barristers, solicitors, jurors and witnesses enjoy an absolute immunity from any form of civil action being brought against them in respect of anything they say or do in court during the course of a trial. This is not because the law regards any of these with special tenderness but because the law recognises that, on balance of convenience, public policy demands that they shall all have such an immunity. It is of great public importance that they shall all perform their respective functions free from fear that disgruntled and possibly impecunious persons who have lost their cause or been convicted may subsequently harass them with litigation.[4]

During *Rondel v Worsley* it had been no part of the case for either party that any distinction was to be drawn between the liability of a barrister for professional negligence in that part of his work that is done in the court itself and work that he does out of court. Notwithstanding this, their Lordships' speeches contained considered observations regarding the extent of a barrister's immunity for matters taking place outside court and in his chambers. Strictly, such observations were 'obiter dicta', but really their Lordships had had to consider the whole matter of a barrister's immunity to arrive at their decision upon the case, and the observations are, therefore, of considerable persuasive authority.

A later case has given the House of Lords the opportunity of specifically considering those observations which stated that a barrister's immunity from suit extended to the preliminary work connected with a court case such as the drawing up of pleadings. *Saif Ali v Sydney Mitchell & Co*[5] directly concerned a consideration of the immunity and its extent in relation to a barrister's pre-trial advice upon parties to litigation and pleadings in a civil matter.

The facts were that Mr Ali was injured in a motor accident in March 1966 when he was a passenger in a van struck by a car driven by Mrs B, owned by Mr B. Mrs B subsequently pleaded guilty to driving without due care and attention. Both Mr Ali and Mr B consulted the defendant solicitors in 1967 concerning a claim in respect of the accident. In 1968 the defendants instructed a barrister to settle proceedings on behalf of Mr Ali and the driver of the van, and to

4 *Sutcliffe v Thackrah* [1974] AC 727 at 757, per Lord Salmon.
5 [1980] AC 198, [1978] 3 All ER 1033, HL.

advise upon the matter. A writ was settled with a statement of claim basing the claim for damages against Mr B as the owner of the car, Mrs B driving as his agent at the time of the accident. The writ was issued in November 1968, and before the three year time limit expired in March 1969, the defendants again consulted the barrister about the claims of Mr B's insurers that the van driver was partly to blame for the accident, and that Mrs B was not driving as her husband's agent. The barrister advised no change in the writ or the statement of claim, and the writ was served on Mr B in August 1969. The action did not proceed very far, and in April 1974 was discontinued. Any claim of Mr Ali's against both the van driver and Mrs B were now time-barred.

A few months later, Mr Ali issued a writ against the defendant solicitors claiming damages for their breach of professional duty and negligence, in that they did not advise him to take proceedings against the van driver and Mrs B. The defendant solicitors then joined the barrister to the proceedings claiming an indemnity from him. He, in turn, applied to have the matter against him struck out as disclosing no reasonable cause of action, and it was this issue of law that came before the House of Lords.

The House held, by a majority of three to two, that the claim should not be struck out for the facts alleged concerned conduct of a barrister outside the sphere of immunity granted to barristers. A barrister's immunity from suit for negligence in respect of his conduct of litigation on the ground of public policy was an exception to be applied only in the area to which it extended. This immunity was not limited to what was done in court, but included some pre-trial work, though not all, for the protection should not be given any wider application than was absolutely necessary in the interests of the administration of justice. Interlocutory and other pre-trial proceedings come within the scope of the protection, but all other pieces of pre-trial work should be tested as to whether it was so intimately connected with the conduct of the cause in court that it could fairly be said to be a preliminary decision affecting the way that cause was to be conducted when it came to a hearing. For pre-trial work that did not satisfy the test, and for advisory work and pure paper work, like other professionals, a barrister may be liable for loss or damage suffered by his lay client by reason of a proven breach of duty of care and skill or negligence.

Lords Wilberforce, Diplock, and Salmon quoted with approval a passage by McCarthy P in the New Zealand Court of Appeal:[6]

> I cannot narrow the protection to what is done in court: it must be wider than that and include some pre-trial work. Each piece of pre-trial work should, however, be tested against the one rule; that the protection exists

6 *Rees v Sinclair* [1974] 1 NZLR 180.

only where the particular work is so intimately connected with the conduct of the cause in court that it can fairly be said to be a preliminary decision affecting the way that cause is to be conducted when it comes to a hearing. The protection should not be given any wider application than is absolutely necessary in the interests of the administration of justice, and that is why I would not be prepared to include anything which does not come within the test I have stated.

Company directors

The company director is an officer of the company,[7] and, in that capacity, owes a duty of care to his company, apart from other duties and responsibilities required of him under the Companies Acts 1948–81. No contractual provision or clause in the company's articles which attempts to indemnify a director in respect of negligence or any breach of duty will be of any validity,[8] but a court may exercise a power to relieve the director of liability for negligence.[9] The court will only exercise this power if the director has acted honestly and reasonably and that, having regard to all the circumstances of the case, including those connected with his appointment, he ought fairly to be excused for the negligence or breach of duty, either in whole or in part, on such terms as the court thinks fit. Thus, a director may be relieved from liability for applying his company's money to an *ultra vires* purpose, where the director was acting on counsel's opinion that the purpose was *intra vires* the company.[10] On the other hand, the court refused to grant relief to a director who had permitted his co-director to hold a very large amount of the company's money for several months without inquiry (in the event, the co-director had misappropriated the money).[11]

The mere imprudence of a director in the exercise of powers clearly conferred upon him does not render him liable for any resulting losses, for the law requires that, as with other professionals, he must be proved to have been negligent in the exercise of his powers.[12] Thus he may exercise his powers of delegation to other responsible persons in the company, and this was illustrated in *Dovey v Cory*[13] where a director of a joint stock company engaged in banking assented to payments of dividends out of capital and to advances on improper security, was held by the House of Lords not to have been

7 Companies Act 1948, s. 455.
8 Ibid, s. 205.
9 Ibid, s. 448.
10 *Re Claridge's Patent Asphalte Co Ltd* [1921] 1 Ch 543.
11 *Re City of London Insurance Co Ltd* (1925) 41 TLR 521.
12 *Overend and Gurney Co v Gibb and Gibb* (1872) LR 5 HL 480 at 495, per Lord Hatherley LC.
13 [1901] AC 477, HL.

negligent of his duties as a director. On the facts, their Lordships were satisfied that he had honestly relied on the judgment, information, and advice of the chairman and general manager of the bank, and was misled by their statements. He had no cause to suspect that these persons were otherwise than of great integrity, skill and competence, and he was, therefore, not negligent.

The speech of Lord Halsbury LC provides an insight into judicial opinion upon charges of neglect aimed at directors of companies:[14]

> The charge of neglect appears to rest on the assertion that Mr Cory, like the other directors, did not attend to any details of business not brought before them by the general manager or the chairman, and the argument raises a serious question as to the responsibility of all persons holding positions like that of directors, how far they are called upon to distrust and be on their guard against the possibility of fraud being committed by their subordinates of every degree. It is obvious if there is such a duty it must render anything like an intelligent devolution of labour impossible. Was Mr Cory to turn himself into an auditor, a managing director, a chairman, and find out whether auditors, managing directors, and chairmen were all alike deceiving him? That the letters from the auditors were kept from him is clear. That he was assured that provision had been made for bad debts, and that he believed such assurances, is involved in the admission that he was guilty of no moral fraud; so that it comes to this, that he ought to have discovered a network of conspiracy and fraud by which he was surrounded, and found out that his own brother and the managing director (who have since been made criminally responsible for frauds connected with their respective offices) were inducing him to make representations as to the prospects of the concern and the dividends properly payable which have turned out to be improper and false. I cannot think that it can be expected of a director that he should be watching either the inferior officers of the [company] or verifying the calculations of the auditors himself. The business of life could not go on if people could not trust those who are put into a position of trust for the express purpose of attending to details of management. If Mr Cory was deceived by his own officers − and the theory of his being free from moral fraud assumes under the circumstances that he was − there appears to me to be no case against him at all.

Thus, the manner in which the work within the company is to be distributed between the board of directors and the staff is a business matter to be decided on business lines. Companies legislation has refrained from attempting to lay down a statutory code of the conduct of company management. Judges also agree that this is sensible, as Lord Macnaghten said in *Dovey v Cory*:[15]

> I do not think it desirable for any tribunal to do that which Parliament has abstained from doing − that is, to formulate precise rules for the

14 Ibid at 485–486.
15 Ibid at 488.

guidance or embarrassment of businessmen in the conduct of business affairs. There never has been, and I think there never will be, much difficulty in dealing with any particular case on its own facts and circumstances; and, speaking for myself, I rather doubt the wisdom of attempting to do more.

Although no precise code can be formulated to cater for the multifarious situations that arise within companies and the exercise of powers by directors, the courts will consider certain matters to determine the duties of the particular directors:[16]

In order . . . to ascertain the duties that a person appointed to the board of an established company undertakes to perform, it is necessary to consider not only the nature of the company's business, but also the manner in which the work of the company is in fact distributed between the directors and the other officials of the company, provided always that this distribution is a reasonable one in the circumstances, and is not inconsistent with any express provisions of the articles of association.

Where directors exercise their power to remunerate a fellow director, yet take no trouble to ascertain the factual basis of his claim for a very large sum of money as expenses, their laxity may well amount to negligence by virtue of the enormity of the claimed expenses.[17]

In discharging his duties, a director must, of course, act honestly, and must also exercise some degree of both skill and diligence. Or, put in more exact terms:[18]

If directors act within their powers, if they act with such care as is reasonably to be expected from them, having regard to their knowledge and experience, and if they act honestly for the benefit of the company they represent, they discharge both their equitable as well as their legal duty to the company.

Apart from the proposition that certain duties, having regard to the company's articles of association and to the exigencies of business, may properly be delegated to other officials of the company, provided the directors have no grounds to suspect the integrity of such officials, there are two more general propositions that may be made concerning the determination of the question of directors' negligence. These additional propositions were identified by Romer J in the case of *Re City Equitable Fire Insurance Co Ltd* and were confirmed by the Court of Appeal.[19] The first is that a director need not exhibit in the performance of his duties a greater

16 *Re City Equitable Fire Insurance Co Ltd* [1925] 1 Ch 407 at 427, per Romer J.
17 *Merchants Fire Office Ltd v Armstrong* (1901) 17 TLR 709, CA.
18 *Lagunas Nitrate Co v Lagunas Syndicate* [1899] 2 Ch 392 at 435, CA, per Lindley MR.
19 [1925] 1 Ch 407, CA.

degree of skill than may reasonably be expected from a person of *his* knowledge and experience. Romer J instanced that a director of a life assurance company does not guarantee that he has the skill of an actuary or of a physician.[20] It can be seen that the test of skill and care is rather different to that applied to other professionals, in that it is more subjective upon the actual knowledge and skill that each director has, rather than by an objective test of the standards of the ordinary practitioner as adopted to architects, for example. It will be a natural result of the test, that a director who is also a qualified accountant or lawyer will be expected to exercise a degree of skill commensurate with his specialist learning and experience, and any other specialist knowledge of a director, relevant to a questioned act or omission, will be taken into account by the court in determining the question of negligence. Thus, what may be negligent on the part of one director, is not necessarily negligent on the part of a co-director privy to the same act or omission.

The second additional proposition identified by Romer J, is that a director is not bound to give continuous attention to the affairs of his company if he is a non-executive director − 'His duties are of an intermittent nature to be performed at periodical board meetings, and at meetings of any committee of the board upon which he happens to be placed. He is not, however, bound to attend all such meetings, though he ought to attend whenever, in the circumstances, he is reasonably able to do so.'[1]

Being pertinent to the case before him, Romer J also enunciated and adopted some principles relative to the duties of directors in relation to the application of the company's funds:

(a) A director who signs a cheque that appears to be drawn for a legitimate purpose is not responsible for seeing that the money is in fact required for that purpose, or that it is subsequently applied for that purpose, assuming, of course, that the cheque comes before him for signature in the regular way, having regard to the usual practice of the company. This is because a director must, of necessity, trust the officials of the company to perform properly and honestly the duties allocated to them.

(b) Before any director signs a cheque, or parts with a cheque signed by him, he should satisfy himself that a resolution has been passed by the board, or committee of the board (as the case may be), authorising the signature of the cheque; and where a cheque has been signed between meetings, he should obtain the confirmation of the board subsequently to his signature. The authority given by the board should not be for the signing of numerous cheques to an aggregate amount, but a proper list of the

20 Ibid at 428.
 1 Ibid at 429.

individual cheques, mentioning the payee and the amount of each, should be read out at the board meeting or committee meeting, and subsequently transcribed into the minutes of the meeting.

(c) It is the duty of each director to see that the company's moneys are from time to time in a proper state of investment, except so far as the articles of association may justify him in delegating that duty to others.

(d) Before presenting their annual report and balance sheet to their share-holders, and before recommending a dividend, directors should have a complete and detailed list of the company's assets and investments prepared for their own use and information, and ought not to be satisfied as to the value of their company's assets merely by the assurance of their chairman, however apparently distinguished and honourable, nor with the expression of the belief of their auditors, however competent and trustworthy.

In conclusion, therefore, it can be said that the exercising of a power that is in fact *ultra vires*, either his own powers to act, or those of the company as specified in its memorandum and articles of association, will generally render the director who purports to exercise that power liable for its consequences, in negligence. A mere error of judgment in the valid exercise of an *intra vires* power will not, of itself, result in the personal liability of the director, for negligence will have to be proved. The proper test to be applied is that the director exercised the degree of skill and care that was to be reasonably expected from a person of his knowledge and experience. Thus, a particular skill of a director in e.g. the law or accountancy, will be taken into account when determining the issue of negligence. Lastly, it can be seen from the dicta quoted above, that the courts are very aware of the necessity to recognise that directors must be entitled to delegate matters to responsible company officials, and cannot keep an eye on everything. Indeed, the degree of skill and care to be exhibited by a non-executive director clearly recognises that the line of responsibility must be organised upon practical, but at all times reasonable, business lines.

Engineers

There is no restriction in law on the use of the description 'engineer', but the term is usually used by members of the many professional institutes which require the passing of professional exams prior to becoming a professional member of the institute. The functions of an engineer can be likened to those of an architect, in that his duties will include the designing of structures and buildings, and the supervising of construction by contractors. Unlike architects, though, engineers will often be involved in pre-construction works at the site, including such matters as the draining of the land prior to the building process. Engineers also tend to specialise, thus there are institutes for the specialisms of civil engineering, mechanical engineering, structural engineering, chemical engineering, electrical engineering, mining, and many others.

Just as architects owe a duty of care to those likely to be affected by their advice during the supervision of construction by contractors,[2] so do engineers owe a similar duty. In *Driver v William Willett (Contractors) Ltd*[3] a building worker was injured on site and sued his employers, the contractors, and a firm of consulting safety and inspecting engineers. The engineers had been engaged by the contractors to advise them as to the observance of safety requirements in relation to the relevant building and other regulations, and also to promote the safe conduct of work generally on the contractors' sites. A site hoist was used to raise scaffold boards, and this had been done for some time, without a direction from the site engineer that the system was unsafe. The plaintiff worker was injured one day when a scaffold board fell.

Rees J held that the engineers' duty was, as experts, to inspect the site of the building operations at regular intervals and to advise the contractors as to the observance of safety regulations and as to the promotion of the safe conduct of work. His lordship was satisfied from the evidence that the engineers could reasonably foresee that the contractors' workmen would be endangered if safety regulations were not observed or the work was not safely conducted. Their duty of care had been breached by their failing to advise the contractors to have the hoistway enclosed by wire mesh as soon as their inspector at the site observed that the hoist was used for carrying scaffold boards and long timbers. There seemed no doubt that the contractors would have accepted such advice and carried out the remedial measures necessary, and, accordingly, the engineers would be apportioned 60 per cent of the liability, and the contractors, being the plaintiff's employers, would be 40 per cent contributorily negligent.

Even where there are no express terms of the contract of engagement, it will be an implied term that the engineer will give instructions and information to his employer's builder within a reasonable time. This view was expressed by Diplock J (as he then was) in the following terms:[4]

> It is clear . . . that to give business efficacy to the contract, details and instructions necessary for the execution of the works must be given by the engineer from time to time in the course of the contract and must be given

2 *Clay v A J Crump & Sons Ltd* [1964] 1 QB 533, [1963] 3 All ER 687, CA.
3 [1969] 1 All ER 665.
4 *Neodon Ltd v Borough of Swinton and Pendlebury* (1958) 5 BLR 34.

in a reasonable time. In giving such instructions, the engineer is acting as agent for his principal, . . . and if he fails to give such instructions within a reasonable time, [his employer] is liable for damages in breach of contract [to the builders]. What is a reasonable time does not depend solely upon the convenience and financial interests of the [builders]. No doubt it is in their interest to have every detail cut and dried on the day the contract is signed, but the contract does not contemplate that. It contemplates further details and instructions being provided, and the engineer is to have a time to provide them which is reasonable having regard to the point of view of him and his staff and the point of view of [his employer], as well as the point of view of the [builders].

The nature and extent of a consulting engineer's duty towards his employer's contractor was considered in *Oldschool v Gleeson (Construction) Ltd*,[5] where the court was of the clear opinion that it is the consulting engineer's plain duty to produce a suitable design for the works which will achieve what the building owner requires, and it is further his duty to ensure that that design is carried out. What of this latter aspect? Can the engineer, or, indeed, should the engineer instruct the contractors of his employer as to the manner of execution of the contract works? In the instant case, the consulting engineer had observed the demolition and excavation, having designed the redevelopment. During demolition a party wall collapsed causing damage to a neighbouring building, and the building owner sued the contractor and the consulting engineer for an indemnity in respect of this damage. The judge said that the consulting engineer neither had a duty nor a right to instruct the contractors as to the manner that they execute their contract works. Also, that even if it is the law that when a consulting engineer knows or ought to know that the contractors are failing to take proper precautions in the absence of which there is a risk of damage to property, he owes those contractors a duty to take care to prevent such damage occurring, then his duty does not extend beyond warning the contractors to take the necessary precautions.

> I do not think that the consulting engineer has any duty to tell the contractors how to do their work. He can and no doubt will offer advice to contractors as to various aspects of the work, but the ultimate responsibility for achieving the consulting engineer's design remains with the contractors. To take the present case as an example, I have no doubt that it was the contractors' duty to set whatever shoring might have been necessary. It was also for them to decide upon the sequence of excavation that was to be adopted and how such excavation was to be temporarily supported if required . . . If the contractors had said, for example, that they planned to excavate first down to footing level along the whole length of the party wall and thereafter to excavate the rest . . . the consulting engineer might well have pointed out the undesirability or even

5 (1976) 4 BLR 103.

the danger of adopting that course; but I do not think that he was under a duty to direct the contractors, for instance, to excavate in strips up to the party wall. It was the responsibility of the contractors to decide upon the method and sequence of excavation so as to achieve the consulting engineer's design; but if, for example, they planned to excavate the hoist pit without any temporary support, and so informed the consulting engineer, then as a matter of common sense the consulting engineer would intervene to prevent that which was described as 'an act of incredible folly'.[6]

In summarising the duties of an engineer in relation to design and supervision in the normal contract of engagement of an engineer, the judge expressed them in the following terms:

> I take the view that the duty of care which a . . . consulting engineer owes to a third party is limited by the assumption that the contractor who executes the works acts at all times as a competent contractor. The contractor cannot seek to pass the blame for incompetent work onto the consulting engineer on the grounds that he failed to intervene to prevent it . . . The responsibility of the consulting engineer is for the design of the engineering components of the works and his supervisory responsibility is to his client to ensure that the works are carried out in accordance with that design. But if . . . the design was so faulty that a competent contractor in the course of executing the works could not have avoided the resulting damage, then on principle it seems to me that the consulting engineer responsible for that design should bear the loss.[7]

Thus, if an engineer employed to prepare plans for a building to be erected, neglects to measure the site, but prefers to act on unauthorised information, resulting in the design being effectively useless, this will amount to professional negligence, and the engineer will be liable for any damage which his client suffers in consequence.[8] The issue has even been extended beyond this to a finding in law that an engineer, if engaged to estimate the expense of certain works, must ascertain for himself the nature of the soil on the site and should not rely on an investigation of some other person, even if that person had previously been engaged by the engineer's employer to ascertain that very matter.[9] The design responsibilities of an engineer are not, it can be seen, to be taken lightly.

Such an observation is rendered almost flippant when one considers an engineer's involvement in 'package deal' contracts for the provision of buildings or structures. In *Independent Broadcasting Authority v BICC Construction Ltd*,[10] EMI Ltd had tendered to 'supply and deliver' a very large television mast for Emley Moor in

6 Ibid at 123.
7 Ibid at 131.
8 *Columbus Co Ltd v Clowes* [1903] 1 KB 244.
9 *Moneypenny v Hartland* (1826) 2 C & P 378.
10 (1980) 14 BLR 1, HL.

Yorkshire. EMI's tender incorporated BICC's design, and in fact was stated in response to the IBA's invitation to tender, to be a quotation for 'design, supply and delivery' of the mast. The contract was awarded to EMI, who sub-contracted it to BICC, including specifications for design criteria of the cylindrical mast. One of the issues in this case was whether BICC, as designers, had been negligent in respect of considering ice-loading, which had subsequently led to the collapse of the mast two years after erection. The fact that BICC, as design sub-contractors, owed a duty of care directly to IBA was not in issue in the House of Lords, nor was the fact that a letter of assurance of the design from BICC to IBA would render BICC liable for negligent misstatement, if the design was, in fact, inadequate. The evidence in the case was that cylindrical masts had not been designed to such a height anywhere in the world, and BICC contended that work on such masts was 'both at and beyond the frontier of professional knowledge at that time'. It was clear that no one had considered the effect of asymmetric ice loading in conjunction with vortex shedding at low wind speeds, for it was assumed in the light of experience with lattice masts, that ice on the stays would cause no problem. The House was of the opinion that that assumption was unwarranted and therefore BICC had been negligent in their design, and had made a negligent misstatement to IBA that the mast would not oscillate dangerously.

The other issue in this important case was whether a main-contractor can make himself contractually liable for the negligence of his sub-contractor. The House held that EMI's tender for the 'design, supply and delivery' of the mast had been accepted on that basis by IBA, and, accordingly, EMI had made themselves contractually responsible for the design, and thus contractually liable to IBA for BICC's negligent design. Although not argued in the House, it was implied in their Lordship's speeches that EMI would be able to obtain an indemnity from BICC in respect of their liability to IBA.

It can be seen, therefore, that any party involved in building work can find himself in a position where he has contractually rendered himself liable to another party for work or advice in fact given by his sub-contractor. Despite the possibility of claiming an indemnity from the sub-contractor, this is a matter that engineers should bear in mind when involved in construction projects – particularly in that their professional indemnity insurers may take the view that the policy does not cover the legal defence of claims where no actual claim for negligence is made against the engineer himself.

A related area is the development of the law in the direction of increasing the duties and liabilities of professional persons, such as engineers, in relation to the provision of articles for use, as distinct from pure advice. The Court of Appeal in *Greaves & Co*

(Contractors) Ltd v Baynham Meikle & Partners[11] had held that, in the circumstances of the case, the consulting engineers had warranted that they would design a warehouse fit for the purpose for which it was required, even though they were only supplying a design, and not a completed article. The building as designed was not fit for its known purpose, i.e. trolley trucks could not operate in it because the vibrations caused the floor to crack, and the engineers were held liable to the contractors who had engaged them to design the warehouse building. The Court of Appeal did, however, state that no general principle of law was being espoused, but that this was a decision upon the particular facts of the case. In itself, that judgment seemed to extend the liability of engineers from what had been previously understood to be their responsibilities, but, because of the special facts of the case, did not appear to place engineers in a worse position than other professional men who may, likewise, in special circumstances, guarantee results. In the *IBA* case, however, Lord Scarman, obiter, made his views known that he regarded the duties placed upon professionals who finally produce an article to be higher than where only advice is given without relation to any article to be produced. His Lordship quoted two passages from the judgment of du Parcq LJ in *Samuels v Davis*:[12]

> if someone goes to a professional man . . . and says 'Will you make me something which will fit a particular part of my body?' . . . and the professional gentleman says: 'Yes', without qualification, he is then warranting that when he has made the article it will fit the part of the body in question.

(This case was concerned with the making of a pair of dentures by a dentist for a patient.) And,

> If a dentist takes out a tooth or a surgeon removes an appendix, he is bound to take reasonable care and to show such skill as may be expected from a qualified practitioner. The case is entirely different where a chattle is ultimately to be delivered.

Lord Scarman then went on to say:

> I believe the distinction drawn by Lord Justice du Parcq to be a sound one. In the absence of any term (express or to be implied) negativing the obligation, one who contracts to design an article for a purpose made known to him undertakes that the design is reasonably fit for the purpose. Such a design obligation is consistent with the statutory law regulating the sale of goods.

Being obiter, this opinion of Lord Scarman is only of persuasive force in the courts, and at this point in time it can only be said that it will require further cases to be taken before the courts for it to be

11 [1975] 3 All ER 99, [1975] 1 WLR 1095, CA.
12 [1943] KB 526 at 529 and 530, CA.

seen whether English law is truly now viewing the building of structures and the like, in the same light as the sale of a pair of shoes or a coffee grinder, for instance.

Lastly, of course, where an engineer is involved in work which is in connection with the provision of a dwelling, he will be under a statutory duty, under the Defective Premises Act 1972, to do the work in a professional manner so that the dwelling is fit for habitation, unless the dwelling is covered by an NHBC certificate.[13]

Estate agents

Estate agency work may be undertaken by anyone who wishes to commence practice as such, for there is no legal necessity to belong to any of the several institutes that have a professional membership in relation to this work. However, under the Estate Agents Act 1979, from May 1982[14] the Director of Fair Trading has powers to prohibit unfit persons from undertaking estate agency work e.g. the buying and selling of properties on behalf of property owners. Pure estate agency work does not include any surveying or valuation work, although many persons combine all three activities. This section will deal only with the professional negligence aspect of estate agency work, the other aspects being considered under a subsequent section.

In relation to the sale of property, it has been held to be an implied, even if not express, term of the contract of engagement of an estate agent who is granted the sole selling agency, that the estate agent will use his best endeavours to bring about a sale.[15] Lord Goddard CJ was of the view that there must be such an implied term, otherwise, why should a property owner employ a sole agent? It seemed to his Lordship that if a sole agent is employed, the contract must be that the estate agent would do his best to find a purchaser and would be committing a breach of his contract if he did not do something. The sole agent must act in response to the property owner's hope that the sole agency would stimulate the estate agent to greater efforts, or else he would be professionally negligent in failing to abide by the implied term to use his best endeavours to find a purchaser by, e.g. advertising the property extensively.

Even in the absence of a stipulation for the sole agency, many estate agents' contracts specifically state that they will use their best endeavours to find a purchaser. A duty will then arise to use reasonable care and it is owed to their client, the property owner. Furthermore, so long as he has the house on his books, it is the estate agent's duty to have regard to the interest of his client and not to

---

13 See above, under 'Architects'.
14 Estate Agents Act 1979 (Commencement No 1) Order 1981 (SI 1981/1517).
15 *Mendoza & Co v Bell* (1952) 159 Estates Gazette 372.

do anything contrary to it e.g. if an estate agent receives a good offer, it is his duty to inform his client about it, and it would be contrary to his duty to merely reject it and turn it down without telling the client about it. So what is the standard of care expected of an estate agent so that he does not breach his professional duty to his client?

In *Prebble & Co v West*,[16] Miss West owned two houses, numbers 11 and 12 in a square in London. She wished to sell them both, and put the matter into the hands of Prebble & Co, estate agents, who specifically contracted to use their best endeavours to introduce an applicant who was ready, willing and able to purchase. In the event, number 11 took a year to sell, and number twelve took fifteen months. When sued for their agency commission, Miss West counter-claimed that they had been negligent. Regarding number 11 she alleged that purchasers had been interested after only six months, but that the estate agents had not pursued the sale properly, because when the prospective purchasers told the agents that they were put off by the cost of repairs necessary, the agents accepted it. Miss West alleged that, this being a normal purchasing ploy to beat the price down, the agents should not have accepted it as a genuine loss of potential purchase. The Court of Appeal had a contrary view, and held that as Prebble & Co honestly believed that those potential purchasers had decided not to proceed, which was reasonable in the circumstances, then they were not negligent in failing to take the matter further.

With regard to number 12, Miss West alleged that the estate agents were wrong to tell the prospective purchaser (who, in fact, became the actual purchaser) that the premises were soon becoming vacant, for this was contrary to their instructions from her. This, she claimed, prejudiced negotiations and she should be compensated for their negligence. Again, however, the Court of Appeal held that there was nothing amiss with what Prebble & Co had done. If the purchaser had visited the premises, he would have seen that they were empty, and, in any event, it is quite reasonable and proper for an estate agent to tell a prospective purchaser that the premises are empty.

Thus, it seems that even in instances where the estate agent is not granted a sole agency, he owes a duty of care to his client not to prejudice the client's interest in anything he does in pursuance of the contract to find a purchaser. But what if the estate agent merely sits back and does nothing? There is strong authority that the client will have no remedy for contractual negligence in the absence of an agreement by the estate agent to use his best endeavours to procure a purchaser, which, for instance will be the case by implied term upon

16 (1969) 211 Estates Gazette 831, CA.

a sole agency contract. In *Luxor (Eastbourne) Ltd v Cooper*,[17] Lord Russell said:

> Contracts by which owners of property, desiring to dispose of it, put it in the hands of agents on commission terms, are not (in default of specific provisions) contracts of employment in the ordinary meaning of the words. No obligation is imposed on the agent to do anything.[18]

This decision was followed in *Ryan v Pilkington*,[19] some eighteen years later, but both these cases did not consider the duty of care owed in tortious negligence, which was only re-recognised by the courts in the subsequent case of *Hedley Byrne & Co Ltd v Heller & Partners Ltd*,[20] and the developing line of cases stemming therefrom. It is therefore submitted that the present state of the law is that where a property owner relies upon the statements of his estate agent that he will act as his agent to find a purchaser, total inaction will render the estate agent liable to a claim of negligence in tort, in the same way that negligent performance of the service will.

A claim in tort was brought against an estate agent in *Mayer v Pluck*.[1] This was for the tort of malicious falsehood, not negligence, against an estate agent, Pluck, who had falsely and deliberately told an auctioneer that Mr Mayer's house was built on an underground stream that caused flooding in the property. Having failed to sell Mr Mayer's house, Mr Pluck intended by this remark to dampen the sale of the house by auction, and then himself offer Mr Pluck a very low sum for the house. His scheme worked in that, because of the rumour he had spread, the house did not reach its reserve price of £12,000. Mr Pluck immediately offered Mr Mayer £5,000 for the house, which was rejected, and caused Mr Mayer to break a contract for the construction of a new house elsewhere. The court held the estate agent liable for the expenses of the breaking of the contract and abortive fees for the purchase of the new site. This may, perhaps, be rightly regarded as a case on the extreme of breach of professional duty by an estate agent, as not really involving 'negligence' at all, but is surely an illustration of the fact that an estate agent should not put his own interests against those of his client.

When given the responsibility of letting commercial property, it has been held that it is a negligent breach of contract for an estate agent not to measure up accurately the premises which are to be let. In *Carreras Ltd v D E and J Levy*,[2] the defendant estate agents were

---

17 [1941] AC 108, HL.
18 Ibid at 124.
19 [1959] 1 All ER 689, [1959] 1 WLR 403.
20 [1964] AC 465, [1963] 2 All ER 575, HL.
1 (1972) 223 Estates Gazette 33.
2 (1970) 215 Estates Gazette 707.

engaged by the plaintiffs to find them office accommodation in London, and negotiate the lease of suitable premises. Premises were found and the landlord's agents informed the defendants that there was 26,996 square footage of office space, and the lease was negotiated on that basis. After taking possession, the plaintiffs had the premises accurately measured, and found them to be only 26,048 square feet. The defendants admitted that their failure to verify the lessor's figure was a breach of their contractual duty of care to the plaintiffs to ascertain the measurements of the premises with accuracy. The defendant estate agents would therefore be liable for any loss or damage suffered by their clients in consequence of their negligence. In the circumstances of this case, there were no damages awarded against the estate agents because the plaintiffs could not prove that the true measurements would have enabled them to negotiate a lesser total rental with the landlord.

When acting for a lessor, it is the duty of the estate agent entrusted with the letting, to find a suitable tenant. This requires the seeking of character references, a financial reference, and the deposit of a sum for possible dilapidations or the payment of rent in advance to being given possession of the leasehold premises. These are the findings of Faulks J in *Brutton v Alfred Savill, Curtis and Henson*.[3] The plaintiff had engaged the defendant estate agents to find some 'nice people' to lease her house in London, at a rent of about £30 per week, with a deposit against dilapidations of £100 as the house had just been redecorated. Prospective tenants saw an employee of the defendants who was given responsibility for this letting, and a couple came forward called Mr and Mrs Brook, who wanted to rent the house almost immediately. The employee took some references from Mr Brook. A satisfactory reply came from a chartered accountant; no reply was received from another person; and his bank refused to say anything. The employee did not regard these references as satisfactory, so considered Mrs Brook as the prospective tenant. Enquiries revealed that she had a Bentley motor car; her bankers regarded her as 'respectable and trustworthy'; and another firm of estate agents said that they could speak 'very highly' of Mrs Brook as she had taken a flat through them previously.

On the appointed day, the employee attended at the flat to find Mr and Mrs Brook talking to the plaintiff, who was tidying up prior to their arrival. The employee then let Mrs Brook sign the tenancy agreement, and only then requested payment of the deposit and rent in advance. Mr Brook replied that he had forgotten his cheque book, and asked to pay the next day. The employee looked to the plaintiff, but sought no specific instructions from her. The plaintiff, Mrs Brutton, had said nothing in response, so the employee let Mr and

Mrs Brook into possession of the flat. No rent was subsequently paid, and it took many months and over £750 legal costs to regain possession of the house, and Mrs Brutton sued the defendant estate agents for breach of contract and negligence, in the sum of these costs by which she was out of pocket. Faulks J held that the defendants were liable in that sum to the plaintiff for their professional negligence in permitting prospective tenants to have possession of their client's house without payment of the deposit and advance rent, but did not appear to consider that they had in any way been negligent in dealing with the references, for they had correctly dismissed Mr Brook as a possible tenant because of the lack of a bank reference.

In conclusion, therefore, it must be emphasised that estate agents owe a duty of care to their clients, and must exercise reasonable skill and care in all their dealings on their clients' behalf. What must be done will obviously vary upon the nature of the agency work undertaken, the specific contractual terms of engagement, and, as always, the general practice of estate agents, which is the measuring rod to be applied to a particular allegation of negligence in performing professional services. If standards are not met, the estate agent will be exposed to claims for breach of contract and/or in tort for negligence, in respect of resulting loss or damage. It will be rare for an estate agent to be liable to a third party, e.g. a purchaser of a house he is selling, for negligent misstatements will mostly be uttered with the ostensible authority of his principal (the client), who will be responsible for this.

Solicitors

It is not legal for a person to call himself a solicitor, unless he has qualified, by both passing examinations set by the governing body, the Law Society, and serving a period in articles in the office of a practising solicitor, and duly been admitted to the Roll of Solicitors of the Supreme Court. The Law Society requires a further period of legal experience to be gained before granting a solicitor a practice certificate, which, on the one hand entitles the solicitor to practice individually on his own account, but also compulsorily to insure his professional risks via the Law Society's special scheme of insurance.[4] In relation to such risks, apart from the Unfair Contract Terms Act 1977, a provision of the Solicitors Act 1974 prohibits any term being introduced in a contract of engagement which purports to limit a

4 See ch 6 re the special Law Society Scheme, and Solicitors Act 1974, ss. 20 to 27 regarding unqualified persons acting as solicitors, and s. 37 regarding compulsory insurance.

solicitor's liability for negligence with regard to contentious work.[5] This section discusses the liability of solicitors for negligence, and is concerned with the liability of the solicitor in private practice, rather than a solicitor employed as a company legal adviser or local authority solicitor.

The solicitor must exercise the skill and care in attending to his duties as would a reasonably competent member of his profession, and this was clearly recognised in 1825 when Abbott CJ explained the test to be applied in the following terms:[6]

> The real question upon the evidence is, whether you think the expense was brought on the parties by the inadvertence of the plaintiff? No attorney is bound to know all the law; God forbid that it should be imagined that an attorney, or a counsel, or even a judge is bound to know all the law; or that an attorney is to lose his fair recompense on account of an error, being such an error as a cautious man might fall into.

Subsequent cases have revealed that the law requires a high standard of legal expertise from the solicitor, and, whilst not expecting a knowledge of all the law, expects the solicitor to recognise where his skill or learning is lacking. Not only the law itself must be known, but also the means of obtaining legal redress and the rules of court procedure. Thus, in a case determined only a few years after the above, the succeeding Lord Chief Justice stated that a solicitor, in general –

> is liable for the consequences of ignorance or non-observance of the rules of practice of this court . . . Whilst on the other hand, he is not answerable for error in judgment upon points of new occurrence, or of nice or doubtful construction, or of such as are usually entrusted to men in the higher branch of the profession of the law.[7]

That last remark refers to the obtaining of a barrister's (counsel's) opinion upon such matters as the doubtful construction of, e.g. a clause in a commercial lease. It follows that a solicitor will, in the majority of cases, satisfy his duty of care to his client by obtaining counsel's opinion upon difficult points of law or construction. But even within his office, a solicitor will be responsible to ensure that his staff draw his attention to such difficulties. Accordingly, in *Richards v Cox*,[8] a solicitor was held liable when a client was told by the solicitor's clerk that her claim was excluded by a clause in a motor policy. The exception clause was of a novel form and had not been encountered before, and it posed a difficult question of interpretation. In the event, the clerk's interpretation was found to be

5 Solicitors Act 1974, s. 60(5).
6 *Montriou v Jeffreys* (1825) 2 C & P 113 at 116.
7 *Godefroy v Dalton* (1830) 6 Bing 460 at 468, per Tindall CJ.
8 [1943] 1 KB 139, CA.

erroneous, and it was held that the solicitor was vicariously liable for his clerk's negligence — the clerk should have recognised that, being a novel and difficult clause to construe, he should have referred it to his employing solicitor.

A solicitor will equally be liable for failing to advise his client of certain matters. Thus, in *Sykes v Midland Bank Executor and Trustee Co Ltd*[9] the defendants were solicitors to a firm of architects and surveyors who took an underlease on office premises. In the underlease was a prohibition against change of user of the premises upon any subsequent assignment of the underlease by the firm, without the permission of both the lessors and the superior lessors (the actual landlords). The solicitors approved this underlease, and, despite knowing that the firm might wish to assign or sublet in the future, did not explain this clause at all. In the event, five years later, the firm wished to sublet part of the premises to a firm of engineers' importers and exporters. The superior landlords refused to consent to the change of user of the premises, and the firm was unable to find a suitable sub-tenant for three years. Karminski LJ expressed the solicitor's duty in conveyancing matters in this way:

> [The solicitor] should have expressly drawn to his clients' attention that the freeholders had an absolute right to refuse consent to a change of user. Clients rely on their solicitors to draw their attention to unusual clauses or dangers in conveyancing matters. This is so even if the clients concerned are experienced professional men, including architects and surveyors. The solicitor is consulted as an expert in conveyancing matters. Those in other professions have usually no knowledge or experience in this field; that is why they consult solicitors. I have no doubt at all that (the solicitor's) failure to call his clients' attention to clause 2 (xi) was in breach of his duty as a solicitor to these clients, and, therefore, negligent.[10]

This duty to inform does not go so far as to require a solicitor who advises a client from time to time on certain matters to advise him of material dates in the client's agreements with others. Without specific instructions, a solicitor is not under a duty to tell his client, e.g. that a break-clause in a lease will operate on a certain date in the future and then remind him when that date arrives.[11] A solicitor must, however, properly explain matters, and should not leave his client with the wrong impression about a matter he has entrusted to the solicitor. Therefore, if a solicitor is instructed to obtain a transfer of a drinking licence to a club's new premises, which, although normally a straightforward matter, runs into difficulties, the solicitor must ensure that his client fully appreciates that no liquor may be served until the difficulty is sorted out. Failure

9 [1971] 1 QB 113, CA.
10 Ibid at 130.
11 *Yager v Fishman & Co and Teff and Teff* [1944] 1 All ER 552, CA.

so to do will be a breach of professional duty to his client, and the solicitor will have to indemnify his client for any costs and penalties that may result from a conviction of serving liquor on unlicensed premises.[12]

It will, of course, be a matter of fact as to what the scope of the advice sought by a solicitor is in a given set of circumstances, and a solicitor, like any other professional, is not expected to advise on matters for which his services have not been retained.[13] Persons, in the very nature of things, often seek advice from their solicitor which is not limited to legal advice, but includes a small or large element of business or practical advice. If the solicitor accepts the basis of his retainer in such circumstances, then he will owe a duty of care to his client for these matters also. In *Neushul v Mellish and Harkavy*,[14] a solicitor was engaged to advise the plaintiff about raising money to put into a business venture of a man with whom she was infatuated. The solicitor also, in fact, acted for the very company in which she wished to invest her money, and he knew the company was not prospering. Furthermore, he had acted in the past for the man, who basically posed as an American of wealth. The plaintiff had failed to obtain financial assistance from her bank manager, who described the man as 'the most obvious con-man I have ever seen', but the solicitor then helped her obtain a high interest loan on the security of her property. The man returned to the USA with the money and never returned or repaid the money, and so the plaintiff suffered financial loss and sued the solicitor for failing to warn her about the man.

The Court of Appeal upheld the finding of professional negligence against the solicitor, and Danckwerts LJ explained the reasoning:

> The duty normally owed by a solicitor to his client only extend[s] to legal advice, [but] he might also undertake to advise on business matters, and he then owes a duty to advise competently, fully and not misleadingly. It [is] often difficult in a given situation to disentangle legal and business or practical advice, and a solicitor who was carrying out a transaction for a client was not justified in expressing no opinion when it was plain that the client was rushing into an unwise, not to say disastrous, adventure. In any case, it [is] plain that, in the present case, H [the solicitor] had been advising the plaintiff on the business side as well as on the conveyancing aspect of the transaction. H had, indeed, been in an impossible position, and should not have consented to act for the plaintiff . . . In advising the plaintiff, H, by reason of his knowledge of the financial affairs of F [the man], had put himself in hopeless difficulties, and, in fact, had merely given her an inadequate warning.

12 *Ashton v Wainwright* [1936] 1 All ER 805.
13 *Duchess of Argyll v Beuselinck* [1972] 2 Lloyd's Rep 172.
14 (1967) 111 Sol Jo 399, CA.

A solicitor has even been found liable to a client by causing her mental distress in failing to properly conduct litigation on the client's behalf. In *Heywood v Wellers*[15] the plaintiff was a woman who was being molested by a former man friend. She went to a firm of solicitors and saw an unqualified litigation clerk whom she believed to be a solicitor of that firm. He, at her request, wrote a letter to the man asking him to desist, but this merely caused an intensification of the molestation. The plaintiff again saw the clerk, and he suggested the obtaining of a county court injunction, and stated that it would only take three weeks and cost about £25. The plaintiff accepted this advice and instructed the institution of these proceedings, and paid the estimated £25 costs. During the next eleven months the clerk initiated proceedings in the High Court, not the county court, which, because of errors and omissions, proved wholly ineffective, for the plaintiff continued to be molested by the man. When she had paid £175 and was asked to pay a further £100 towards the costs totalling £446, she instructed the firm to drop the case, and, shortly thereafter sued the firm for professional negligence, claiming £170 of costs actually paid and £150 as damages for distress caused by the mishandling of the case.

The Court of Appeal held that she was entitled to the return of the costs she had paid which had been thrown away in the abortive proceedings for the injunction, and £125 to compensate her for the vexation, anxiety and distress and the continued molestation, which were the direct and foreseeable consequences of the solicitors' failure to obtain the relief which it was the sole purpose of the injunction proceedings to secure. The facts revealed a clear breach of the solicitors' duty to their client by their vicariously negligent conduct of the litigation.

There is no doubt that a solicitor enjoys the same immunity from action on the grounds of public policy, as does a barrister (above) in relation to the conduct and management of court proceedings whilst acting as an advocate.[16] A solicitor may act as an advocate for his client in the county court, in magistrates' courts, and, in certain circumstances, in the crown court. No special immunity from suit therefore exists in relation to matters that cannot be said to be a preliminary decision affecting the way that cause is to be conducted when it comes to hearing.[17] Thus, where a solicitor negligently fails to ascertain all the relevant facts pertinent to an intended action, he enjoys no immunity from action, and so in *Losner v Michael Cohen & Co*[18] the Court of Appeal found a solicitor liable to his client when

15 [1976] QB 446, [1976] 1 All ER 300, CA.
16 *Rondel v Worsley* [1969] 1 AC 191, [1967] 3 All ER 993, HL; *Saif Ali v Sidney Mitchell & Co* [1980] AC 198, [1978] 3 All ER 1033, HL.
17 The test in *Rees v Sinclair* [1974] 1 NZLR 180, approved in *Saif Ali*, above.
18 (1975) 119 Sol Jo 340, CA.

he failed to ascertain the true owner of some dangerous dogs that had attacked his client. Because of this omission, the proceedings in the magistrates' court had to be dismissed by the court, and so the solicitor had failed to adequately carry out his client's instructions, and was liable to his client in damages. A solicitor will likewise be liable in failing to take note of the limitation periods;[19] bringing proceedings in a court which has no jurisdiction to hear the matter;[20] permitting judgment to be entered against his client in default of a defence being entered when engaged to defend that action;[1] and failing to watch the court list, so that his client is unrepresented at the hearing.[2]

A solicitor will also be liable to non-clients who rely upon his exercise of due care upon an action in negligence, and suffer loss thereby. So, in *Ross v Caunters*,[3] the beneficiary of a will being drawn up by a solicitor for his client is a person to whom he owes a duty of care to carry out his client's instructions properly. The solicitors in this case had failed to warn the testator that neither a beneficiary nor a beneficiary's spouse should witness the signing of the will, and the testator had asked a beneficiary's spouse to witness the will. The beneficiary claimed damages against the solicitors for negligence in respect of the loss of the benefits given to her by the will after the testator's death. The solicitors had admitted their negligence, but had contended that they owed no duty of care to the plaintiff beneficiary. Megarry VC held that a duty was owed on common law principles, and her claim for pure financial loss should succeed against the solicitors for their negligence, for she was a person within the solicitors' direct contemplation as being likely to be injured by their failure to carry out the testator's instructions.

Stockbrokers

A stockbroker must obey his client's instructions or be liable to him for any loss or damage that flows from breach of those instructions. In *Jarvis v Moy, Davies, Smith, Vandervell & Co*,[4] on 25 March, the defendant stockbrokers were instructed by the plaintiff to buy 300 Canadian Pacific shares at not more than $43, unless it was possible to obtain backwardation facilities at a cheaper rate than formerly. The stockbrokers bought 300 Canadian Pacific shares on 27 March

---

19 *Kitchen v Royal Air Force Association* [1958] 2 All ER 241, [1958] 1 WLR 563, CA; *Fletcher & Son v Jubb, Booth and Helliwell* [1920] 1 KB 275, CA.
20 *Williams v Gibbs* (1836) 5 Ad & El 208; *Cox v Leech* (1857) 1 CBNS 617.
 1 *Godefroy v Jay* (1831) 7 Bing 413.
 2 *Burgoine v Taylor* (1878) 9 Ch D 1.
 3 [1980] Ch 297, [1979] 3 All ER 580.
 4 [1936] 1 KB 399.

at $43 each, but by the next contango or settlement day upon the London Stock Exchange, 6 April, the shares had fallen to $41. The plaintiff sued the defendants alleging breach of duty in that they should have waited until the contango day to purchase the shares, and, because they had not, the plaintiff was $600 out of pocket. Judgment was given in favour of the plaintiff for this premature exercise of their mandate as brokers.

A stockbroker may also be liable to repay his client's money and his brokerage commission if he does not purchase shares in exact accordance with his instructions. In *Lamert v Heath*,[5] the defendant, a sharebroker, was instructed by the plaintiff to purchase 280 'Kentish Coast Railway scrip'. He duly bought 280 share certificates which were signed by the company's secretary, but, at a later date, the company's directors denied the genuineness of the scrip, alleging that it was issued by the secretary without authority. The plaintiff therefore sued the defendant for the recovery of the price of these false shares and for return of his commission which had therefore not been earned. Again, the court found in the plaintiff's favour.

A client's instructions are not undertaken to be carried out at all events, and a stockbroker only undertakes to use due and reasonable diligence to endeavour to execute his instructions. This was the court's finding in *Fletcher v Marshall*,[6] but in the circumstances did find the stockbroker in breach of his duty to his client. The plaintiff had employed the defendant, a sharebroker in Manchester, and lodged money in his hands, to procure for him fifty shares in a certain railway company. The defendant, without disclosing the name of his client, entered into a contract with H, another sharebroker, to purchase them for him. According to the usage of the Stock Exchange at Manchester, there were two 'settling days' in each month, on which all transactions between brokers, and between them and their principals, were to be settled. H did not perform his contract with the defendant by the next settling day, so the plaintiff requested the return of his money. The defendant refused to return the money, so the defendant sued for its return, on the ground that the defendant no longer had any right to hold onto the money, not having performed his instructions with due diligence. The court held the broker liable to make a return of the deposited moneys.

If a client gives an order to his agent stockbroker in such uncertain terms as to be susceptible of two different meanings, and the stockbroker bona fide adopts one of them and acts upon it, it is not competent of the client to repudiate that act as unauthorised because he

5 (1846) 15 M & W 486.
6 (1846) 15 M & W 755; and in *Briggs v Gunner* (1979) 129 NLJ 116, it was held that a stockbroker is under no general duty to pass comment on the wisdom or otherwise of his client's investment policy.

meant the order to be read in the other sense of which it is equally capable. It is a fair answer to such an attempt to disown his authority to tell the client that the departure from his intention was occasioned by his own fault, and that he should have given his order in clear and unambiguous terms. Thus, in *Loring v Davis*,[7] where the client wrote a letter to his brokers concerning a share transfer that was running into difficulties stating that 'I wish you clearly to understand that whatever position you may have to assume with regard to them [the shares] I consider myself fully bound to support you', the stock-brokers were held as fully entitled to interpret that letter as meaning that they were still his brokers with regard to the transaction and could act, on his behalf, in the way they considered best.

Although a stockbroker is bound by the custom of the Stock Exchange of which he is a member, he cannot plead that he has obeyed instructions to sell shares until a valid contract of sale is concluded, even if it is the custom of his Exchange to ignore statutory provisions regarding the making of a valid contract of sale. Accordingly, in *Neilson v James*[8] a stockbroker sold shares to a jobber on the Bristol Stock Exchange, but in accordance with the custom of that Stock Exchange, the bought and sold notes between the stockbroker and the jobber omitted to state the name of the registered proprietor of the shares as required by statute. Thus the contract of sale was void in law at that time, and the stockbroker's client was held to be entitled to claim damages for his loss sustained upon the winding-up order of the company after the date when a valid sale of the shares should have been concluded by the stockbroker on his behalf.

To assist their clients who choose to play the 'genteel casino' of the Stock Exchange, stockbrokers may 'carry over' an account to another account day on the Stock Exchange. A stockbroker, whilst not bound or obliged to carry over,[9] must give notice to his client if he is not, and he is entitled to carry them over on the fortnightly settlements at the prices fixed by the jobbers, debiting his client with the losses, if any, on each such carrying over. Apart from this being the general usage of the Stock Exchange, if a client is sent accounts of what is being done, as is normally the case, the stockbroker does not breach his contract with the client or exercise a power outside his authority, until such time as his client specifically revokes the broker's authority to carry over.[10] Furthermore, a stockbroker is fully entitled to sell either part or the whole of an account as against

---

7 (1886) 32 Ch D 625; following *Ireland v Livingston* (1872) LR 5 HL 395.
8 (1882) 9 QBD 546, CA.
9 *Re Hewett, ex p Paddon* (1893) 9 TLR 166 at 167, CA, per Lord Esher MR, obiter.
10 *Campbell & Co v Brass* (1891) 7 TLR 612.

his client once the client has intimated that he cannot take up the shares in his account, either in whole or in part.[11]

A stockbroker will be liable, in common with other agents, to parties with whom he deals, for acting in breach of his warrant of authority as purported authorised agent of his client. In *Starkey v Bank of England*[12] a sum of Consols was standing in the joint names of F W Oliver and his brother Edgar in trust for others. F W Oliver wrote to a firm of stockbrokers of which the appellant was a member, enclosing an application to the Bank of England to issue a power of attorney from F W and Edgar Oliver to the appellant and his partner to transfer the Consols, and requesting the brokers to lodge the application with the bank. The appellant having lodged it, the bank issued to the brokers a power of attorney to sell and transfer, and sent notices to F W and Edgar Oliver at the addresses given in the application that a power of attorney had been applied for. No notice reached Edgar Oliver. The brokers forwarded the power to F W Oliver, who returned it to the brokers executed by him, and purporting to be executed by Edgar. The brokers, believing that all was right, sold the Consols, and the power was lodged at the bank by the appellant who afterwards signed the 'demand to act' endorsed on the power and executed the transfer to the purchaser. A similar transaction afterwards took place with regard to a transfer of bank stock.

After F W Oliver's death two years later, it was discovered that the signatures of Edgar Oliver to the powers of attorney were forgeries and that he knew nothing of the transactions. Edgar Oliver therefore sued the Bank of England for restitution of the Consols and a sum equal to the dividends which had accrued since the transfers, and the bank in turn sought an indemnity from the stockbrokers for breach of warranty of authority. The House of Lords held the stockbrokers liable for this act which was committed without authority, albeit innocently and believing themselves to be duly empowered.

Similarly, in *Yeung Kai Yung v Hong Kong and Shanghai Banking Corporation*,[13] innocent stockbrokers were sent forged share transfer deeds concerning shares which had in fact been stolen, and duly transferred the shares. Upon subsequent recovery of the shares by the true owner, the stockbrokers were held liable to indemnify the bank which had carried out their instructions for re-registration of the shares.

---

11 *Cullum v Hodges* (1901) 18 TLR 6, CA.
12 [1903] AC 114, HL.
13 [1980] 2 All ER 599, [1980] 3 WLR 950, PC.

Surveyors and valuers

There are several institutes for surveyors and valuers, but there is no general requirement for an individual to be a member of any institute or possess professional qualifications to carry on the practice or business of surveying or valuing property.

If engaged to inspect property and to give a general opinion upon a property, but not to make a detailed survey, a surveyor will still be liable if he does not discover the presence of dry rot, woodworm and settlement.[14] Equally, if a surveyor is instructed by a prospective purchaser of a property to survey the house and gives it a 'clean bill of health', and, indeed, values it at above the purchase price, he will be liable for negligently failing to discover that the house was slipping on its foundations to such an extent that, within five years, the house has become valueless.[15] In another case, a surveyor was held liable to his client for failing to appraise him of the risk of dehydration and settlement created by the presence of poplar trees growing near to the house his client was intending to purchase, and the fact that the house was built upon ground with a clay sub-soil. The surveyor had not even noticed cracks and other signs indicating shrinkage.[16] Where an old property had ties, a surveyor was held negligent in not drawing his client's attention to them, the ties being so deficient that within months of his client's purchase of the house, large cracks had appeared by the ties.[17]

It will be useful to look at one illustration to see the sequence of events leading to a finding of negligence against a surveyor. In *Freeman v Marshall & Co*,[18] the plaintiff was interested in a certain property that she wished to convert into flatlets as an investment property. She herself inspected the property on two occasions, and then called upon the defendant firm, being carried on by a Mr Marshall, to carry out a survey of the property's basement where she had noticed damp. Being satisfied as to the general state of the rest of the property, she did not instruct him to carry out a full structural survey. Mr Marshall carried on the business of estate agent, valuer and surveyor, though in fact had never received any formal training or passed any professional examination in surveying. He was a member of the Valuers Institution, but this was by election and not by examination. He did have some thirty years experience in estate agency work, though, and claimed a working knowledge of structures. Holding himself out in the practice of a surveyor, of course means that he is to be judged by the standards of a reasonably competent surveyor.

14 *Philips v Ward* [1956] 1 All ER 874, [1956] 1 WLR 471, CA.
15 *Morgan v Perry* (1973) 229 Estates Gazette 1737.
16 *Daisley v B S Hall & Co* (1972) 225 Estates Gazette 1553.
17 *Lees v English & Partners* (1977) 242 Estates Gazette 293.
18 (1966) 200 Estates Gazette 777.

The plaintiff attended at the property with Mr Marshall, and pointed out the damp in the basement to him, and asked him what it was. He replied that there was not very much damp, and that it was due to condensation, so if the basement was kept properly aired there would be no trouble from it. The plaintiff relied on Mr Marshall's opinion, bought the property and was at pains to keep the basement properly aired. After a year it was manifest that something was seriously wrong, and the plaintiff called in a chartered surveyor who discovered rising damp and dry and wet rot, and extensive repairs were done to the basement. Accordingly, the court found Mr Marshall liable for professional negligence, and awarded the plaintiff a sum equal to the costs of repairs and the lost rent from the basement flatlets whilst the repairs were carried out.

The function of a quantity surveyor is to measure the work or otherwise ascertain the amount due from his employer to a building contractor. Normally, when issuing interim and final certificates, a quantity surveyor will not be acting in an arbitral capacity without a specific contractual provision to that effect, and will therefore be liable for a breach of his duty to act fairly in making his valuation.[19] Thus, in *Tyrer v District Auditor for Monmouthshire*[20] a surcharge imposed upon Tyrer was upheld in respect of his negligence in approving excessive quantities and prices in some contracts with a firm of building contractors made by the Monmouthshire Council which employed him to check the quantities and prices.

Valuers must have a practical working knowledge of the law relating to the exercise of their profession, so that they may perform their duties in a proper fashion. In *Jenkins v Betham*[1] valuers were asked to value some ecclesiastical property as between an incoming and outgoing incumbent. Negligently and erroneously, not appreciating the difference, the valuers based their valuation as between an incoming and outgoing tenant, not incumbent, and were held liable for their negligence. Similarly, in *Weedon v Hindwood, Clarke and Esplin*[2] the defendant valuers were found wanting in their relevant legal knowledge. Here, the valuers had been retained to act for their client in compulsory purchase negotiations. Just prior to the commencement of negotiations, the Court of Appeal had held altered the law as to the date on which property should be valued when being compulsorily purchased. Neither the valuers, nor the local district valuer appeared to be aware of this decision, and were equally lacking in knowledge of the House of Lords' decision to uphold the

19 *Sutcliffe v Thackrah* [1974] AC 727, [1974] 1 All ER 859, HL.
20 (1973) 230 Estates Gazette 973.
 1 (1855) 15 CB 168.
 2 (1974) 234 Estates Gazette 121.

ruling that was actually made during the time negotiations were being undertaken. This alteration in the law was to the great benefit of the owners of property being compulsorily acquired, and the valuers were subsequently held liable for their negligence resulting in financial loss to their client.

> The question of valuation must to a great extent be a matter of opinion, and must depend upon the valuer's experience, but it is difficult to believe that a careful valuer in making a valuation does not endeavour to get some data on which to work . . . There are questions which can be asked, . . . for instance, what the person has paid for the property.

This is how Goddard LJ analysed the problem of the court in determining whether an expression of, what in effect is, an opinion, regarding the value of a property, may be made negligently.[3] The facts of the case before him were that the defendant valuer had inspected his client's property and given a valuation figure. The valuer had not, however, made any local inquiries as to the value of that or similar properties in the area, despite being unfamiliar with the locality. He also failed to enquire of his client the price the property had realised in recent exchanges. Not long thereafter, subsequent to his client obtaining a mortgage on that valuation, the property was sold at a price which was less than half the valuation figure given by the defendant valuer. The Court of Appeal held the valuer to have been negligent in that his knowledge of the locality was insufficient and he ought to have taken steps to inform himself of the value of similar properties. His failure so to do was a breach of his duty of care to his professional client.

The sale of a property at about one-third of the valuation occurred in *Kenney v Hall, Pain and Foster*. The valuation had, in fact, been made by one of the defendant valuers' employees who had very limited experience in the valuation of property and was totally unqualified. He had even given the valuation in direct breach of his instructions, which were that if he were asked to give a firm opinion as to asking price or value, he should refer the matter back to one of the firm's qualified partners. Goff J accepted that the mere fact that a valuation proved to be wrong was insufficient evidence, but felt that this valuation was so wide of the mark that it could, therefore, be properly described as erroneous. The employee certainly lacked still, and had failed to take, reasonable care by not referring the valuation back to his office. The defendant firm was therefore liable in negligence to the plaintiff who had relied on the valuation made to him.

One other point of law arose in this case, and that concerned the issue of whether or not the defendants owed the plaintiff a duty of care, because they had not charged him for the valuation – it had been given gratuitously. Counsel for the defendants had conceded that a duty of care was owed, and Goff J stated that he thought this was rightly conceded. His Lordship said:[4]

> It makes no difference whether or not they intended to charge a fee for their services. In point of law they could have done so, because whenever a professional man renders services to another at his request he is, in the absence of a contrary intention, entitled to charge for those services. So when [a valuer] is asked to place a value on property with a view to sale he will, in the absence of a contrary intention, be entitled to charge for such valuation; though if he is instructed thereafter to act as [estate] agent for the vendor on the sale of the property, the valuation will ordinarily be treated as part of the services rendered towards the earning of the commission in the event of a successful sale, in which event a separate fee for the valuation will be waived.

Finally, in relation to valuations, a valuer owes a duty of care to third parties who may reasonably come to rely on the valuation. Thus, in *Cann v Willson*,[5] an intending mortgagor sought a valuation of his house from the defendant firm of valuers, who were also informed that their valuation was to be passed on to the intending mortgagee. A valuation was made, which was subsequently proved to have overvalued the house, when a forced sale on default of the mortgage payments by the mortgagor was made. The mortgagee sued the valuers for negligence, and Chitty J held the valuation to have been negligent – the defendants were in breach of a duty of care to the mortgagee whom they knew would place reliance on their valuation. In the reverse situation, where the intending mortgagee instructs valuers, the valuers will owe a duty of care to the intending mortgagor who relies on a valuation that says the property is good for security to the sum of the valuation, because it is within the reasonable contemplation of the valuers that the valuation figure will be passed on to intending purchasers (i.e. mortgagors) of the property. This was the finding of Park J in *Yianni v Edwin Evans & Sons*.[6]

In conclusion, it can be said that although the law accepts, as is the case with other professions, that a mere error of judgment may not be negligent, surveyors and valuers, whether actually qualified or not, must exercise reasonable skill, of a degree to be expected from experienced persons holding themselves out as professional surveyors or valuers, to avoid liability for negligence upon an erroneous

---

4 (1976) 239 Estates Gazette 355, 429; see also *Singer and Friedlander Ltd v John D Wood & Co* (1977) 243 Estates Gazette 212, and *Corisand Investments Ltd v Druce & Co* (1978) 248 Estates Gazette 315.

5 (1888) 39 Ch D 39; approved in *Hedley Byrne & Co Ltd v Heller & Partners Ltd* [1964] AC 465, [1963] 2 All ER 575, HL; cf *Eagle Star Insurance Co Ltd v Gale and Power* (1955) 166 Estates Gazette 37.

6 [1981] 3 All ER 592, [1981] 3 WLR 843.

report. And potential plaintiffs are both immediate clients, and purchasers of the property reported on – although, in the case of valuations in particular, the distance in time from the date of the report will be a matter going to reasonableness of the plaintiff's reliance on the report, for it is common knowledge that the price of property is very prone to fluctuations.

Chapter 2

An outline of the law of insurance

Introduction

Modern insurance law has developed from three sources – insurance practice, the common law, and statute. This body of law can be said to be concerned with two areas, the first being the formation of a valid contract of insurance, the second being the determination of the rights and duties of the respective parties to the contract.

The primary grouping consists of a definition of an insurance contract; the requirement for the insured to have an insurable interest; the parties to the contract; offer; acceptance; agreement; and payment of the premium by the insured to the insurer.

The secondary grouping consists of the principle of utmost good faith ('uberrima fides'); rules regarding non-disclosure and misrepresentation of material facts; warranties and conditions within the policy; interpretation and construction of the policy; the principle of indemnity; insurers' rights of subrogation; and contribution between policies.

The principles cited in this chapter relate to contracts for the insurance of professional negligence risks, otherwise known as professional indemnity insurances, and must not be understood as necessarily of application to other insurance contracts, albeit that many points of general principle are embodied herein and are drawn from case-law relating to a variety of insurance contracts. The purpose of this chapter, therefore, is confined to a presentation of an outline of insurance law in so far as it relates to this variety of contract of insurance.

Definition of the insurance contract

The courts have struggled for a complete definition of 'a contract of insurance' for over two hundred years. One of the earliest judicial pronouncements was 'Insurance is a contract upon speculation',[1] and it was not until the turn of this century that an authoritative definition of an insurance contract was given. This was in the leading case of *Prudential Insurance Co v Inland Revenue Commissioners*,[2] where Channell J said:

> Where you insure a ship or a house you cannot insure that the ship shall not be lost or the house burnt, but what you do is insure that a sum of money shall be paid upon the happening of a certain event. That I think is the first requirement in a contract of insurance. It must be a contract whereby for some consideration, usually but not necessarily for periodical payments called premiums, you secure to yourself some benefit, usually but not necessarily the payment of a sum of money, upon the happening of some event. Then the next thing that is necessary is that the event should be one which involves some amount of uncertainty. There must be either uncertainty whether the event will ever happen or not, or if the event is one which must happen at some time there must be uncertainty as to the time it will happen. The remaining essential is that . . . the insurance must be against something. A contract which would otherwise be a mere wager may become an insurance by reason of the assured having an interest in the subject-matter – that is to say, the uncertain event which is necessary to make the contract amount to an insurance must be an event which is prima facie adverse to the interest of the assured. The insurance is to provide for the payment of a sum of money to meet a loss or detriment which will or may be suffered upon the happening of the event . . . A contract of insurance, then, must be a contract for the payment of a sum of money, or for some corresponding benefit such as the rebuilding of a house or the repairing of a ship, to become due on the happening of an event, which event must have some amount of uncertainty about it, and must be of a character more or less adverse to the interest of the person effecting the insurance.

A few years later, however, this definition was found to be inadequate by the Court of Appeal in *Gould v Curtis*.[3] With regard to the adversity of the event insured, Buckley LJ had this to say:[4]

> If the policy be one such as a fire policy, or a marine policy on a vessel, it is a policy of indemnity, an obligation to indemnify. In insurances of that class I agree that what you look at is to see whether there has occurred an event adverse to the person who is insured, such as that, having suffered a loss by reason of that adverse event, he is to be indemnified by the sum which is guaranteed to him under the policy. The same is not true of a policy of life insurance. A policy of life insurance is not a policy of indemnity, but is a policy upon a contingency. Death cannot for this purpose be appropriately described as an adverse event . . . for it is not in the sense that it occasions pecuniary loss, which is what is meant in the case of a fire or marine policy.

1 Per Lord Mansfield in *Carter v Boehm* (1766) 3 Burr 1905.
2 [1904] 2 KB 658 at 663, 664.
3 [1913] 3 KB 84, CA.
4 Ibid at 95.

This distinction between indemnity and contingency insurances has been followed by the courts,[5] and it can clearly be seen that contracts for the insurance of professional negligence risks fall within the category called indemnity insurances, for the purpose of the insurance is to indemnify the insured professional against pecuniary loss (legal damages and costs) arising out of an adverse event (the professional's negligent act, error or omission which causes loss to be suffered by his client or a third party). Hence the generic name of these insurance contracts − professional indemnity insurances. Other indemnity insurances commonly encountered are Motor Insurance; Public Liability Insurance; Employers' Liability Insurance; and, more recently, Product Liability Insurance.

It should be noted that Channell J's definition refers not only to the payment of money, but also to the payment of 'some corresponding benefit', and so the provision of a car, or a driver and a car, has been held to be a benefit under a contract of insurance,[6] but not the discretionary provision of legal advice and an indemnity.[7] The benefits, then, must be contractually forthcoming under the terms of the insurance policy, and not merely at the discretion of the insurer.

Channell J's definition remains relatively unscathed, and a wholly satisfactory definition of a contract of insurance may never be evolved. In the words of Megarry V-C; 'Plainly it is a matter of considerable difficulty. It may be that it is a concept which it is better to describe than attempt to define.'[8]

One other point to be mentioned at this stage is that there is no requirement in English common law for a contract of insurance to be made in writing. It can be made orally, or partly in writing and partly orally, provided valuable consideration is given for it,[9] but in Scotland contracts of insurance must be made in writing, being 'obligationes litteris'.

Insurable interest

Prior to the Life Assurance Act 1774, gambling and wagering contracts were not prohibited by English law,[10] and so were enforceable in the courts. They were not void simply because they were wagers

---

5 See *West Wake Price & Co v Ching* [1957] 1 WLR 45 at 51, per Devlin J; and *Medical Defence Union Ltd v Dept of Trade* [1980] Ch 82 at 89, per Megarry V-C.
6 *Dept of Trade and Industry v St Christopher Motorists Assn Ltd* [1974] 1 All ER 395, [1974] 1 WLR 99.
7 *Medical Defence Union Ltd v Dept of Trade* [1980] Ch 82.
8 Ibid at 95.
9 *Bhugwandass v Netherlands India Sea and Fire Insurance Co of Batavia* (1888) 14 App Cas 83; *Murfitt v Royal Insurance Co Ltd* (1922) 38 TLR 334.
10 But for marine insurances, see the Marine Insurance Act 1745.

made without interest. The 1774 Act, however, altered the position and thenceforth rendered 'null and void to all intents and purposes whatsoever' all insurances effected on lives or other events wherein the person for whose benefit or on whose account the policy has been effected, has no interest.[11] Such purported insurances, being in substance wagering and gambling agreements, have thus been rendered unenforceable at law, and it is for this reason that the Act's common title is rather misleading and is therefore often referred to as the Gambling Act 1774.

It was this effect of the 1774 Act that gave rise to Channell J's inclusion of the ingredient of the insured having an interest in the subject matter of the insurance. The Act's requirement for an insurable interest overrides any provision in an insurance contract that purports to make the policy incontestable,[12] and 'Anybody who sues on a policy can only sue in respect of his own interest unless by special provisions, the law allowing it, the policy is made for the sake of another, or unless some statute says the policy shall enure for the benefit of somebody else.'[13]

What, then, constitutes a legally recognised insurable interest? The classic definition was given by Lawrence J in *Lucena v Crauford*:[14]

> A man is interested in a thing to whom advantage may arise or prejudice happen from the circumstances which may attend it . . . and whom it importeth that its condition as to safety or other quality should continue: interest does not necessarily imply a right to the whole or a part of a thing, nor necessarily and exclusively that which may be the subject of privation, but the having some relation to, or concern in the subject of the insurance, which relation or concern by the happening of the perils insured against may be so affected as to produce a damage, detriment, or prejudice to the person insuring; and where a man is so circumstanced with respect to matters exposed to certain risks or damages, or to have a moral certainty of advantage or benefit, but for those risks or dangers, he may be said to be interested in the safety of the thing.

In professional negligence insurance the subject matter of the insurance is legal costs and damages awarded to an aggrieved party against the insured professional. This clearly envisages that the happening of this peril will 'produce a damage, detriment, or prejudice to the person insuring', and is therefore an insurable interest, and in this case the interest is a straightforward pecuniary interest.

In all indemnity insurances, the insurer undertakes to indemnify the insured against pecuniary loss caused by or occasioned by a

---

11 Life Assurance Act 1774, s. 1.
12 *Anctil v Manufacturers Life Insurance Co* [1899] AC 604, PC.
13 Per Phillimore J in *Cosford Union v Poor Law and Local Government Officers' Mutual Guarantee Assn Ltd* (1910) 103 LT 463 at 465.
14 (1806) 2 Bos & PNR 269 at 302, HL.

particular defined risk. With regard to insurances covering professional negligence risks, the purpose of the indemnity is to enable the insured to recoup his loss arising from his negligent act, error or omission, and he may only recover to the extent of this interest. This is self-evident, but may also be supported by the words of Devlin J (as he then was) in a case involving an accountant's professional negligence policy:[15]

> The essence of the main indemnity clause − as indeed of any indemnity clause − is that the assured must prove a loss. The assured cannot recover anything under the main indemnity clause or make any claim against the underwriters until they have been found liable and so sustained a loss. If judgment were given against them for the sum claimed, they would undoubtedly have sustained a loss.

Under the basic indemnity clause, then, it can be seen that no claim on the insurance is strictly valid until judgment is entered against the insured. Most professional indemnity policies, however, contain what is known as a 'QC clause' which widens the scope of the policy and provides additional cover (see chapter 4, below).

The parties to the insurance contract

The insured

Throughout English contract law any individual or legal body may enter into a valid contract, subject only to a few limitations upon their contractual capacity. Insurance contracts are likewise bound by the common law rules with the additional requirement of insurable interest discussed above.

Insurers who grant policies to minors i.e. persons under eighteen years of age,[16] will be liable for the losses, but, for his part, the minor will only be bound by his obligations if the contract is for his benefit as a whole,[17] which it probably will not be if the premium absorbs nearly all of his income.[18]

Where the insured was drunk at the time of the making of the contract of insurance, he may be granted relief from enforcement of the contract if he can show that his condition was known to the other e.g. the insurer's agent,[19] and provided he has not ratified the contract after becoming sober.[20]

Where an insured is sued to perform his obligations under the insurance contract e.g. pay the premium, he may set up a defence

---

15 *West Wake Price & Co v Ching* [1957] 1 WLR 45 at 49.
16 Family Law Reform Act 1969, s. 1.
17 *Clements v London and North Western Rly Co* [1894] 2 QB 482, CA.
18 *Imperial Life Insurance Co v Charlebois* (1902) 22 CLT 417.
19 *Imperial Life Assurance Co of Canada v Audett* (1912) 1 WWR 819.
20 *Matthews v Baxter* (1873) LR 8 Exch 132.

that he was insane or of unsound mind when the contract was made. He must, however, in order to succeed in this defence, show that at the time of the contract his condition was known to the insurer or the insurer's agent.[1]

For the capacity of a partner to bind his partners, see chapter 1.

The insurer

The carrying on of all insurance business in the United Kingdom is regulated by the Insurance Companies Acts 1974 and 1981, but basically it can be said that a policy of insurance may be under-written by an individual, or by a company formed in compliance with the companies legislation.

The capacity of an insurance company to enter into insurance contracts is dependent upon:

(a) The terms of its memorandum of association or other instrument constituting it.

Any insurance policy not authorised by such terms is *ultra vires* and cannot be enforced by the company against the insured,[2] and the insured can only enforce the policy if he acted in good faith and the policy was decided upon by the directors of the insurance company.[3]

(b) Authorisation by the Secretary of State to carry on insurance business of the specified class or classes.[4]

With regard to professional indemnity insurance, the relevant authorisation must be for General Business (as against Long Term Business e.g. life assurance) of the 'General liability' class.[5] Applications for authorisation may be submitted by insurance companies based anywhere in the world, but different considerations will apply depending upon whether the head office is in the United Kingdom, in a member state of the EEC, or elsewhere.[6] Once authorised, the insurance company is regulated by a statutory regime regarding its accounts, its solvency and the conduct of its insurance business.[7] The Secretary of State has extensive powers of intervention where, for instance, he considers that the company may be unable to meet its liabilities, he may 'take such action as appears to him to be appropriate for the purpose of protecting policyholders or potential

1 *Imperial Loan Co Ltd v Stone* [1892] 1 QB 599, CA.
2 *Joseph v Law Integrity Insurance Co Ltd* [1912] 2 Ch 581, CA, following *Flood v Irish Provident Assurance Co Ltd and Hibernian Bank Ltd* (1910) 46 ILT 214, CA (Ireland).
3 European Communities Act 1972, s. 9(1).
4 Insurance Companies Act 1981, s. 2(1).
5 Ibid, Sch 2, Part I, class no. 13.
6 Ibid, ss. 7, 8 and 9.
7 See Insurance Companies Act 1974, Parts II and III (as amended by the Insurance Companies Act 1981, Sch 5, Part I).

policyholders of the company'. Other powers of intervention give the Secretary of State power to impose the following requirements in relation to authorised insurance companies:[8]

(a) restrictions on new business;
(b) requirements about investments;
(c) maintenance of assets in the United Kingdom;
(d) custody of assets;
(e) limitation of premium income;
(f) actuarial investigations;
(g) acceleration of information required by accounting provisions;
(h) information and production of documents.

So far as liability insurances are concerned, only an individual who is a member of Lloyd's may carry on general insurance business without authorisation by the Secretary of State for Trade,[9] and all members of Lloyd's must comply with certain requirements contained in the Insurance Company Acts 1974 and 1981. For instance, Lloyd's underwriters must carry all insurance premiums they receive to a trust fund which has been approved by the Secretary of State, and they must have their accounts audited annually.[10]

As a general introduction to the business at Lloyd's it may be said that underwriting members of Lloyd's combine together in varying numbers (from two to several hundred) to form syndicates, each with its own managing agent. This managing agent appoints one member, or 'name' as they are known, to be the 'active' underwriter on behalf of the names in the syndicate. He then conducts insurance business in his 'box' in the underwriting room at Lloyd's. Within the syndicate the agreement is that each name will bear a definite proportion of the risk accepted by the active underwriter on behalf of the syndicate.

A Lloyd's policy may be underwritten by one or more syndicates, but each name is liable solely for his own subscription to the policy, and not for sums underwritten by his fellow names in the syndicate.[11] The policy is, therefore, in effect, not one contract but a number of separate contracts between names (Lloyd's underwriters) and the insured. One name, however, may bring representative proceedings or sue on the policy without the need to join the other names.[12]

The Corporation of Lloyd's is under no legal liability to make good sums defaulted upon by one or more of its underwriting

---

8 Ibid, ss. 28–37.
9 Insurance Companies Act 1981, s. 2(2).
10 See Insurance Companies Act 1974, s. 73 (as amended by Insurance Companies Act 1981, Sch 5, Part I).
11 *Tyser v Shipowners' Syndicate (Reassured)* [1896] 1 QB 135; *Rozannes v Bowen* (1928) 32 Ll L Rep 98 at 101, CA.
12 *Scott v Tuff-Kote (Australia) Pty Ltd* [1976] 2 Lloyd's Rep 103, NSW Sup Ct.

members under any policy,[13] although in practice a voluntary fund is maintained.

A person seeking a Lloyd's policy may only place the risk in 'the Room' through the agency of a Lloyd's broker.[14] Such brokers must meet certain requirements and have been approved by the Committee of Lloyd's to gain this exclusive right of direct access to Lloyd's underwriters in their 'boxes'. It will often be the case that the person's own insurance brokers are not Lloyd's brokers, and in these instances the insurance broker will gain the agency of a Lloyd's broker to place the risk in Lloyd's.

Using accepted abbreviations to condense the details of the risk to be insured on to one or two sheets of paper, known as a 'slip', the Lloyd's broker will seek out one or more syndicates who are willing to subscribe to the policy upon negotiated terms and proportions. Once the syndicate's 'active' underwriter has initialled the slip, he binds all the members or names of his syndicate, upon the agreed terms and proportions.[15] When the slip has been fully subscribed, the Lloyd's Policy Signing Office (LPSO) executes a policy in conformity with the slip, on behalf of the contracting syndicates. The effect of the issue of the policy from the LPSO is that each member of each syndicate is bound as if he had personally signed it.[16]

Within the professional indemnity insurance market, there are what are known as 'Master Policy' schemes, whereby the underwriting company or Lloyd's syndicate will empower a broker to issue cover directly to the applicant on its behalf. The issued policy is usually known as a 'Certificate of Insurance', and will bear the substance of the terms and conditions of the Master Policy on its reverse side. These 'Certificates', however, will only be issued by the broker upon the standard terms and rates of premium of the Master Policy, any proposed variations upon these will have to be referred back to the underwriters. Where the Master Policy emanates from members of Lloyd's, it will, of course, have passed through the LPSO.

The offer for insurance

It is not true to say that it is the person seeking insurance who will always be the party making the offer for a contract of insurance, it may, in a particular instance, be the insurer.

---

13 *Industrial Guarantee Corpn Ltd v Corpn of Lloyd's* (1924) 19 Ll L Rep 78.
14 *Julien Praet & Cie SA v H G Poland Ltd* [1960] 1 Lloyd's Rep 416 at 433, per Pearson J.
15 *Thompson v Adams* (1889) 23 QBD 361.
16 *Eagle Star Insurance Co Ltd v Spratt* [1971] 2 Lloyd's Rep 116 at 124, per Lord Denning MR.

An offer for insurance must be capable of acceptance by the other party. To be capable of acceptance, the offer must be complete in all material respects regarding details of the risk, duration of the risk, the amount and subject matter of the insurance, the rate of premium to be charged, and the terms and conditions attaching to the insurance cover. Without these material terms having been agreed between the parties, the offer will be incomplete and thus incapable of acceptance.[17]

In the usual course of events there will be negotiations between the insurer and the person seeking the insurance cover (or his insurance broker), these discussions having been initiated by either party. For instance, an architect may have been sent a leaflet advertising facilities for professional negligence insurance by an insurer (or broker acting as insurer's agent) and he makes inquiries as a result of this prompt. It is not unknown for brokers to advertise the availability of professional indemnity insurance in professional journals. Alternatively, he may have gone to his own broker and, through him, initiated inquiries concerning the availability and terms of such insurance from one or more insurers. These insurers may, in turn, submit variations in material terms of the insurance, and these variations will, in law, constitute counter-offers.[18] The final, complete offer of insurance, then, may, equally easily, in fact be made by the proposer or the insurer following protracted negotiations.

With regard to the duration of the risk, in liability insurances generally, it is the normal practice to issue insurance policies for one year only, and professional indemnity insurances are no exception to this practice of annual contracts. A new contract of insurance will have to be entered into at the end of each twelve month period of cover.

The rate of premium to be charged by insurers to cover the risk is obviously an essential term of the proposed contract of insurance, and no offer can be complete without either the actual premium being ascertained, or, at least, a certain arrangement for determining the premium having been defined between the parties.[19] Hence, where cover is needed urgently, it may be granted by insurers 'at a rate to be agreed' ('t.b.a.'), but this is not a common practice in professional negligence insurance.

The amount of the insurance must also be certain, and, as in the case of other liability insurances, will be an indemnity of the insured's pecuniary loss up to a specified limit. In professional indemnity insurances, this limit may be defined in either of two ways. There may be a limited sum specified as applying to the aggregate of all

17 *Allis-Chalmers Co v Maryland Fidelity and Deposit Co* (1916) 114 LT 433, HL.
18 *Canning v Farquhar* (1886) 16 QBD 727, CA.
19 *Hyderabad (Deccan) Co v Willoughby* [1899] 2 QB 530.

claims made during the year of insurance (e.g. £1m limit payable on the policy on all claims during the year) or may be a maximum sum to be applied to each and every claim made under the policy during its operation (e.g. £ $\frac{1}{2}$ m limit on each and every claim made in the year of insurance).

The subject matter of professional negligence policies will, needless to say, primarily be the pecuniary loss suffered by the insured professional person by reason of a judgment for legal damages and costs being awarded against him, by virtue of a negligent act, error or omission committed in the conduct of his professional practice. There may well be, however, additional risks forming parts of the whole subject matter of the insurance. This must be determined in the offer, e.g. cover for libel and slander, for the offer to be completely constituted.

As regards the terms and conditions of the insurance other than those described above, a court will not necessarily require these to be defined in the offer in order to hold that a valid contract for insurance can be concluded, upon acceptance of the offer. Where, for instance, a proposer has filled in and signed a proposal form of a particular insurer, and has forwarded the proposal to that insurer, the court will readily infer that the proposer's offer was for insurance on the usual, or standard, terms of cover issued by that insurer for that type of insurance. Indeed, a court may go so far as to hold that a completed and signed proposal constitutes a complete offer even where no premium has been specifically determined in the offer, on the ground that the proposer impliedly has accepted that the usual, or standard, premium for that insurance will apply.[20] This may particularly be held to be the case where a professional man sends a completed and signed proposal form, applicable to a particular professional indemnity 'scheme' cover, back to the scheme insurers.

A few last remarks about the offer of insurance concern the revocation of the offer. As in general contract law, the offeror for insurance (be he proposer or insurer) may withdraw or revoke his offer at any time before it is accepted. This will render the offer incapable of acceptance by the party to whom the offer is made.[1] Even if not withdrawn by a positive act, the offer will only remain open for acceptance until either a time specified in the offer, or, otherwise, for a reasonable time since it was made.[2] To be operative, a withdrawal of offer must be communicated by the offeror to the offeree prior to any valid acceptance by him of the offer.[3] This rule

20 *General Accident Insurance Corpn v Cronk* (1901) 17 TLR 233.
 1 *Dickinson v Dodds* (1876) 2 Ch D 463, CA.
 2 *Ramsgate Victoria Hotel Co v Montefiore* (1866) LR 1 Exch 109.
 3 *Byrne v Van Tienhoven* (1880) 5 CPD 344.

has a particular effect upon notices of withdrawal made by post – the withdrawal does not operate from the time of posting, but only from when the offeree's mind has been brought to it.[4]

Acceptance of the offer

As explained above, the offer may, upon the facts of a particular case, actually be made by either party negotiating for a contract of insurance. It follows, naturally, that the acceptance may flow from either the proposer or the insurer depending upon the circumstances.

The first governing principle of acceptance is that an offer can only be accepted by a party to whom the offer is made.[5] Secondly, the offeree must accept the offer unqualifiably in every material regard. Thirdly, the offeree must communicate his acceptance to the offeror.

A conditional or qualified acceptance will only operate as a counter-offer, which will not conclude the contract of insurance.[6]

Communication of the acceptance to the person making the offer is an important aspect. There must be something said or something done by the person to whom the offer is made, to signify his acceptance of the offer and so conclude a binding contract. Mere silence or non-communication does not denote acceptance.[7] An acceptance must be brought to the notice of the offeror, and an attempted oral acceptance is not communicated if it is 'drowned by an aircraft flying overhead', or if the attempted acceptance is spoken into a telephone or sent on a teleprinter after the line has failed. On the other hand, if the offeror does not 'catch' the telephone acceptance, or the ink on the offeror's teleprinter fails, the acceptance is communicated.[8]

The situation is rather different, however, where the offeror either authorises or specifies acceptance by post. In these circumstances, acceptance will be held to have been validly communicated once a properly addressed letter of acceptance has been posted, even if it is never received by the offeror.[9] Furthermore, a court will presume that an offer made through the post may be accepted by post, unless the offeror exclusively specifies some different mode of acceptance, and also that where acceptance by post may reasonably be considered

4 *Henthorn v Fraser* [1892] 2 Ch 27, CA.
5 *Carlill v Carbolic Smoke Ball Co* [1893] 1 QB 256, CA.
6 *Re Yager and Guardian Assurance Co* (1912) 108 LT 38.
7 *Felthouse v Bindley* (1862) 11 CBNS 869, affd (1863) 1 New Rep 401; *Powell v Lee* (1908) 99 LT 284.
8 *Entores v Miles Far East Corpn* [1955] 2 QB 327 at 333, CA, per Denning LJ, obiter.
9 *Dunlop v Higgins* (1848) 1 HL Cas 381.

to have been within the contemplation of the parties, this mode of acceptance may be used.[10]

Where the offer is made by the proposer, there are five main ways by which the insurer may signify his acceptance:

(i) *By a formal acceptance*

An unqualified and unconditional acceptance of the offer terms concludes a binding contract of insurance. Thereby, the insurers are bound to issue, and the proposer to accept, a policy that accords in every way with the offer.[11]

(ii) *By the issue of a policy*

The issue of a policy will be regarded as conclusive evidence that the insurers have accepted the proposal. Where a policy is valid only when executed by the company seal, the acceptance is completed by the execution of the policy,[12] and it is immaterial that the policy is retained by the insurers.[13]

(iii) *By initialling a 'slip'*

As previously discussed the initialling of a 'slip' by underwriting members of Lloyd's, or an insurance company, which is subscribed to one hundred per cent of the risk, operates as a binding acceptance of the proposal from which the underwriters cannot resile,[14] although there is some doubt of the legal status of a partially subscribed 'slip'.

(iv) *By acceptance of the premium*

Where the insurers have received and retained the premium for the insurance, but have not otherwise communicated an acceptance of the offer contained in the proposal, a presumption may be raised, in the absence of contrary evidence, that the insurers have made an acceptance by their act of retention of the premium.[15] Consequently, the insurers will be liable for a loss within the terms of the insurance contracted.

(v) *By the conduct of the insurer*

Even where no premium has been paid by the proposer, nor any policy of insurance issued, the facts may lead a court to find an

10 *Household Fire and Carriage Accident Insurance Co Ltd v Grant* (1879) 4 Ex D 216, CA.
11 *Solvency Mutual Guarantee Co v Freeman* (1861) 7 H & N 17; *Adie & Sons v Insurances Corpn Ltd* (1898) 14 TLR 544.
12 *M'Elroy v London Assurance Corpn* (1897) 24 R (Ct of Sess) 287 at 290, per Lord Maclaren.
13 *Xenos v Wickham* (1866) LR 2 HL 296.
14 *Thompson v Adams* (1889) 23 QBD 361; *Jaglon v Excess Insurance Co Ltd* [1972] QB 250; *General Reinsurance Corpn v Forsakringsaktiebolaget Fennia Patria* (1981) Times 31 October.
15 *Mead v Davison* (1835) 3 Ad & El 303; *Canning v Farquhar* (1886) 16 QBD 727, CA.

acceptance of the proposal, and therefore a binding contract of insurance. For instance, a demand for payment of the premium will conclude the contract,[16] subject to any special term of the insurance that the policy is only to operate from the date of receipt of the premium, prior to which time the insurers will not be 'on risk'.

Where the offer is made by the insurer, the proposer may accept the offer verbally or in writing, or by his insurance broker. In practice, insurers usually insist upon receiving a completed and signed proposal form, together with the proposer's formal agreement to pay the premium.

The question of unqualified acceptance of the offer is considered in the next heading.

Agreement

The communication of a purported acceptance of an offer of insurance will not conclude a binding contract unless the acceptance corresponds with all the terms of the offer to which it relates.

An acceptance must correspond with the offer in the following sense; the acceptance must be without any material variation in terms, and must be unconditional, otherwise it will not be regarded as a valid acceptance in law, but as a counter-proposal or counter-offer.[17] A distinction must be drawn here between a departure from the terms of the offer, and the mere expression of the same terms in different words, or the expression of a term which if unexpressed would have been implied. Therefore, a contract of insurance may still be completed upon the issue of a policy containing terms or conditions not previously alluded to by either party, provided the issued policy contained nothing other than the insurer's ordinary or standard terms and conditions. This is because the proposer will be deemed to be contracting on these standard terms and conditions without a contrary intention being expressed during negotiations.[18]

If the acceptance does not accord in every material respect with the offer, the parties are at cross-purposes in reality, and any premiums paid in the mistaken belief that a binding contract of insurance was in operation are recoverable by the proposer in an action for money had and received to the insurer's use. An illustration of this would be the completion of a proposal form by a professional person for a policy of professional indemnity insurance including legal defence and libel and slander extensions, and, without more, the insurers issue to him a bare professional indemnity policy without these extensions, and the proposing professional pays the premium requested in

16 *Xenos v Wickham* (1866) LR 2 HL 296 at 308, per Pigott B.
17 *Canning v Farquhar* (1886) 16 QBD 727, CA.
18 *General Accident Insurance Corpn v Cronk* (1901) 17 TLR 233.

the covering letter. In these circumstances the proposer may be able to obtain repayment of the premium paid,[19] provided the payment of the premium was not, in fact, an acceptance by the proposer of the tendered policy which was a counter-offer. This latter aspect can cause difficulties.

What if the proposer receives the policy and, upon a cursory examination, it appears to be an acceptance of his completed proposal form but is, in fact, a counter-proposal as would appear if the policy was read carefully? Would the retention of the policy and the payment of premium upon it be regarded as an acceptance by him of the insurer's counter-offer?

The answer is that these acts would be viewed as an acceptance of the counter-offer if:[20]

(a) the proposer is able to read; and

(b) he has had ample opportunity to scrutinise the policy; and

(c) he could reasonably be expected to discover the variations upon a careful examination of the policy.

The view has been expressed, however, that it would be otherwise if the proposer were led by the insurer's agent, or by a letter accompanying the policy, to believe that the policy did contain terms corresponding with his offer, so that he need not trouble to read it.[1]

The above comments are, of course, only relevant to a situation where a completed proposal form has been sent to the insurer by the proposer and he receives back a purported acceptance by means of the issue of a policy. Where the contract of insurance has already been concluded by reason of, for example, a formal letter of acceptance from the insurer, the issue of the policy will not be an acceptance of the proposal, but rather an act in performance of the previously concluded contract of insurance. This distinction is very important, for in the latter circumstance the proposer is entitled to have any discrepancy between the issued policy and the agreed terms of the contract rectified, by the court if necessary,[2] and the insurer is still entitled to call for payment of the premium under the concluded insurance contract.[3]

The court's role in rectification of a policy issued in purported performance of a concluded contract of insurance has been explained by Bankes LJ:[4]

19 See *Johnston v Prudential Assurance Co* [1946] IAC Rep (1938–49) 59.
20 *Provident Savings Life Assurance Society v Mowat* (1902) 32 SCR 147, Can SC.
1 Ibid at 160, per Taschereau J.
2 *Fowler v Scottish Equitable Life Insurance Society and Ritchie* (1858) 28 LJ Ch 225.
3 *Solvency Mutual Guarantee Co v Freeman* (1861) 7 H & N 17.
4 A *Gagniere & Co Ltd v Eastern Co of Warehouses Insurance* (1921) 8 Ll L Rep 365 at 366–367, CA.

[Counsel] says it is not a correct view to suggest that it is a mutual mistake that has to be established. I view that contention with considerable sympathy. It seems to me much more accurate to say that if you prove the parties have come to a definite parol (verbal) agreement, and you then afterwards find in the document which was intended to carry out that definite agreement that something other than that definite agreement has been inserted, then it is right to rectify the document in order that it may carry out the real agreement between these parties . . . [with] that which it is sought to insert in the document instead of the agreement which appears there . . .

Finally, in this section concerning agreement between the parties, attention must be drawn to the well-established principle of law that one party to a contract will be estopped from pleading that in his own mind he was not in agreement with the other party, and so did not accept the offer put forward by that party, if his conduct, viewed objectively, is that of a man who in fact did conclude a contract.[5] This doctrine is known as the requirement for *consensus ad idem* (agreement upon the matter) to form a valid contract. The clearest example of a party being estopped by his conduct from denying that full agreement has been reached is where he signs a contractual document. Thus, where a proposer completes and signs a proposal form for an insurance that has been accurately explained to him, but does not care to read the proposal carefully, he is bound to accept the policy issued pursuant to this accepted proposal. He will not be able to plead that a mistake on his part as to the nature of the contract avoids the insurance or rendered the proposal incapable of acceptance, i.e. make a plea of *non est factum*, for on the objective test of his conduct, he meant to be bound by the document to which he appended his signature.[6]

The basis of the doctrine of estoppel has long been that where someone, by his words or conduct, wilfully causes another to believe in the existence of a certain state of things, and induces him to act on that belief, or to alter his own previous position, the former is precluded from averring against the latter a different state of things as existing at the same time.[7] Furthermore, a party who negligently or culpably stands by, and allows another to contract on the faith of a fact he cannot contradict, cannot afterwards dispute that fact in an action against the party whom he has himself assisted in deceiving.[8]

Payment of the premium

The premium is the price for which the insurer undertakes to pay the sum insured upon the occurrence of the insured event. In contract

5 See *Provident Savings Life Assurance Society v Mowat* (1902) 32 SCR 147, Can SC, where many authorities are cited.
6 *Gardner v Hearts of Oak Assurance* [1928] IAC Rep 21.
7 *Pickard v Sears* (1837) 6 Ad & El 469.
8 *Gregg v Wells* (1839) 10 Ad & El 90.

law, the term consideration is used rather than price, and any consideration sufficient to support a simple contract may constitute the premium in a contract of insurance,[9] e.g. a promise to pay a premium.

The amount of the premium is purely a matter decided upon by negotiation between the parties to the contract, and, although the consideration for the contract may be something other than money, it is normal practice for the premium to be payable in money to the insurer or his authorised agent. The obligation upon the insured is prima facie to pay cash,[10] but the insurer may accept a cheque, promissory note or bill of exchange in whole or part payment of the premium. In these latter circumstances, the question arises as to whether the insurer has accepted that mode of payment absolutely, or conditionally upon the document being honoured when presented on its due date. This issue is one for a jury at trial of the action,[11] but there will be a presumption of absolute acceptance if the insurer has accepted payment by negotiable instrument for his own convenience.[12]

Insurers are not, then, bound to accept a cheque in payment of a due premium,[13] unless they have expressly or impliedly authorised that mode of payment. For example, if an insurer writes to the insured and asks the insured 'when remitting' to enclose the invoice, the insurer will be understood to have impliedly authorised the insured to pay them by sending the money through the post in the ordinary ways in which money is remitted by post i.e. not in cash unless a small amount.[14] A previous course of dealing between the insured and the insurer may also give rise to a presumption of authorisation of payment by cheque or other negotiable instrument.

Insurers may also, expressly or impliedly, authorise payment of the premium by instalments, and this is not uncommon where professional indemnity insurance is concerned, due to the large size of some premiums, without which arrangement a heavy burden might be placed upon the professional practice's cash flow.

Premiums are also often paid to agents authorised by the insurer to receive payments of premiums on his behalf. In these cases, payment in a form other than cash will not bind the insurer, unless that mode has been authorised by the insurer, until the agent has in fact received payment in cash. Moreover, an arrangement whereby the

9 See *Prudential Insurance Co v IRC* [1904] 2 KB 658, especially at 663.
10 *London and Lancashire Life Assurance Co v Fleming* [1897] AC 499 at 507, PC.
11 *Goldshede v Cottrell* (1836) 2 M & W 20.
12 *Anderson v Hillies* (1852) 12 CB 499.
13 *Bridges v Garrett* (1870) LR 5 CP 451.
14 *Mitchell-Henry v Norwich Union Life Insurance Society Ltd* [1918] 2 KB 67, CA.

agent gives the insured credit is not effective unless payment by an authorised mode is made during the days of grace.[15]

An insurance intermediary may agree to advance his client the money for the premium and pay it to the insurer on behalf of the insured, and, under such an arrangement, the insurer will be bound when he receives such payment, even by way of settlement of accounts between the insurer and that insurance intermediary.[16] The insured, however, must have an actual agreement to this effect with his broker or agent, in order to benefit from that mode of payment of the due premium, otherwise the intermediary will be acting outside the scope of his authority to conclude a contract on behalf of the insured.[17]

As already explained, the contract for insurance may be concluded by the parties without a requirement that the premium shall first be paid, but rather that the insured undertakes that he will pay the agreed premium. In these circumstances, the insurer is on risk from the agreed commencement of the policy, and if the insured event occurs thereafter, the insurer will be liable under the policy, notwithstanding that he has not yet received the premium from the insured. It will not matter whether the contract of insurance was completed by the initialling of a fully subscribed 'slip' at Lloyd's,[18] or by the issue of a policy by an insurance company.[19]

Often, though, insurers make it a condition precedent to the attachment of liability under the policy, that the premium has been paid, or even a condition subsequent that the policy can be avoided by the insurers if the premium is not paid within the specified period.[20] Such a condition may be stipulated in the policy,[1] in a letter of acceptance of the insured's proposal,[2] or by some other means. The courts will enforce this contractual condition,[3] unless the insurer has waived compliance with the condition upon a first premium or any renewal premium.[4]

A policy may require prepayment of the premium and, contrary to the true situation, also recite receipt of it, but this alone will not be construed by the court to be a waiver of the condition,[5] other than in a policy made by deed where the doctrine of estoppel will apply.[6]

15 *Acey v Fernie* (1840) 7 M & W 151.
16 Ibid at 155, per Lord Abinger CB.
17 Ibid at 155, per Parke B.
18 *Thompson v Adams* (1889) 23 QBD 361.
19 *Roberts v Security Co Ltd* [1897] 1 QB 111, CA.
20 *Bamberger v Commercial Credit Mutual Assurance Society* (1855) 15 CB 676.
 1 *Roberts v Security Co Ltd* [1897] 1 QB 111, CA.
 2 *Looker v Law Union and Rock Insurance Co Ltd* [1928] 1 KB 554.
 3 *Phoenix Life Assurance Co v Sheridan* (1860) 8 HL Cas 745.
 4 *Equitable Fire and Accident Office Ltd v Ching Wo Hong* [1907] AC 96, PC.
 5 Ibid at 100.
 6 *Roberts v Security Co Ltd* [1897] 1 QB 111, CA.

The principle of *uberrima fides*

> There is no class of documents as to which the strictest good faith is more rigidly required in courts of law than policies of assurance.[7]

This fundamental principle of insurance law that each party to an insurance contract must observe the utmost good faith – *uberrima fides* – has been applied for hundreds of years, and if it is not observed by one of the parties, the contract of insurance may be avoided by the other party.

The principle has been explained in many learned judgments. In 1766, Lord Mansfield uttered the following:[8]

> The special facts, upon which the contingent chance is to be computed, lie more commonly in the knowledge of the insured only: the underwriter trusts to his representation, and proceeds upon confidence that he does not keep back any circumstance in his knowledge, to mislead the underwriter into a belief that the circumstance does not exist, and to induce him to estimate the risk as if it did not exist. The keeping back of such a circumstance is a fraud, and therefore the policy is void. Although the suppression should happen through mistake, without any fraudulent intention; yet still the underwriter is deceived, and the policy is void; because the risk run is really different from the risk understood and intended to be run at the time of the agreement . . . The governing principle is applicable to all contracts and dealings. Good faith forbids either party by concealing what he privately knows, to draw the other into a bargain, from his ignorance of that fact, and his believing the contrary . . .

In 1879, Jessel MR said:

> The first question to be decided is, what is the principle on which the Court acts in setting aside contracts of insurance? As regards the general principle I am not prepared to lay down the law as making any difference in substance between one contract of assurance and another. Whether it is life, or fire, or marine assurance, I take it good faith is required in all cases, and though there may be certain circumstances from the peculiar nature of marine insurance which require to be disclosed, and which do not apply to other contracts of insurance, that is rather, in my opinion, an illustration of the application of the principle than a distinction in principle.[9]

And in 1928, Scrutton LJ observed:

> It has been for centuries in England the law in connection with insurance of all sorts, marine, fire, life, guarantee and every kind of policy, that, as the underwriter knows nothing and the man who comes to him to ask him to insure knows everything, it is the duty of the assured, the man who desires to have a policy, to make a full disclosure to the underwriters

---

7 *Mackenzie v Coulson* (1869) LR 8 Eq 368 at 375, per James V-C.
8 *Carter v Boehm* (1766) 3 Burr 1905 at 1909.
9 *London Assurance v Mansel* (1879) 11 Ch D 363 at 367.

without being asked of all the material circumstances, because the under-writer knows nothing and the assured knows everything. That is expressed by saying that it is a contract of the utmost good faith – *uberrima fides*.[10]

This duty of the utmost good faith is, then, cast upon both the parties to the insurance contract, and all representations made by them during negotiations to induce the other party to conclude a contract of insurance must be true. Thus, the insurer must correctly represent the period the risk will be covered,[11] and the proposer must not only be completely honest, but also must make full disclosure of all facts material to the insurance.

The question of materiality of particular facts is considered in the next section.

Non-disclosure and misrepresentation

In the English law of contract, the general rule is that a contracting party is under no duty to disclose material facts known to him but not to the other party: there is no duty of good faith on the parties when they enter into a contract.[12] Contracts of insurance, though, are an exception to this general rule, and it has recently been said that: 'Full disclosure is of the very essence . . .' of a contract of insurance.[13] This means that the insurer should be informed of every material circumstance within the knowledge of the proposer, the proper question being whether the particular circumstance was in fact material, not whether the proposer believed it to be so.[14]

> In cases of insurance a party is required not only to state all matters within his knowledge, which he believes to be material to the question of the insurance, but all which in point of fact are so. If he conceals anything that may influence the rate of premium which the underwriter may require, although he does not know it would have that effect, such concealment entirely vitiates the policy.[15]

And in the Court of Appeal it has been observed that:

> No class of case occurs to my mind in which our law regards mere non-disclosure as invalidating the contract, except in the case of insurance. That is an exception which the law has wisely made in deference to the plain exigencies of this particular and most important class of trans-actions. The person seeking to insure may fairly be presumed to know all

10 *Rozanes v Bowen* (1928) 32 Ll L Rep 98 at 102.
11 *Duffel v Wilson* (1808) 1 Camp 401.
12 *Keates v Cadogan* (1851) 10 CB 591; *Fletcher v Krell* (1873) 42 LJQB 55.
13 *Lee v British Law Insurance Co* [1972] 2 Lloyd's Rep 49 at 57, CA, per Karminski LJ.
14 *Lindeneau v Desborough* (1828) 8 B & C 586 at 592, per Bayley J.
15 *Dalglish v Jarvie* (1850) 2 Mac & G 231 at 243, per Rolfe B.

the circumstances which materially affect the risk, and, generally, is, as to some of them, the only person who has the knowledge; the underwriter, whom he asks to take the risk, cannot, as a rule, know and but rarely has either the time or the opportunity to learn by enquiry, circumstances which are, or may be, most material to the formation of his judgment as to his acceptance or rejection of the risk, and as to the premium which he ought to require.[16]

What, then, is the test of materiality?

The rule in relation to marine insurance was established by 1832,[17] and was embodied in the Marine Insurance Act 1906. The Court of Appeal has recently affirmed that the rule is the same for non-marine risks as for marine risks,[18] and this decision has since been followed.[19]

Section 18 of the Marine Insurance Act 1906 provides:

(1) The assured must disclose to the insurer, before the contract is concluded, every material circumstance which is known to the assured, and the assured is deemed to know every circumstance which, in the ordinary course of business, ought to be known by him. If the assured fails to make such disclosure, the insurer may avoid the contract.

(2) Every circumstance is material which would influence the judgment of a prudent insurer, in fixing the premium, or determining whether he will take the risk.

It has been emphasised in a recent case that the test is whether the insurer can show that the fact which was not disclosed *would* have affected the judgment of a prudent insurer, and not merely that it *might* possibly have done so.[20] A line of authority[1] that the test was whether a reasonable man, in the position of the assured and with the knowledge of the facts in dispute ought to have realised that they were material to the risk, has now, therefore, been overruled.

In non-marine insurances, the proposer is usually asked to complete and sign a proposal form containing a list of questions, and a court will presume that all such questions refer to material facts,[2] but other facts will not become immaterial simply because no question

---

16 *London General Omnibus Co Ltd v Holloway* [1912] 2 KB 72 at 85, CA, per Kennedy LJ.
17 *Elton v Larkins* (1832) 5 Car & P 385.
18 *Lambert v Co-Operative Insurance Society Ltd* [1975] 2 Lloyd's Rep 485, CA.
19 *Woolcott v Sun Alliance and London Insurance Ltd* [1978] 1 All ER 1253, [1978] 1 WLR 493; and *Reynolds and Anderson v Phoenix Assurance Co Ltd* [1978] 2 Lloyd's Rep 440.
20 *Reynolds and Anderson v Phoenix Assurance Co Ltd* [1978] 2 Lloyd's Rep 440 at 456–457.
1 See, for example, *Joel v Law Union and Crown Insurance Co* [1908] 2 KB 863, CA.
2 *Glicksman v Lancashire and General Assurance Co Ltd* [1927] AC 139 at 144, per Viscount Dunedin.

was asked about them. The general rule regarding the fact's influence upon the judgment of a prudent insurer in determining the premium, or influencing his decision to accept the risk, will still apply.

With reference to professional negligence insurance, the insurer's proposal form will generally contain questions concerning the following:

(a) Name and address(es) of proposer(s).
(b) Style or title of business or practice.
(c) Full addresses of all places of business or practice.
(d) Profession.
(e) Give qualifications, age and experience of all partners of the practice.
(f) How long has the business or practice been established, and how long has each partner been a principal?
(g) Give details of age and experience of all unqualified staff.
(h) Have any claims been made against any member of the practice or business, either in the present firm or a previous firm? If yes, please give details.
(i) Is any proposer aware of any circumstances that may give rise to a claim for negligence, error or omission? If yes, please give details.
(j) Give names of all previous insurers.
(k) Has any proposal for professional insurance in respect of any proposer hereto been declined or been made subject to special terms? If yes, please give details.

Despite the onerous nature of the duty of disclosure upon the insured, the situation is ameliorated somewhat by some seven categories of facts which need not be disclosed to the insurer:

1 *Facts within actual or presumed knowledge of insurer*
An insurer cannot insist that the policy is void because the insured did not tell him what he actually knew, no matter what way he came by that knowledge,[3] nor that he had abundant means of knowing from his previous knowledge coupled with the particulars given by the insured.[4]

2 *Facts outside actual or presumed knowledge of insured*
The insured can only be expected to disclose material facts which are within his actual knowledge or which he ought to have known in the ordinary course of his business.[5] Where the insured fails to make reasonable inquiries to discover a material fact, this will show a lack of

3 *Carter v Boehm* (1766) 3 Burr 1905 at 1910, per Lord Mansfield.
4 *Bates v Hewitt* (1867) LR 2 QB 595.
5 Marine Insurance Act 1906, s. 18(1).

uberrima fides on his part, even if unintentional, for he will have neglected his duty towards his insurer. What are reasonable enquiries will depend upon the circumstances of each case.[6]

3 Facts within constructive knowledge of the insurer
An insurer cannot plead non-disclosure if there has been reasonably sufficient disclosure by the insured, so that the insurer can see if he requires further information, which he can obtain either by asking the insured,[7] or by inquiry from an immediately available source.[8]

4 Facts as to which insurer waives information
Waiver of disclosure of material facts will not be inferred too readily, or else the obligation to disclose would be destroyed.[9] The test is whether a normally prudent insurer would have been put on inquiry as to some precise detail by reason of the information disclosed.[10]

5 Facts tending to diminish the risk
It has long been understood that an insurer does not need to be told of facts which lessen the risk agreed and understood to be accepted by the express terms of a contract of insurance. Thus, if an insurer insures for a period of a year, he need not be told of any circumstance to show that the risk will only run for six months.[11]

6 Spent convictions
The Rehabilitation of Offenders Act 1974 entitles a proposer for insurance to withhold from the insurer information about convictions that have become 'spent' after the expiry of the relevant 'rehabilitation period', which varies in length according to the seriousness of the sentence. Under section 4 of the Act, a spent conviction is to be treated 'for all purposes in law' as though it had never happened, and the person who has the spent conviction is to be treated as though he had not committed or been charged with the offence in question. Thus an insurer will not be able to avoid a contract of insurance on the grounds of non-disclosure of a spent conviction or the facts surrounding it.

---

6 *Australia and New Zealand Bank Ltd v Colonial and Eagle Wharves Ltd* [1960] 2 Lloyd's Rep 241.
7 *Freeland v Glover* (1806) 7 East 457.
8 *Foley v Tabor* (1861) 2 F & F 663 at 672, per Erle CJ.
9 *Greenhill v Federal Insurance Co Ltd* [1927] 1 KB 65 at 85, CA, per Scrutton LJ.
10 *Anglo-African Merchants Ltd v Bayley* [1969] 1 Lloyd's Rep 268 at 278, per Megaw J.
11 See *Carter v Boehm* (1766) 3 Burr 1905 at 1910, per Lord Mansfield.

7 Facts covered by or dispensed with by a warranty

Any circumstance which it is superfluous to disclose by reason of any express or implied warranty, need not be disclosed to the insurer,[12] for the insurer will be fully protected by the warranty.[13]

The duty of disclosure extends to agents of the insured utilised to conclude a contract of insurance on the insured's behalf. When such an agent or intermediary is brought into contact with an insurer, the latter transacts on the basis that he has disclosed every material circumstance within his personal knowledge, whether it be known to his principal or not.[14]

The duty to disclose material facts only applies up to the moment at which a binding contract of insurance is concluded,[15] and conditions precedent to the validity of the contract (e.g. a specification for payment of premium before insurer is on risk) are of great importance in the determination of the time the contract is concluded.

Professional negligence policies only subsist, in the main, for a period of one year, in common with other liability insurances, but will be renewable for a like period on the tender and acceptance of the appropriate renewal premium. Such renewal will be the conclusion of a new contract of insurance, so it follows that on renewal of a policy, the insured is obliged to disclose any change of circumstance or any occurrence material to the risk, which has happened since the making of the lapsing contract.[16] The renewal of the policy is impliedly made on the understanding that the statements in the original proposal are still accurate.[17]

Actual concealment by the insured of a fact he knows to be material to the risk is fraud, and the contract of insurance is voidable at the election of the insurer. The effect is the same, however, in the event of innocent non-disclosure by the insured;[18] once the insurer knows all the facts and has had a reasonable time in which to make up his mind, he must, once and for all, make his election whether to carry on with the contract or avoid it.[19] Thus, where an insurer learns that a fact has been concealed, or incompletely disclosed, and then accepts further premiums on the same policy, he loses his right to avoid it.[20]

12 Marine Insurance Act 1906, s. 18(3)(d).
13 *De Maurier (Jewels) Ltd v Bastion Insurance Co Ltd and Coronet Insurance Co Ltd* [1967] 2 Lloyd's Rep 550.
14 *Blackburn Low & Co v Vigors* (1887) 12 App Cas 531 at 541, per Lord Watson; *Blackburn Low & Co v Haslam* (1888) 21 QBD 144.
15 *Cory v Patton* (1872) LR 7 QB 304; *Lishman v Northern Maritime Insurance Co* (1875) LR 10 CP 179; *Canning v Farquhar* (1886) 16 QBD 727, CA.
16 *Re Wilson and Scottish Insurance Corpn Ltd* [1920] 2 Ch 28.
17 *Pim v Reid* (1843) 6 Man & G 1 at 25, per Cresswell J; *Looker v Law Union and Rock Insurance Co Ltd* [1928] 1 KB 554.
18 *Elton v Larkins* (1832) 5 C & P 86.
19 *Simon, Haynes, Barlas and Ireland v Beer* (1945) 78 Ll L Rep 337.
20 *Hemmings v Sceptre Life Assn Ltd* [1905] 1 Ch 365.

In a case concerning a solicitor's professional negligence policy,[1] it was held that improper dealing by the insured solicitor with his client's account was a circumstance material to the risk insured, and the facts should have been disclosed. The insurer had discovered the facts, but then held discussions with the insured concerning his liability. The court held that the insurer had not made his election to affirm or disaffirm the policy within a reasonable time, and so entitled the insured solicitor to act in the belief that the policy was being recognised as in force. The insurer's own solicitor suggested to the insured that the advice of a King's Counsel should be obtained, upon which advice the insured subsequently settled the claim based on the improper dealings. So acting to his detriment, the court held that the insurer was estopped from electing to disaffirm the indemnity policy.

Facts or statements material to the risk that do not become a matter of contract may also be misrepresented during negotiations and, here again, insurance law diverts from the general law of contract. Under the Misrepresentation Act 1967, the remedies of rescission and/or damages are made available to a party induced to enter into a contract by a fraudulent, innocent or negligent misrepresentation, and, although these remedies are open to insurers, equity regards such misrepresentations by an insured as a breach of the duty of utmost good faith:

> If there is information given, be it quite innocent, which is not a matter of contract, and never becomes a matter of contract, yet, nevertheless, if it is inaccurate, it can be used to avoid the policy or policies in question.[2]

This special rule of insurance law appears to be unaffected by the 1967 Act,[3] and really overlaps with the rules relating to non-disclosure.

Warranties and conditions

It is general practice for contracts of insurance to contain a number of conditions, both as to the existence or continuation of a certain state of affairs, and as to the performance or non-performance of some act by the insured.[4] Such stipulations or conditions are known in insurance law as 'warranties' and form a category of condition quite unlike warranties in the sense as understood in general contract

---

1 *Simon, Haynes, Barlas and Ireland v Beer* (1945) 78 Ll L Rep 337.
2 *Graham v Western Australian Insurance Co Ltd* (1931) 40 Ll L Rep 64 at 66, per Roche J.
3 See *Everett v Hogg, Robinson and Gardner Mountain (Insurance) Ltd* [1973] 2 Lloyd's Rep 217.
4 Marine Insurance Act 1906, s. 33(1).

law or in the Sale of Goods Act 1979. In insurance law, a 'warranty' is a term of the contract of insurance which must be strictly complied with and upon any breach of which, however minor, the insurer is entitled to repudiate the contract from the date of the breach of the warranty.[5]

Warranties may be incorporated into an insurance contract either expressly (e.g. 'the insured warrants . . .') or impliedly (e.g. by use of a phrase such as 'it is a condition precedent that . . .'), and breach will produce the same result irrespective of the mode of incorporation.

A breach of a warranty as to a past or present fact occurs at the commencement of the insured period, and therefore an insurer will be able to reject all claims under the policy for the contract will be avoided 'ab initio'. By contrast, a breach of a promissory warranty, or warranty of a continuing nature, which takes place during the currency of the policy will entitle the insurer to reject claims for losses occurring after the breach, but he will remain liable for losses occurring prior to the breach.

The ascertainment of warranties is not an easy matter, the situation being complicated by many insurers' indifferent use of the words 'warranty' and 'condition'. This causes additional confusion to an insured who is trying to construe his policy accurately in terms of truly fundamental terms (warranties), and other less important terms that do not relate to the very existence of the contract or the validity of claims made under the policy.

The difficulties encountered by insured persons in understanding the provisions of their policies receive judicial sympathy, as can be seen from this judgment of Lord Wright in a case concerning a motor liability policy:[6]

> The question turns entirely upon the construction of the contract. The narrow issue is whether there was a warranty or condition of the policy that the vehicle should be used exclusively for delivery of coal by the [insured] and, as a minor issue, for delivery of the [insured's] own coal, in connection with their business as coal merchants. The policy is in a form which has in its general scheme long been in use by insurance companies, though the general scheme has exhibited many variations, some major and some minor, in detail. In that scheme there is a proposal form, signed by the assured, containing various particulars and answers to various questions, and a declaration that the answers are to be the basis of the contract and an agreement to accept the company's policy. The policy itself contains a recital incorporating the proposal and declaration and it sets out the risk insured, certain exceptions and conditions and a schedule

---

5 *Pawson v Watson* (1778) 2 Cowp 785 at 787, per Lord Mansfield; *De Hahn v Hartley* (1786) 1 Term Rep 343, affd (1787) 2 Term Rep 186; Marine Insurance Act 1906, s. 33(3).
6 *Provincial Insurance Co Ltd v Morgan* [1933] AC 240 at 251–252, HL.

embodying various particulars. Though this general scheme of policy has been, as it were, sanctified by long usage, it has often been pointed out by judges that it must be very puzzling to the assured, who may find it difficult to fit the disjointed parts together in such a way as to get a true and complete conspectus of what their rights and duties are and what acts on their part may involve a forfeiture of the insurance. An assured may easily find himself deprived of the benefits of the policy because he has done something quite innocently but in breach of a condition, ascertainable only by the dovetailing of scattered portions.

In that case, the House of Lords held that questions in the proposal form relating to the purposes for which the lorry was to be used, and the nature of the goods to be carried, together with a declaration that the answers in the proposal form would be the basis of the contract, formed a promissory warranty as to the use of the lorry. However, occasional use of the lorry for hauling timber rather than coal was not a breach of that warranty, there being no warranty as to the *exclusive* use of hauling coal.

That case may be distinguished from another decision of the House of Lords relating to a similar clause[7] which stated 'the proposal shall be the basis of the contract and be held as incorporated therein'. Their Lordships held that these words did convert answers in the proposal into warranties or conditions of the policy, and the policy could be repudiated from its commencement date (i.e. *ab initio*) because the insured had inadvertently given the wrong address for the garaging of the vehicle.

Warranties have met harsh criticism from some members of the . House of Lords. For instance, in a case involving repudiation of a claim by insurers on the strength of the terms of a 'basis of the contract' clause, Lord Wrenbury expressed his view that:[8]

> I think it a mean and contemptible policy on the part of an insurance company that it should take the premiums and then refuse to pay upon a ground which no one says was really material. Here, upon purely technical grounds, they having in point of fact not been deceived in any material particular, avail themselves of what seems to me to be the contemptible defence that although they have taken the premiums, they are protected from paying.

Warranties are often framed in terms of a condition precedent to the liability of the insurer, rather than to the validity of the contract, so that the insurer may repudiate the particular claim and not the whole policy, and so be entitled under the policy to retain the premium, which would otherwise be returnable to the insured.

---

7 *Dawsons Ltd v Bonnin* [1922] 2 AC 413, HL.
8 *Glicksman v Lancashire and General Assurance Co Ltd* [1927] AC 139 at 144–145, HL.

Insurers have been held to be fully entitled to stipulate for the future performance of obligations by the insured,[9] and wherever these duties are expressed in clear words, the courts will enforce them, as they have done in the following instances:

(a) 'No claim under this policy shall be payable unless the terms of this condition shall have been complied with';[10]
(b) 'Any communication whatever relating to the accident must be forwarded to the [insurer] immediately on receipt thereof'[11] (it will be immaterial that the communication was relayed to the insured's broker who then failed to pass it on to the insurer);[12]
(c) 'The company shall be under no liability hereunder in respect of any loss which has not been notified to the company within fourteen days of its occurrence'.[13]

However, it is not a breach of the condition 'That the insured shall not by himself, or his agent, make any admission of liability to any person in respect of whom indemnity might be claimed under the policy', if the insured's employee admits liability without the authorisation of his employer, the insured.[14] This is because the insured has not contravened the precise, literal demands of the condition, and he is required to do no more than comply strictly with it.[15]

A warranty or condition may also be expressed in the policy as an 'exception', and, again, the effect of this term or stipulation will have to be construed. Non-compliance with an 'exception' or 'exclusion' clause which is, in fact, a warranty, will accordingly permit the insurer to repudiate the claim,[16] although, of course, the insurer may otherwise be protected by the exception clause being a term of definition of the contract of insurance, and matters within the exception are thereby automatically outside the ambit of the policy.

Express and implied warranties or conditions that are generally incorporated in contracts of professional indemnity insurance may, for clarification, be divided into three groups:

1 *Conditions precedent*
(a) that the insured shall comply with his duty of disclosure;
(b) that all statements made by the insured during negotiations shall be true;

---

9 *Woolfall and Rimmer Ltd v Moyle* [1942] 1 KB 66, CA.
10 *Welch v Royal Exchange Assurance* [1938] 1 KB 757.
11 *Hassett v Legal and General Assurance Society Ltd* (1939) 63 Ll L Rep 278.
12 *Vezey v United General Commercial Insurance Corpn Ltd* (1923) 15 Ll L Rep 63.
13 T H *Adamson & Sons v Liverpool and London and Globe Insurance Co Ltd* [1953] 2 Lloyd's Rep 355.
14 *Tustin v Arnold & Sons* (1915) 84 LJ KB 2214.
15 *Hide v Bruce* (1783) 3 Doug KB 213.
16 *Piddington v Co-Operative Insurance Society Ltd* [1934] 2 KB 236.

(c) that the subject matter of the insurance is adequately described;
(d) that the insured has an insurable interest in that subject matter.

2 *Conditions subsequent*
(a) that the insured shall not alter the risk as defined in the proposal;
(b) that the insured shall not effect a similar policy with other insurers;
(c) that either or both of the parties may determine the contract on notice;
(d) that the insured shall not fraudulently make a claim under the policy.

3 *Conditions precedent to the liability of insurers*
(a) that the premium shall be paid;
(b) that notice and particulars of claims against the insured shall be provided within a prescribed time;
(c) that the insured shall contest a claim for professional negligence if a jointly-appointed Queen's Counsel advises that there is a reasonable prospect of defending the claim;
(d) that the insured shall assist the insurer to investigate and ascertain the cause and extent of the neglect, error or omission;
(e) that disputes as to the liability of the insurer under the policy shall be referred to arbitration;
(f) that there shall be contribution from other insurances covering the same risk;
(g) that no admission of liability or offer or promise of payment shall be made without the written consent of the insurer.

Construction of the policy

The principle rule of construction in interpreting contracts of insurance was clearly stated by Lord Ellenborough CJ as long ago as 1803 when he said:[17]

> In the course of the argument it seems to have been assumed that some peculiar rules of construction apply to the terms of a policy of assurance which are not equally applicable to the terms of other instruments and in all other cases: it is therefore proper to state upon this head, that the same rule of construction which applies to all other instruments applies equally to this instrument of a policy of insurance, viz. that it is to be construed according to its sense and meaning, as collected in the first place from the terms used in it, which terms are themselves to be understood in their plain, ordinary, and popular sense, unless they have generally in respect to the subject-matters, as by the known usage of trade, or the like, acquired a peculiar sense distinct from the popular sense, of the same

17 *Robertson v French* (1803) 4 East 130 at 135–136.

words; or unless the contract evidently points out that they must in the particular instance, and in order to effectuate the immediate intention of the parties to that contract, be understood in some other special and peculiar sense. The only difference between policies of assurance, and other instruments in this respect, is, that the greater part of the printed language of them, being invariable and uniform, has acquired from use and practice a known and definite meaning, and that the words super-added in writing (subject indeed always to be governed in point of con-struction by the language and terms with which they are accompanied) are entitled nevertheless, if there should be any reasonable doubt upon the sense and meaning of the whole, to have a greater effect attributed to them than to the printed words, inasmuch as the written words are the immediate language and terms selected by the parties themselves for the expression of their meaning, and the printed words are a general formula adopted equally to their case and that of all other contracting parties upon similar occasions and subjects.

The proper construction to be placed upon words in an insurance contract is a matter of law for the court,[18] and the doctrine of binding precedent will be applied by the court in appropriate circumstances − 'If a construction had already been put on a clause precisely similar in any decided case, we should defer to that authority.'[19] However, decisions upon the construction and meaning of words in previously decided cases must not be taken as authoritative unless the language and the circumstances are substantially identical.[20] This has been aptly described by one member of the Court of Appeal − 'Authorities may determine principles of construction, but a decision upon one form of words is no authority upon the construc-tion of another form of words.'[1] It may also be mentioned that where there is no English decision upon the exact form of words in ques-tion, a court may have regard to decisions upon those words in other jurisdictions, but how much weight it will give to such a decision will be determined by the status of that court, and the quality of reason-ing behind the judgment.

The policy as a whole will be construed so as to give a reasonable interpretation to it, as well as to particular words or phrases, and 'the true construction of a document means no more than that the court puts on it the true meaning, and the true meaning which the party to whom the document was handed or who is relying on it would put on it as an ordinarily intelligent person construing the words in the proper way in the light of relevant circumstances.'[2] Thus, words used

18 *Simond v Boydell* (1779) 1 Doug KB 268.
19 *Glen v Lewis* (1853) 8 Exch 607 at 618, per Parke B.
20 *Re Calf and Sun Insurance Office* [1920] 2 KB 366 at 382, CA, per Atkin LJ.
 1 *Re Coleman's Depositories Ltd and Life and Health Assurance Assn* [1907] 2 KB 798 at 812, CA, per Buckley LJ.
 2 *Hutton v Watling* [1948] Ch 398 at 403, CA, per Greene MR.

will be given their literal construction,[3] but, as one past Lord Chancellor has added:[4]

> two rules of construction now firmly established as part of our law may be considered as limiting those words. One is that words, however general, may be limited with respect to the subject-matter in relation to which they are used. The other is that general words may be restricted to the same genus as the specific words that precede them.
>
> There is perhaps a third consideration which cannot be overlooked, and that is that where the same words have for many years received a judicial construction it is not unreasonable to suppose that parties have contracted upon the belief that their words will be understood in what I will call the accepted sense. And it is to be remembered that what Courts have to do in construing all documents is to reach the meaning of the parties through the words they have used.

In its task of construing the whole policy, and its terms and conditions, in their ordinary and natural meaning, the court may only give effect to the intention of the parties as evidenced by the written words of the policy, and any other document incorporated with it,[5] (commonly the signed proposal form). The general rule that oral evidence may not be received by the court applies to contracts of insurance as fully as to any other contract reduced to written form.[6] Oral evidence may be adduced, however, relating to the surrounding facts and circumstances, but only to show what were the facts which the negotiating parties had in their minds,[7] or to prove a custom or usage or particular meaning of words used which is not contrary to the meaning of the express words.[8]

In the case of ambiguity or inconsistency between particular terms or clauses of the policy, the court will adopt the more reasonable interpretation to carry out 'that which is just and honest and businesslike',[9] and in so doing will have regard to the whole policy to reconcile the inconsistencies. The grammatical interpretation of operative clauses will prevail over recitals,[10] but the recital may provide assistance in the interpretation of operative words.[11] Equally, where the proposal form is incorporated with the policy by

3 *Cory v Burr* (1883) 8 App Cas 393 at 405, HL, per Lord Fitzgerald.
4 *Thames and Mersey Marine Insurance Co Ltd v Hamilton Fraser & Co* (1887) 12 App Cas 484 at 490, HL, per Lord Halsbury LC.
5 *South Staffordshire Tramways Co v Sickness and Accident Assurance Assn* [1891] 1 QB 402, CA; *Yorkshire Insurance Co Ltd v Campbell* [1917] AC 218, PC.
6 *Hare v Barstow* (1844) 8 Jur 928; *Davies v National Fire and Marine Insurance Co of New Zealand* [1891] AC 485, PC.
7 *Bank of New Zealand v Simpson* [1900] AC 182, PC.
8 *Birrell v Dryer* (1884) 9 App Cas 345, HL.
9 *Lion Insurance Assn v Tucker* (1883) LR 12 QBD 176 at 190, CA, per Brett MR.
10 *Anglo-International Bank Ltd v General Accident Fire and Life Assurance Corpn Ltd* (1934) 48 Ll L Rep 151.
11 *Blascheck v Bussell* (1916) 33 TLR 74, CA.

an express provision, reference to the proposal may resolve ambiguities, but the policy, being the later document in time, will prevail.[12] As Lord Wright has said in the House of Lords:[13]

> No doubt the proposal conditions and the express conditions of the policy must be read together and, as far as may be, reconciled, so that every part of the contract may receive effect. But if there is a final and direct inconsistency, the positive and express terms of the policy must prevail.

One last tenet of construction is that where the words of a document are ambiguous in their grammatical and ordinary interpretation, they are to be construed against rather than in favour of the party who prepared the document.[14] This is known as the *contra proferentem* rule. Insurance policies are, of course, generally provided by insurers and, because this general rule of construction applies to contracts of insurance,[15], it follows that 'in dealing with the construction of policies, whether they be life, or fire, or marine policies, an ambiguous clause must be construed against rather than in favour of the (insurer)'.[16]

It must be emphasised that the *contra proferentem* rule only comes into operation in a case of real ambiguity and cannot be invoked to defeat the clear meaning of the words used.[17]

By way of illustration of the court's interpretation of policies in giving effect to the parties' intentions as expressed in the words used in the policy, reference may be made to cases where professional indemnity policies have been considered.

With regard to a solicitor's professional indemnity policy, the operative words 'claims . . . by reason of neglect, omission or error . . .' have been held not to include loss sustained by a solicitor entering into an illegal agreement,[18] nor from his clerk's fraudulent receipt of money from a client.[19]

The same operative words in an accountant's professional indemnity policy have been construed as not including a claim based upon both fraud of an employee and negligence of the insured accountants,[20] nor a claim brought against the insured simply for money had and received to his own use.[1]

12 *Kaufman v British Surety Insurance Co Ltd* (1929) 33 Ll L Rep 315.
13 *Izzard v Universal Insurance Co Ltd* [1937] AC 773 at 780, HL.
14 *Tarleton v Staniforth* (1794) 5 Term Rep 695 at 699, per Lord Kenyon.
15 *Houghton v Trafalgar Insurance Co Ltd* [1954] 1 QB 247, [1953] 2 All ER 1409, CA.
16 *Re Etherington and Lancashire and Yorkshire Accident Insurance Co* [1909] 1 KB 591 at 596, CA, per Vaughan Williams LJ.
17 *Alder v Moore* [1960] 2 Lloyd's Rep 325, CA.
18 *Haseldine v Hosken* [1933] 1 KB 822, CA.
19 *Davies v Hosken* [1937] 3 All ER 192.
20 *West Wake Price & Co v Ching* [1956] 3 All ER 821, [1957] 1 WLR 45.
 1 *Whitworth v Hosken* (1939) 65 Ll L Rep 48.

The principle of indemnity

The purpose of liability insurance is to insure the proposer against financial loss arising by reason of his becoming liable to pay damages to a third party for breach of a duty towards him in contract or in tort. In terms of professional indemnity insurance, the aim, as the name implies, is to cover loss incurred by the insured professional by reason of a judgment against him or her for damages for a breach of contract or tortious duty, committed in the conduct of his or her practice of the profession. The obligation of insurers to indemnify the insured can only arise upon the happening of the insured event as specified in the contract of insurance, and the liability to a third party must arise out of events within the scope of the policy, and not be specifically excluded under its terms or conditions.

The fundamental rule of indemnity – that the insured shall recover no more than his loss – is a rule of universal application throughout the law of insurance. This rule was enunciated by Brett LJ in *Castellain v Preston*:[2]

> In order to give my opinion upon this case, I feel obliged to revert to the very foundation of every rule which has been promulgated and acted on by the courts with regard to insurance law. The very foundation, in my opinion, of every rule which has been applied to insurance law is this, namely, that the contract on insurance contained in a marine or fire policy is a contract of indemnity, and of indemnity only, and that this contract means that the assured, in case of a loss against which the policy has been made, shall be fully indemnified, but shall never be more than full indemnified. That is the fundamental principle of insurance, and if ever a proposition is brought forward which is at variance with it, that is to say, which either will prevent the assured from obtaining a full indemnity, or which will give to the assured more than a full indemnity, that proposition must certainly be wrong.

If an act of neglect or culpable error is committed by the insured's employee which causes financial loss to be suffered by the insured only, this loss will not be recoverable under a professional indemnity policy. Mere loss incurred by the insured because of his own negligence or that of his employee is outside the scope of the policy, for the purpose of the policy is to indemnify the insured against his liability to third parties for negligent acts or omissions – this is the loss envisaged under the policy – not a loss suffered by the insured without the incursion of liability to another party caused by the act of neglect.[3]

---

2 (1883) 11 QBD 380 at 386, CA.
3 *Goddard and Smith v Frew* [1939] 4 All ER 358; *Walton v National Employers' Mutual General Insurance Assn Ltd* [1974] 2 Lloyd's Rep 385, NSW Sup Ct.

Related to this reasoning is the *proximity rule*, which requires the insured loss to have resulted from the risk insured (e.g. negligence). The court is 'bound to look to the immediate cause of the loss or damage, and not to some remote or speculative cause'.[4] Thus the proximate cause of a loss is not simply the last of a series of events, but the dominant,[5] direct,[6] operative and effective[7] cause of the loss. The rule of proximity has been explained as being an implied term of the liability policy which arises from the very nature of the bargain and must therefore be presumed to be nothing more nor less than the real meaning of the parties to a contract of insurance.[8] This concept of proximate cause, then, relates back to the whole question of construction of the policy which records the negotiated contract of insurance.

Indemnification of a loss must mean just that, and the insured may not recover more than his actual loss arising from the risk insured against. The policy will, however, contain a limit upon each claim, or, alternatively, a limit on the amount recoverable in any one year upon claims notified to the insurer in that period of insurance (an 'aggregate limit' clause), and an insured cannot recover more than these contractual limits even if his loss is greater.

Some professional indemnity policies also contain special terms which modify the basic rule of indemnification of the insured for the amount of his actual loss. For instance, there may be a 'franchise clause' whereby it is agreed that if a claim which would otherwise be payable under the policy does not exceed a specified amount, no sum will be recoverable under the policy; but if the claim exceeds that specified amount, the whole loss will be recoverable under the policy, up to the policy limit. That clause is to be distinguished from what is called an 'excess clause' whereby the insured must himself bear the first £x of each and every loss claimed under the policy, i.e. he is his own insurer for the first layer of each claim payable under the policy. Other variations may be encountered, for example, an annual limit to be self-insured by the insured, after which the insurer will pay the whole of each claim. Obviously, the premium charged by the insurer will reflect in some way the different level of risk accepted by the insurer.

It is an ordinary principle of insurance law that an insured person cannot by his own deliberate act cause the event upon which the insurance money is payable. It is both contrary to public policy as

---

4 *Everett v London Assurance* (1865) 19 CBNS 126 at 133, per Willes J.
5 *Leyland Shipping Co Ltd v Norwich Union Fire Insurance Society Ltd* [1918] AC 350 at 363, HL, per Lord Dunedin.
6 *Becker, Gray & Co v London Assurance Corpn* [1918] AC 101 at 114, HL, per Lord Sumner.
7 *P Samuel & Co Ltd v Dumas* [1924] AC 431 at 447, HL, per Viscount Cave.
8 *Becker, Gray* case, above, at 112, per Lord Sumner.

applied by the courts, and insurers will also be presumed not to have agreed to pay on that happening.[9] Thus, where a solicitor suffered loss to a third party by reason of a champertous agreement (then a crime), which he intentionally entered into, he was held to be unable to recover the loss under his professional indemnity policy.[10] So also will losses caused by an insured's own dishonest act, or that of his employee, be irrecoverable under the policy.[11] The intention of the policy is also spelt out in the operative clause of the policy, which refers to losses from an act of 'neglect, error or omission', and this, too, lends to the construction of the policy itself as excluding dishonest, criminal, fraudulent or other deliberate misconduct from its ambit.

When does the insured become entitled to claim his indemnity from the insurers? Obviously, contractual conditions or warranties relating to the notification of the claim to the insurer, and to the rendering of every assistance in investigating the loss claimed, will have to be complied with, together with any other conditions precedent to the liability of the insurer, e.g. payment of the agreed premium. General insurance law does not require the insured to pay the third party's claim, and perhaps ruin himself in so doing, before being entitled to seek relief from his indemnifying insurer. The court will come to the insured's aid and exercise its equitable jurisdiction to permit the insured to seek the specific enforcement of the policy by a recalcitrant insurer, to oblige the insurer to relieve him of liability up to the limits specified in the policy.[12]

Of great importance to the insured seeking to protect himself against all financial loss arising out of a claim for professional negligence being made against him, is whether his legal costs of resisting the claim will be included in the indemnity provided by his policy. If the insured were adjudged at fault, and therefore liable to the third party who suffered by reason of his act of neglect, error or omission, it would seem reasonable that costs awarded against the insured in the action should be covered by his insurer's indemnity.[13] However, the legal costs could be very large, perhaps even greater than the award of damages in some cases, and therefore the insured would rightly feel that his effective level of protection is not the limit specified in the policy, but rather the amount remaining after the costs awarded to the third party and his own costs, for that sum only would represent funds available under the policy to meet the damages award. And what if the claim of negligence were successfully

9 *Beresford v Royal Insurance Co Ltd* [1938] AC 586 at 595, [1938] 2 All ER 602 at 604, HL, per Lord Atkin.
10 *Haseldine v Hosken* [1933] 1 KB 822, CA.
11 *Davies v Hosken* [1937] 3 All ER 192.
12 See *Johnston v Salvage Assn and McKiver* (1887) 19 QBD 458, CA.
13 *Xenos v Fox* (1869) LR 4 CP 665.

defended? Would any legal costs not recovered from the plaintiff third party have to be borne by the insured, or would they be recoverable when the risk insured, i.e. negligence, has not been proved to have occurred?

It is because of these arguments that professional indemnity policies always have a special clause stating that all the legal costs and expenses incurred with the written consent of the insurer, will be recoverable under the policy, whether or not the claim against the insured professional succeeds. This indemnity regarding costs is generally stated to be provided in addition to the agreed limit of the policy, so the policy limit refers to the sum available wholly to apply to an award of damages against the insured. A variation on the theme is for the costs to be shared between the insured and the insurer in a predetermined proportion or quantity.

Subrogation

As a natural result of the fundamental principle of indemnity in insurance contracts (cf life assurance), the insurer, once he has admitted the insured's claim and has paid the sum payable under the policy,[14] becomes entitled to be subrogated to the position of the insured in respect of the loss. This arises from a general equitable right which arises whenever one person indemnifies another for a loss pursuant to a legal obligation to do so,[15] and has also been considered an implied term of the contract of insurance.[16]

The doctrine of subrogation has been expressed by the Court of Appeal to be as follows:[17]

> as between the underwriter and the assured the underwriter is entitled to the advantage of every right of the assured, whether such right consists in contract, fulfilled or unfulfilled, or in remedy for tort capable of being insisted on or already insisted on, or in any other right, whether by way of condition or otherwise, legal or equitable, which can be, or has been exercised or has accrued, and whether such right could or could not be enforced by the insurer in the name of the assured by the exercise or acquiring of which right or condition the loss against which the assured is insured, can be, or has been diminished.

This equitable doctrine or implied term, despite its wide effect of placing the insurer in the shoes of the insured, does have limitations.

14 *Mason v Sainsbury* (1782) 3 Doug KB 61.
15 *Burnand v Rodocanachi & Sons & Co* (1882) 7 App Cas 333 at 339, HL, per Lord Blackburn.
16 *Yorkshire Insurance Co Ltd v Nisbet Shipping Co Ltd* [1962] 2 QB 330 at 339–340, per Diplock J.
17 *Castellain v Preston* (1883) 11 QBD 380 at 387, CA, per Brett LJ; Cotton and Bowen LJJ concurred.

It might be thought that an insurer could insist upon the insured pursuing such rights as the insured has against other parties who contributed to the loss, or in some other way take these rights of action into account when settling with the insured his payment under the policy. This is not possible under the normal rights of subrogation for the insured must first make full payment under the policy.[18] It follows from this that an insurer is not precluded from later insisting upon the exercise of rights of subrogation although he had not so requested prior to payment under the policy.[19] An insurer will also not be subrogated to the rights of the insured which are unconnected with the subject matter of the insurance,[20] but he will be entitled to all rights of the insured which arise from the loss and those by which the loss will be diminished.

A recent decision of the Court of Appeal imposes a further limit on an insurer's right to subrogate. Although, in principle, it might be thought that an insurer could exercise, by subrogation, the right of the insured to recover a loss caused by the negligence of his employee from that employee,[1] the Court of Appeal has taken the view that equity will not permit the doctrine of subrogation to be used in this way, and a term excluding this course of action could be implied in the contract of insurance.[2] It was thought that such a burden upon an employee would be unjust and would lead to industrial unrest. Since this decision, professional indemnity policies tend to bear a specific clause waiving any subrogation rights against a negligent employee if the insured so requests.

Contractual terms will override the doctrine, and it is general practice for all insurers to insert conditions in the policy which give them the right to pursue claims against other parties in the insured's name, and also the right to full control of such proceedings, prior to payment of sums due under the policy. It is understandable that insurers wish to become involved in litigation against their insured in the case of professional indemnity policies, but due to the fear of many professional persons insuring thereunder that this might lead to a conflict of interest between themselves and their insurer, (when an insurer may be content to settle a claim of negligence for a small amount, rather than resist such a claim, whereas the professional insured has his standing in the profession to consider), a special clause has been devised and is widely adopted. This 'Q.C. clause'

---

18 *Dickenson v Jardine* (1868) LR 3 CP 639; *Collingridge v Royal Exchange Assurance Corpn* (1877) 3 QBD 173.
19 *West of England Fire Insurance Co v Isaacs* [1897] 1 QB 226, CA.
20 *Sea Insurance Co v Hadden* (1884) 13 QBD 706, CA.
 1 See *Lister v Romford Ice and Cold Storage Co Ltd* [1957] AC 555, [1957] 1 All ER 125, HL.
 2 *Morris v Ford Motor Co Ltd* [1973] QB 792, [1973] 2 All ER 1084, CA.

aims to resolve any such conflict of interest between insurer and insured as to the right course of action when negligence is alleged against the insured.

Contractual conditions forbidding the insured from settling or compromising claims made against him without prior consent of his insurer, are inserted to emphasise what is, in fact, a natural consequence of the doctrine of indemnity. An insured person must not renounce or compromise any right he may be able to exercise so as to diminish the insured loss, otherwise he incurs a liability to his insurers to the extent that he has deprived his insurer of his opportunity to recover by exercising subrogation rights.[3]

It may be that an insured recovers a sum in diminution of his loss prior to full indemnity from his insurer, and in such a case, any sums so recovered will be deducted from the sums otherwise payable by the insurer,[4] and any sums paid by the insurer in ignorance of such recoveries must be reimbursed to the insurer so that the insured does not profit from his loss.[5] Conversely, if amounts are recovered by virtue of an insurer exercising by subrogation the rights of the insured, he must account to the insured for such sums recovered, less the costs of recovery, that exceed the amount paid by way of indemnity to the insured. This actually is achieved automatically because the action for recovery will be in the insured's name and a judgment can only be satisfied by the payment of sums awarded to the insured (and so diminish or extinguish his loss to be indemnified under the policy).

The last observations concerning subrogation rights are that where an insurer fully indemnifies an insured for a loss, and then proceeds to enforce the rights to which he has become subrogated, the defendant to that action, which will be in the name of the insured, will not be able to plead in his defence that at that later point in time the insured has no loss (having been indemnified by his insurer), and therefore he, the defendant, can have no damages awarded against him. This would make a nonsense of the fundamental principle of indemnity in insurance contracts, and so 'it is to be considered as if the insurers had not paid a farthing' to the insured.[6] This will also be the case where insurers have indemnified an insured under a policy in the belief that they are liable under the policy, albeit that they were not, in fact, legally liable to pay.[7] Interestingly enough, though, the position is otherwise if the defendant

---

3 *Commercial Union Assurance Co v Lister* (1874) 9 Ch App 483; *Phoenix Assurance Co v Spooner* [1905] 2 KB 753.
4 *West of England Fire Insurance Co v Isaacs* [1897] 1 QB 226, CA.
5 *Castellain v Preston* (1883) 11 QBD 380, CA.
6 *Mason v Sainsbury* (1782) 3 Doug KB 61 at 64, per Lord Mansfield CJ.
7 *King v Victoria Insurance Co* [1896] AC 250, PC.

can show that the policy was not a valid and binding contract, from which no right of subrogation could have arisen.[8]

The defendant is also entitled to treat the insurer as the real plaintiff, although he sues in the name of his insured, and may raise a special defence against the subrogating insurer to defeat the action, which may be a general defence, e.g. the insurer is an alien enemy and cannot maintain the claim,[9] or a particular defence, e.g. that by a term of the policy, the insurer undertook not to proceed against him.[10] This latter defence could presumably be available to an employee sued by a subrogating insurer in contravention of a clause waiving those rights in the policy, or upon proof that his employers (the insured) had requested the waiver to be applied if such was strictly necessary.

Contribution: double insurance

A person is perfectly free under the general law to insure a risk with several insurers, even with each carrying the full amount of the risk. With indemnity insurances, however, as already explained above, the insured may never obtain more than an indemnity of his loss by way of insurance, and this fundamental rule has the necessary result that the insured cannot recover many times over simply by effecting several policies. As a corollary to this, each separate insurer is fully liable to the insured until he has been indemnified. It is no defence for an insurer to point out that other insurers are also liable to the insured if he should claim under their policies rather than his. In the absence of conditions to the contrary, the insured may pursue a full indemnity under any of the several policies he might hold for the same risk, and the insurer will have to indemnify him in full.[11] If he should fail to gain full monetary satisfaction from one insurer, the insured may recover the balance of his loss from one of his other insurers. Once having met his liability, however, the insurer will be able to call upon the other insurers to contribute their share of the loss pro rata, on equitable principles.[12]

To give rise to this equitable 'right of contribution', four matters need to be established:

1 *The insurances must have the same subject matter*
This means that the particular loss must be covered by each policy of insurance for the right of contribution to arise. The various policies

8 *John Edwards & Co v Motor Union Insurance Co Ltd* [1922] 2 KB 249.
9 *The Palm Brach* [1916] P 230.
10 *Thomas & Co v Brown* (1899) 4 Com Cas 186, per Mathew J.
11 *North British and Mercantile Insurance Co v London, Liverpool and Globe Insurance Co* (1877) 5 Ch D 569, CA.
12 *Godin v London Assurance Co* (1758) 1 Burr 489.

may cover other subject matter not common between them without effecting the right to contribution for the relevant loss.[13]

2 *The insurances must cover the same risk*
Although the policies may each cover several perils, it will be sufficient if they all cover the same peril which causes the loss.[14] *Quaere* if the policies are very different in their scope.

3 *The insurances must be for the benefit of the same insured*
The insurances must all cover the same interest of the same insured.[15] This has more importance to property insurance than professional indemnity insurances.

4 *Each policy must be valid and enforceable*
Each insurance must be such that the insured may call upon each insurer, separately, to indemnify him for the loss. This will not be so where the policy is unenforceable due to breach of a condition or warranty,[16] or has not yet attached at the time of the loss.[17] There will be contribution where the policy is avoided only after the loss.[18]

In the practice, policies of insurance now always contain conditions of various types which modify the general right of contribution described above. Some conditions in liability policies provide that if at the time of any claim arising there is any other insurance covering the same risk, the insurer will be liable for no more than his rateable proportion of the claim. The Court of Appeal has recently had to consider an instance where both insurance policies contained this rateable proportion clause, but the policies had different limits of indemnity, and the question arose as to whether the claim should be shared equally by the insurers, or in some manner to reflect their respective maximum liabilities.

The case was *Commercial Union Assurance Co Ltd v Hayden*,[19] and concerned two public liability policies; under theirs, Commercial Union had a maximum liability of £100,000, whereas a Lloyd's syndicate's policy (Hayden representing them all) had a maximum liability of £10,000. The insured had suffered a loss of some £4,425, by way of an award of damages for personal injuries against him. Hayden interpreted the rateable proportion clause on

13 *American Surety Co of New York v Wrightson* (1910) 16 Com Cas 37.
14 Ibid.
15 *Scottish Amicable Heritable Securities Assn v Northern Assurance Co* 1883 11 R (Ct of Sess) 287.
16 *Monksfield v Vehicle and General Insurance Co Ltd* [1971] 1 Lloyd's Rep 139.
17 *Sickness and Accident Assurance Assn v General Accident Assurance Corpn* 1892 19 R (Ct of Sess) 977.
18 *Weddell v Road Transport and General Insurance Co Ltd* [1932] 2 KB 563.
19 [1977] QB 804, [1977] 1 All ER 441, CA.

the basis of each insurer's maximum liability and contributed on
this basis. The Commercial Union contended that a one-half contribution was required, on the basis that an insurer's 'rateable proportion' should be calculated by reference to the independent
liability of each insurer if he had been the only insurer. On this reasoning, Hayden's rateable proportion would only be less than one-
half when the claim exceeded Hayden's independent liability of
£10,000. The Court of Appeal held that the rateable proportion
clause was equally capable of either construction in its literal interpretation, and therefore should be given the meaning more likely to
be intended by reasonable business men. An assumption by the
insurers of an equal level of risk up to the lower level of the two
maximum liability limits was more realistic than an intention to use
those limits, inserted to protect the insurer from exceptionally large
claims, to adjust liability in respect of claims within the limits of both
policies.

Even more recently, the Court of Appeal has had to consider the
situation where clauses in the policies purport to exclude liability if
other insurances cover the same risk. This case was *National
Employers Mutual General Insurance Association Ltd v Haydon*[20] (a
representative Lloyd's underwriter), and in fact concerned double
insurance of professional negligence risks. A certain firm of
solicitors held a professional indemnity policy issued by the plaintiff
company from year to year, until midnight of 24–25 March 1976.
That policy contained a clause which stated that the policy did not
indemnify the insured in respect of any claim made against him for
which 'the insured is or would but for the existence of this policy be
entitled to indemnity under any other policy except in respect of any
excess beyond the amount payable by such other policy'. The clause
therefore sought to provide a position where any other insurer of the
risk would have to pay in full, and they would not pay a penny unless
the loss exceeded the full amount payable under that other policy.
A claim was notified under this policy on the day of its expiry,
24 March 1976.

The Lloyd's policy, sponsored by the Law Society, was of the
Master Policy type, i.e. common terms and rates for all subscribers
of a certain grouping, and became effective after midnight of 24–25
March 1976. It contained retrospective cover for claims 'first made
against the assured or the firm during the period of insurance', and
also an exclusion clause stating that: '. . . this insurance shall not
indemnify the Assured in respect of any loss arising out of any claim
. . . in respect of any circumstance or occurrence which has been
notified under any other insurance attaching prior to the inception
of this [policy]'.

20 [1980] 2 Lloyd's Rep 149, CA.

The question was whether the insurance company could claim a contribution from the Lloyd's underwriters for the claim made on 24 March, because of the latter policy's retrospective cover. The alternative question was whether the Lloyd's policy exclusion clause, on its true construction, effectively excluded any liability of the Lloyd's underwriters for the claim, that claim having been properly notified under the NEM policy, and so overrode the equitable 'right of contribution'.

The Court of Appeal unanimously held that the exclusion clause in the Lloyd's policy did exclude the loss reported under the NEM policy, and that therefore double insurance had not occurred. The clause defined the scope of the cover rather than excluded otherwise valid claims, and therefore contribution did not arise. As can be seen from this decision particularly, difficult questions of construction arise on double insurance.

Chapter 3

The basic policy

Introduction

It would be wrong to suggest that there is any one 'model' professional indemnity policy, from which underwriters, whether insurance companies or Lloyd's underwriters, draw guidance, or, indeed, to which an insured person may refer to compare his policy. That being said, the purpose of this chapter is to attempt to provide a guide to what may be called the 'basic' policy of insurance of professional negligence risks. All policies will, in fact, vary from this basic policy, either in scope or in detailed provisions, and therefore consideration of the basic policy will give the reader a great insight into his own particular policy, as will the next chapter which deals with some of the more commonly found extensions to the principal cover for professional negligence.

The main clauses of the basic policy will each be considered in turn, and will be divided up into their salient parts for analysis where necessary. In practice, the sequence of the various clauses will vary, but this will generally not affect the meaning to be attached to them, unless the legal interpretation or construction of the clause or the policy is in some way varied in the circumstances of the policy.

The recital clause

WHEREAS the person or partnership named in the Schedule (hereinafter called 'the insured' which expression shall include the said persons and any other person or persons who may become a partner in the firm) have made to the Insurer a written proposal containing particulars and statements which it is hereby agreed shall be the basis of this contract and are to be considered incorporated herein and in consideration of the payment of the premium stated within the said Schedule.

This recital clause identifies the parties to the contract of insurance and contains the important 'basis of the contract' condition that is found in nearly all policies of all types. The effect of entering incorrect information on the proposal form will be a breach of this condition or warranty which will entitle the insurer to repudiate the policy,[1] quite apart from any question of breach of good faith (*uberrima fides*) by the insured[2] or non-disclosure of a material fact[3] which might entitle the insured to avoid the policy or claim on those grounds.

The clause also identifies that the consideration for the contract is the payment of the premium, and in this form acknowledges the payment of the required premium. Upon the construction of the clause, the payment of premium is a condition precedent to the validity of the insurance contract, therefore non-payment of the premium will mean that the policy will not attach to the risk, that of professional negligence, until the premium is paid, and the courts will enforce such a condition precedent.[4] The mere fact that the recital clause acknowledges receipt of the premium, when it has not in fact been tendered, will not be treated, without more evidence, as a waiver by the insurer of this condition precedent to the attachment of liability.[5]

Further, with regard to the interpretation of the policy, it must be pointed out that a court will only refer to the recital clause to gain guidance to the interpretation and construction of the policy as a whole, if there is an inconsistency in the interpretation of the words used in the operative clause of the policy.[6] The grammatical interpretation of operative words prevails over recitals.[7] Certainly, this recital will help resolve any difficulty upon who is insured under the policy. For instance, it makes it clear that a person may be an insured under the policy even if he is not named on the Schedule as an insured, if he has become a partner in the insured firm since the beginning of the year of insurance.

The operative clause

NOW THIS POLICY WITNESSETH that the Insurer hereby agrees to indemnify the Insured to the limits specified in the Schedule hereto in respect of any sum or sums which the Insured may become legally liable to pay as damages for breach of professional duty as a result of any claim or claims

1 See *Dawsons Ltd v Bonnin* [1922] 2 AC 413, HL.
2 E.g. *Carter v Boehm* (1766) 3 Burr 1905.
3 See e.g. *London General Omnibus Co Ltd v Holloway* [1912] 2 KB 72, CA.
4 *Phoenix Life Assurance Co v Sheridan* (1860) 8 HL Cas 745.
5 *Equitable Fire and Accident Office Ltd v Ching Wo Hong* [1907] AC 96, PC.
6 *Blascheck v Bussell* (1916) 33 TLR 74, CA.
7 *Anglo-International Bank Ltd v General Accident Fire and Life Assurance Corpn Ltd* (1934) 48 Ll L Rep 151.

made upon the insured during the period of insurance arising out of the conduct of the practice or business described in the Schedule as a direct result of any negligent act, error or omission therein committed by the Insured or their predecessors in the practice or business whenever the same was or alleged to have been committed.

The Insurer will also indemnify any employee of the Insured if the Insured requests in respect of liability for which the Insured would have been entitled to indemnity if the claim had been made against the Insured, provided that such employee shall be subject to the terms and conditions of this policy as if he were the Insured so far as they can apply.

The operative clause of the policy, as it is called, is the main substantive clause which defines the scope of the insurance, and specifies that the nature of the insurance is an indemnity which is subject to certain limits.

'. . . the Insurer hereby agrees to indemnify the Insured . . .'

The fundamental principle applicable to professional indemnity policies, and all other liability policies, is that the insured should be indemnified against financial loss arising from the risk insured against, no more and no less.[8] An insured must never make a profit from his loss, and if the insured can prove no loss, the obligation to indemnify does not arise.[9]

At common law the obligation to indemnify also does not arise where the Insured caused the loss by his own deliberate,[10] criminal,[11] or dishonest[12] act, nor that of his employee, even without specific clauses excluding them.

'. . . to the limits specified in the Schedule hereto . . .'

These words define the extent of the indemnity provided by the insurer, and therefore, in their nature define the scope of the policy. Such contractual stipulations will be recognised and upheld by the courts,[13] and limits expressed to be in the aggregate for all claims under a professional indemnity policy have been held perfectly valid.[14]

Reference will have to be made to the Schedule to see whether the limits are expressed in terms of an aggregate for all claims in the year; or in terms of a limit for each and every claim arising during the period of insurance; or even a combination of the two.

8 *Castellain v Preston* (1883) 11 QBD 380, CA.
9 See *West Wake Price & Co v Ching* [1957] 1 WLR 45 at 49, per Devlin J.
10 *Beresford v Royal Insurance Co Ltd* [1938] AC 586, [1938] 2 All ER 602, HL.
11 *Haseldine v Hosken* [1933] 1 KB 822, [1933] 3 All ER 192, CA.
12 *Davies v Hosken* [1937] 3 All ER 192, (1937) 58 Ll L Rep 183.
13 *Allen v London Guarantee and Accident Co Ltd* (1912) 28 TLR 254.
14 *Forney v Dominion Insurance Co Ltd* [1969] 3 All ER 831, [1969] 1 WLR 928.

'. . . in respect of any sum or sums which the Insured may become legally liable to pay . . .'

These words further define the nature of the indemnity provided by the policy. On their strict, literal construction, the words would exclude any sum or sums which the insured might pay, even on the advice and with the consent of the insurer, on a compromise or 'ex gratia' or 'without admission of liability' settlement. Reference may also be had, however, when construing this part of the operative clause, to the 'Q.C. clause'. The combined effect would lead to an ambiguity in the interpretation of the policy as a whole, which would have to be resolved by a court adopting the more reasonable interpretation to effect 'that which is just and honest and businesslike'.[15] Applying this test, the ambit of the policy would be likely to be construed as including such payments or settlements which had the consent of the insurer, or were made upon the advice of the appointed Queen's Counsel who has considered whether a particular claim should be contested or not with any reasonable prospect of success.

If there is no 'Q.C. clause' in the policy, the construction of the policy upon this point is rather more difficult. Obviously a judgment of the court awarding damages against the insured for professional negligence would be included by the words 'legally liable to pay', but the right to an indemnity under the policy could be rather more contentious. Most probably, though, the final test of the *contra preferentem* rule would be invoked by a court to resolve this case of real ambiguity,[16] and the connivance of the insurer with the insured in any settlement, albeit on an 'ex gratia' or 'without admission of liability' basis, would be damning to any construction of the policy other than that such compromises were to be included in the words 'legally liable to pay'.

'. . . as damages . . .'

The observations above regarding settlements or compromises are also relevant here.

The word 'damages' could also be construed as having a wider meaning than perhaps anticipated. Not only the award of compensation granted against the insured might be regarded as 'damages' in the policy, but also any award of costs against the insured in that action for professional negligence.[17] It would probably be extending the word's meaning too greatly beyond its literal construction,[18] however, to include the insured's costs without a specific clause mentioning the payment of such costs. Most professional negligence

15 *Lion Insurance Assn v Tucker* (1883) 12 QBD 176 at 190, CA, per Brett MR.
16 *Houghton v Trafalgar Insurance Co Ltd* [1954] 1 QB 247, [1953] 2 All ER 1409.
17 See *Xenos v Fox* (1869) LR 4 CP 665.
18 *Cory v Burr* (1883) 8 App Cas 393, HL.

policies will contain such a clause covering the insured's legal costs and expenses.

'. . . for breach of professional duty . . .'

These words indentify the risk that might give rise to the loss insured against. Chapter 1 deals in detail with the question of professional negligence, but it would be correct to link these words directly with the subsequent words 'any negligent act, error or omission' in the operative clause, and it will be convenient to consider the court's interpretation of professional negligence policies under that heading.

'. . . as a result of any claim or claims made upon the Insured during the period of insurance . . .'

Clearly, the terms of this part of the operative clause require that the claim must be made upon the insured during the twelve month period of insurance covered by the policy.

The important feature of this is that it is not the negligent act, error or omission which must occur during that twelve month period, but that the *claim* arising from that negligence or breach of professional duty must be intimated to the insured professional during the insurance period. This basic policy is therefore on a 'claims arising' basis, and not on an alternative basis that is occasionally available where only claims arising from a negligent act, error or omission committed during the currency of the policy. This latter form of cover is of a much more limited scope, because the former covers all claims arising during the policy years, *whenever* the negligent act, error or omission was committed.

This part of the operative clause also ties in with the conditions of the policy requiring notification of claims to the insurer. Such conditions therefore must be complied with to come within the terms of the indemnity provided by the policy.[19]

'. . . arising out of the conduct of the practice or business described in the Schedule . . .'

Attached to the policy will be a Schedule which will identify the profession or business carried on by the insured person or persons. Whilst the non-disclosure of other activities would be a breach of the good faith in insurance contracts entitling the insurer to avoid the policy in any case,[20] these words emphasise that the activities specified to the insurer are the only ones which are covered by the indemnity under the policy. The insurer is further protected from

---

19 *Hassett v Legal and General Assurance Society Ltd* (1939) 63 Ll L Rep 278; *Vezey v United General Commercial Insurance Corpn Ltd* (1923) 15 Ll L Rep 63.
20 *Dalglish v Jarvie* (1850) 2 Mac & G 231; *Lee v British Law Insurance Co* [1972] 2 Lloyd's Rep 49, CA.

paying out for negligence arising from non-specified business or professional activities, by the recital clause which makes the information in the proposal form the 'basis of the contract'.[1]

'. . . as a direct result of any negligent act, error or omission therein . . .'

These words are, of course, the crux of the negligence policy, and it is
therefore not surprising that there has been some considerable
amount of litigation regarding the precise scope and meaning of
these, or similar, words.

In the first of a series of three cases against Lloyd's underwriters
upon professional indemnity policies, a solicitor's indemnity policy
was considered, as in the second, and in the third an accountant's
indemnity policy was at issue.

In *Haseldine v Hosken*[2] a Lloyd's policy of indemnity covering
claims arising from any 'neglect, omission or error' was considered
by the Court of Appeal. The facts of the case were that the plaintiff
insured solicitor had agreed in November 1928 to pay all disburse-
ments in connection with a certain action against a company, including court fees, counsel's fees, etc., and had agreed further not to seek
to recover any professional charges against his client if the action
was unsuccessful. On the other hand, if the action was successful
against the company, Haseldine would recover £200, or 20 per cent
of the award, whichever were the greater. In February 1930, these
amounts were revised to £500 or 40 per cent, respectively, and subsequently the action against the company was lost and costs were
awarded to the company. Haseldine's client was unable to meet the
bill of costs awarded to the company, so the company proceeded
against Haseldine for recovery. He settled this action for £950, and
then claimed to be indemnified under his professional indemnity
policy issued by the defendant representative Lloyd's underwriter.

The Court of Appeal held that Haseldine's agreement with his
client amounted to champerty (which was then illegal). Being illegal
and also contrary to public policy, a claim in respect of loss due to
having contracted it was not maintainable in the English courts. The
court further held that the loss in respect of which the indemnity was
claimed, did not arise by reason of any neglect, omission or error
committed by Haseldine acting as a solicitor in his professional capacity, but rather arose from his entering into a personal speculation,
and this was outside the scope of the professional indemnity policy.

Subsequently, in *Davies v Hosken*[3] the same words had to be construed by Porter J. The facts of this case were that Davies and his

1 See above.
2 [1933] 1 KB 822, CA.
3 [1937] 3 All ER 192, [1937] 58 Ll L Rep 183.

partner had taken over the practice of a Mr Ashford who had died, and had continued to employ Mr Ashford's clerk, a Mr Digby. Certain professional clients had later handed sums of money to Mr Digby for investment on mortgage, and he had in some cases put the money received into his own pocket, and in others he had paid it into the firm's account and had then fraudulently induced the solicitors to draw cheques, which he applied to his own purposes. When these activities were discovered, Davies and his partner paid their clients' claims, prosecuted Mr Digby, and then sought to be indemnified under their professional indemnity policy.

The question before the court was whether this serious loss was within the terms of the policy. Porter J thought that the words 'neglect, omission or error' pointed to an omission rather than a positive act, and therefore he was inclined on that ground to consider that Mr Digby's fraudulent scheme, being a positive set of commission rather than omission, was not within the scope of the policy. Porter J did feel, however, that he would have more difficulty if the operative words had included a reference, additionally, to 'any act . . . .'. At the conclusion of his judgment, Porter J summarised the position:[4]

> [Mr Digby] really set out to make a positive act, to make money by false pretences; that was an act, and not a neglect, omission or error, and there-fore does not fall within the terms of the policy.
>
> For those reasons I think the claim fails. It is unfortunate for Messrs Davies that that should be so, but it is, of course, a question of what the actual words cover. I will not say what they are meant to cover, because neither party thinks exactly, nor can be expected to think exactly, the same about what the words intended to cover. If the words do not cover a particular matter, the insurers are entitled to take the point. In those cir-cumstances the claim fails.

Slightly different material words were considered in *Whitworth v Hosken*[5] which concerned an accountant's indemnity policy. The operative clause referred to losses arising from 'any act of neglect default or error' in the conduct of the insured's business as accoun-tant. The insured firm of accountants was handling the sale of a certain business, through a Mr Kirby who visited an interested party to discuss a possible purchase. One of the insured accountants then wrote to the interested party, who, a day or two later, saw Mr Kirby again and agreed to purchase the offered business. Mr Kirby took a 10 per cent deposit, gave a receipt for this deposit and said an official receipt would follow. This was sent the next day. Three weeks later Mr Kirby called on the purchaser and asked for the balance of the purchase price so as to be ready for completion three days hence. The

4 Ibid at 195 and 186.
5 (1939) 65 Ll L Rep 48.

purchaser, thinking he was dealing with the accredited representative of a reputable firm of chartered accountants, gave a cheque to Mr Kirby for the remaining 90 per cent of the price. Mr Kirby cashed the cheque and absconded with the proceeds.

The judge in this case could find no evidence of any act of 'neglect', 'default', nor 'error' on the part of the insured accountant, for he had done all that he had intended to do, that is, permit Mr Kirby to accept moneys on behalf of the vendor of the business. This being so, there was nothing to bring the matter within the operative words of the policy.

In no instance have the actual words of the 'basic policy' adopted here been considered, but the attitude of the courts can be extracted from those cases, as well as the Court of Appeal's decision in *Goddard and Smith v Frew*.[6] Under an auctioneers' and estate agents' policy, the insured were protected under an indemnity for losses arising from 'any act, neglect, omission, misstatement or error' committed in the conduct of the business. An employee of the firm, over a period of time, embezzled a substantial part of the rents he collected on the firm's behalf, which the firm later had to account for to their client. The Court of Appeal had no doubt that the case turned entirely on the interpretation of the words of the policy, and these did not cover embezzlement by an employee, which was the true proximate cause of the loss. The policy was an indemnity policy against carefully described liabilities, and not a fidelity policy to insure the insured against the dishonesty of their employees.

Variations in wording have been considered in the Supreme Court of New South Wales, Australia, and these decisions are of persuasive authority in the English courts.

In *Simon Warrender Pty Ltd v Swain*[7] a firm of insurance brokers held a policy of indemnity against losses resulting from 'errors or omissions' issued by Lloyd's underwriters. An employee of the brokers deliberately did not effect a policy on a client's fishing boat. The client subsequently suffered loss and recovered this loss from the insurance brokers with the insurer's consent. The question was whether the insurer could escape liability under this errors and omissions policy on the ground that the employee had deliberately not effected the policy on the fishing boat, and so the act was outside the scope of the indemnity policy.

The court held that the intent of the employee was not necessarily to be imputed to his employers, and the insurer did not allege a wilful and deliberate failure on the part of the employers. Therefore, as far as the insurance brokers were concerned, the insurer's plea was that there was a mere failure by them to effect the fishing boat policy, and

6 [1939] 4 All ER 358, CA.
7 [1960] 2 Lloyd's Rep 111.

therefore that failure was an error or omission within the policy.

It is submitted that an English court would not follow that line of reasoning which is at variance with the other cases cited, and would accordingly not have held that this deliberate act of an employee was within the scope of an 'errors and omissions' policy.

Also to be contrasted with that decision is one of the full Supreme Court of New South Wales, *Walton v National Employers' Mutual General Insurance Association Ltd*.[8] In October 1969, a client of the insured stockbrokers instructed them to buy approximately 10,000 shares in X Co. On that date the insured brokers bought more than 10,000 shares for various clients, and booked 9,710 to this client. On the same day, the insured firm forwarded to this client a broker's bought note stating that 10,190 shares had been bought for him. The mistake was due to the carelessness of one of their employees. The client paid the full price for the 10,190 shares. It was six months later that the mistake was discovered, and the insured had to purchase 1,020 shares in X Co to make reparation, the price having greatly increased in the meantime. The insured brokers claimed an indemnity against this loss under a 'Stockbroker's Combined Policy', which insured them, inter alia, against 'any claim for which the Insured is legally liable arising out of negligence' in the conduct of the business.

Distinguishing the *Simon Warrender* case, the court held that the loss did not fall within the policy because it was not in respect of a claim by a client arising out of negligence, but one in respect of damage suffered in the internal management of the stockbroker's business due to the mistake of an employee. In the words of Kerr CJ:[9]

> It is clear that carelessness or negligence of the appellant or his employee did not bring about any breach of contract on the appellant's part which was itself a breach involving carelessness or negligence of the appellant. The appellant argues that he became bound contractually to carry out certain obligations because of the negligence on his employee's part in the employee's relations with him. But the policy does not indemnify the appellant against any loss which he may suffer because of carelessness of his employees . . . In the present case the negligence of the employee did not cause any loss which could become the basis for a claim by the clients in relation to the purchase on October 1, 1969, and the sale thereafter of 10,190 shares. The negligence did not give rise and could not have given rise to any claim by the clients, because, by reason of the negligence, they got the benefit of the full performance of their contract with the appellant and paid the appellant in full on that basis at the price of the day.

8 [1974] 2 Lloyd's Rep 385.
9 Ibid at 388–389.

From the above cases, it is submitted that the words of the 'basic' policy adopted in this chapter, i.e. 'any negligent act, error or omission', would be interpreted by the courts as embracing any act, error or omission within the normal understanding of those words, but all will be understood as being subject to the qualifying word 'negligent'. Within a professional indemnity policy, the court would surely be bound to construe the word 'negligent' as referring to the necessity for some cause of action to lie against the insured professional, arising out of some breach of duty of care. This duty of care could, perhaps, arise in tort (i.e. the tort of negligence), or in contract (i.e. breach of the contractual duty of care owed by a professional person to his client), or further in tort for negligent misstatement. The requirement of a claim being made against the insured professional is of the essence of the professional indemnity policy, for it is not designed to indemnify an insured against all losses caused through the negligence of himself or his staff, but only those losses arising from these sorts of claims which are founded upon the legal liability of the insured to another party, sounding in some form of negligence or breach of duty to that party, arising out of the conduct of the prescribed business or practice.

'. . . committed by the Insured or their predecessors in the practice or business whenever the same was or alleged to have been committed'

The intention of these words is to make it clear that all those participating in the practice or business are protected by the indemnity against claims made upon them during the period of insurance, no matter when the negligent act, error or omission was committed. Thus past partners' negligent defalcations will be covered by the policy, as well as those committed by the present partners or employees that result in a claim being made against the business or practice, or members thereof, during the twelve month period of insurance specified in the schedule to the policy.

Strictly speaking, when a partner retires from the business or practice, the partnership comes to an end, and a new partnership agreement will be formed between the remaining members of the old partnership, possibly with one or more new partners to replace the retiring partner. The wording adopted in this 'basic' policy, therefore, makes it clear that both the business firm or professional practice, and the individual partners are covered by the insurance, whether the partners be 'old', continuing, or 'new'.

It is important to stress, however, that retiring partners will not be covered under the policy in respect of claims made against them personally for their negligent act, error or omission. Only claims made against *the firm*, rather than the retired partner alone, are covered by the wording. For this reason retiring partners often seek what is known as 'run-off' cover to protect them against such personal claims of negligence. This cover is usually available for a single premium payment to cover a six year period, but practice may vary in individual instances.

There is no English decision upon the interpretation of this sort of 'predecessors in business' wording, but there is a decision of the Australian High Court upon a Lloyd's professional indemnity policy which protected a firm of solicitors against claims for negligent acts, errors or omissions committed 'on the part of the Firm or their predecessors in business'.[10]

The facts were that a claim for breach of professional duty was made against a Mr Price, a solicitor practising in partnership with a Mr Ellis, and Mr Price claimed an indemnity under the partnership's professional indemnity policy then in force. Mr Price and Mr Ellis had entered into partnership as from 1 February 1954, and first effected a professional indemnity policy in September 1956. In the proposal for this insurance Mr Price disclosed that there might be a claim made against him in respect of an alleged omission to set an action down for trial within time while practising on his own account. This claim was subsequently proved against Mr Price when it was held that his omission had occurred in March 1952, and Mr Price then sought an indemnity under the policy effected by the partnership. The insurers under this policy, Lloyd's underwriters, disputed their liability, and the question before the court was whether the indemnity covered a claim made, within the year of insurance, against one of the insured, if the claim arose by reason of a negligent act, error or omission committed before the commencement of the partnership.

This particular policy, unlike the 'basic' policy adopted in this chapter, gave a definition of the 'Firm' insured in the recital clause as follows:

> . . . 'the Firm' which expression shall include the aforesaid persons who may at any time and from time to time during the subsistence of this Policy be a partner in the Firm *or any one or more of them* (author's italics).

What fell before the court to construe were the proposal and an insurance certificate upon which was endorsed a copy of the indemnity and the conditions which the policy would contain if issued (i.e. it was a 'master policy' scheme of insurance). A court in construing an insurance contract may only generally have regard to the documents evidencing the contract from which it must interpret the intention of the parties as to the scope of the insurance,[11] and this the

10 *Maxwell v Price* [1960] 2 Lloyd's Rep 155.
11 *Robertson v French* (1803) 4 East 130; and see ch 2, p. 92, above under 'Construction of the policy'.

Australian court did. Dixon CJ first postulated whether either the insured or the insurer had ever considered the scope of the cover under the policy prior to Mr Price's claim, and then said:[12]

> At all events, the question, as I see it, depends upon tracing out the logical effect of the direction to supply the words 'any one or more of them' as included within the meaning of the word 'firm', and then considering whether there is any sufficient ground for implying a restraint upon the application of the words . . . Now, to me it seems that if this is literally and logically applied to the case of David Lee Price, the proviso agrees to indemnify him against any claim for breach of professional duty as solicitor which may be made against him during the period by reason of any negligent act, error or omission whenever or wherever the same was or may have been committed on his part.

Due to this particular definition of the insured firm, then, the court held the insured solicitor to be indemnified against claims made upon him prior to his ever forming the present partnership. This decision of the Australian High Court is not binding upon the English courts, but would be of persuasive authority if a similar set of circumstances arose. It is submitted, however, that liability for negligent acts, errors or omissions committed prior to becoming a partner in the insured firm under the 'basic' policy would not be considered by an English court to be covered, not least because of the absence of any definition of the insured firm referring to 'any one or more of them'. If a 'new' partner requires an indemnity from such possible claims arising from his 'old' practice, then a specific extension of the primary cover will be required from the insurer, for which an extra premium may or may not be requested, depending upon the circumstances, e.g. whether claims are anticipated.

'The Insurer will also indemnify any employee of the Insured if the Insured requests in respect of liability for which the Insured would have been entitled to indemnity if the claim had been made against the Insured, provided that such employee shall be subject to the terms and conditions of this policy as if he were the Insured so far as they can apply.'

The purpose of this part of the operative clause is to make it clear that the insurer will cover situations where an employee of the insured business or practice is sued by a claimant alleging professional negligence rather than the firm. The employers, i.e. the partners of the firm, would not strictly in law be liable to indemnify an employee against the consequences of his own negligent act, error or omission,[13] in practice employers will readily wish to indemnify

12 *Maxwell v Price*, above, at 158.
13 Indeed the converse is true, see *Lister v Romford Ice and Cold Storage Co Ltd* [1957] AC 555, [1957] 1 All ER 125, HL; cf *Morris v Ford Motor Co Ltd* [1973] 2 QB 792, [1973] 2 All ER 1084, CA.

their employees and, moreover, would view it in their interests to have the action properly defended, not wishing it to be popular opinion that they employ incompetent staff. In the normal course of events, therefore, this extension is included in the 'basic' policy at no extra cost to the insured, being a reflection of the desire of proposers to include it. The insurer protects his position, though, by including the necessity of the employee only being covered to the same extent and under the same terms and conditions as the named insured.

The operative clause regarding legal costs

FURTHER it is agreed that the Insurer in addition will pay the costs and expenses incurred with the Insurer's written consent relating to the defence and/or settlement of claims. If a payment in excess of the amount of indemnity available under this Policy is made the Insurer's liability in respect of such costs and expenses of the Insured shall be such proportion of the total costs and expenses incurred as the amount of the indemnity available under the Policy bears to the total amount paid to dispose of the claim against the Insured.

The first sentence of this second operative clause takes the form of an indemnity regarding the legal costs and expenses of the insured that are incurred with the written authority of the insurer. Many professional indemnity policies will not contain such an open-ended indemnification of costs, and the sentence is extended to include a limitation of this costs liability to some specified sum, or even a proportion of the eventual damages or settlement sum payable to the claimant against the insured. Certainly, the desire of professionals seeking this form of insurance is to have at least some measure of cover available to them to meet the large bill of their own legal representatives in the event of a long-fought defence failing, the main body of the costs awarded to the successful claimant being covered by the main indemnity of the policy.[14] Even a successfully defended case will often lead to some shortfall in costs received from the unsuccessful claimant.

What is the effect of the words in this clause 'the Insurer will pay the costs and expenses incurred with the Insurer's written consent relating to the defence and/or settlement of claims'? Is the initial written consent of the insurer sufficient to see the insured through to the bitter end of a long legal wrangle all the way to the House of Lords? Although these words have never been tested in the courts, very similar provisions were considered under another liability policy in *E Hulton & Co Ltd v Mountain*,[15] when Bankes LJ said, obiter:[16]

14 *Xenos v Fox* (1869) LR 4 CP 665.
15 (1921) 8 Ll L Rep 249, CA.
16 Ibid at 250.

In my view, the words of the policy, 'no costs shall be incurred without the consent of the underwriters', literally construed, mean that at every stage of the proceedings involving costs the consent of the underwriters must be applied for. A clause, however, must be construed reasonably. Application for consent was a necessary condition precedent, and it must be shown either that an express application was made and express consent given, or that the necessity for making it was waived, or that the consent was implied.

The application for the consent of the underwriters should be made at every important stage of the proceedings. When the consent was applied for and given for defending an action, if the action resulted in favour of the assured and there was an appeal it would be necessary to apply and obtain consent to oppose the appeal, and if the appeal resulted in a new trial being ordered, application and consent would be necessary before proceeding to defend the new trial.

It is submitted that these views, although expressed obiter in that case, would be applied to any interpretation before a court upon the 'basic' policy wording.

As an interesting corollary to this requirement of consent to the incurring of costs in defending and/or settling a claim against the insured, where claims are made against an insured, the insurer is obliged to discuss the matter with the insured. Where insurers under a third party liability policy defended actions against their insured, in his name but without his consent, having neither consulted the insured nor asked him if he has anything to say as to the advisability of defending the actions, the insurers were held to have incurred a common law liability for all the costs, notwithstanding any conditions in the policy limiting their maximum liability under the policy.[17]

The second sentence of the clause is inserted to avoid liability for all the costs and expenses no matter what the eventual liability of the insured is ajudged to be to the aggrieved third party. In *Knight v Hosken*[18] an estate agents' professional indemnity policy provided that if the insurers required the insured to contest any claim against the insured, they would 'pay all costs, charges and expenses in connection therewith'. Whilst delivering his judgment in this case, Lord Greene MR said that the insurers would be liable for all the costs upon the £5,000 claim, even though the indemnity limit was £2,000, because of the wording of the clause. The case, however, revolved around the issue of whether the insured had agreed to make a contribution to the costs of the claim against him which had gone to the Court of Appeal, so that this agreement would supersede and vary the provision in the policy. In the event, it was held by the Court of

17 *Allen v London Guarantee and Accident Co Ltd* (1912) 28 TLR 254.
18 (1943) 75 Ll L Rep 74, CA.

Appeal that the insured estate agent had not concluded a binding contract to pay a proportion of the appeal costs, therefore the policy provisions were undisturbed with the result that the insurers were fully liable for all the costs involved in defending the claim against the insured. No contract for contributing to the costs was completed because the insured received no consideration for that agreement from the insurers. They were fighting the case for their own benefit, and he received no benefit or forbearance to his use from the insurers which could form legal consideration for a valid agreement.

It is important to note, though, that it was accepted by Lord Greene MR that the insurers were at complete liberty at any stage to turn to the insured and make full settlement to him under the policy, i.e. £2,000, and then have no further part in the proceedings. It therefore seems reasonable to believe that a court will uphold any future right of the insurer to withhold his consent to the incurring of costs under the 'basic' policy wording, provided that this is not an unreasonable course of action in the circumstances, but the insurer would then, of course, have to make a full indemnity of the claim to the insured so he may pay the claimant, forthwith, without the incursion of further legal costs. The insured would then be at liberty to continue the defence of the action at his own expense, holding the moneys paid under the policy in trust for the insurer if the case is successfully defended, or for the claimant if the action is successful.[19]

The proviso clause

> PROVIDED ALWAYS that the Insurer shall be liable only, in respect of any claim hereunder, for that part of the claim (which for the purpose of this clause shall be deemed to include all costs and expenses incurred with the Insurer's written consent) which exceeds the amount stated as 'the Excess' in the Schedule hereto in respect of any one claim or number of claims arising out of the same occurrence and to the same amount in respect of all claims under this policy during any one year of insurance.

This clause is drafted so as to provide an 'aggregate limit' basis to the policy, so that no matter how many claims are validly made under the policy in any year of insurance, the maximum liability of the insurer will be the sum specified as the limit of indemnity in the schedule to the policy. This limit therefore applies as the limit of indemnity recoverable in respect of any one claim made under the policy,[20] and in respect of the aggregate of all claims made in the year of insurance. It may thus be treated as a decreasing fund of indemnity, for as claims under the policy are settled in point of time, there is an ever-decreasing 'pool' of remaining liability under the

---

19 *Castellain v Preston* (1883) 11 QBD 380, CA.
20 See *Allen v London Guarantee*, above.

policy. One huge claim could exhaust the indemnity limit, leaving the insured with no indemnity from insurance for other claims that may arise during that year of insurance.

Overall limits to the insurance contract are perfectly valid, being the bargain struck between the parties in consideration of the premium asked by the insurer.[1] It may even be agreed under the policy that different limits of indemnity will apply in respect of any one claim, e.g. £10,000, with an aggregate limit for the year, e.g. £30,000, overriding the single claim limit in any insurance year.

It can be appreciated that this aggregate basis of limiting liability could leave an insured professional in precarious circumstances if a number of claims happen to be made upon him in any particular twelve month insurance period. Because of this risk, many professionals will be prepared to pay an increased premium in order to gain the benefit of an indemnity policy that has no aggregate limit contained in it, so that any number of valid claims may be made under the policy in any year of insurance. The only limit expressed in the policy will relate to each claim made. Accordingly, this extended basis of cover is called 'each and every claim' basis, and the first part of the proviso clause will be amended to read:

> PROVIDED ALWAYS that the Insurer shall be liable only, in respect of each and every claim hereunder, for that part of the claim (which for the purpose of this clause shall be deemed to include all costs and expenses incurred with the insurer's written consent) which exceeds the amount stated as 'the Excess' in the Schedule hereto and a number of claims arising out of the same occurrence shall be treated as one claim only.

In respect of both forms of proviso clause, two matters call to be explained. The first relates to the 'Excess' which will be found in the schedule attached to the policy. It is customary in professional indemnity policies for the insured to always bear the first proportion of each and every claim made under the policy. There are various reasons put forward for this, and perhaps the most plausible is that the knowledge that being involved in claims for professional negligence will certainly result in his bearing some financial burden, is an incentive to the insured to maintain the highest standards of professional competence within his business or practice, both in relation to his own skill and also with regard to the training and supervision of his staff. This proportion of self-insured Excess is often quite substantial, rarely less than hundreds of pounds, more commonly though, it is expressed in thousands of pounds.

The wording of the proviso clause provides that the specified Excess born by the insured, is to be taken into account when considering the total indemnity claimed under the policy, i.e. damages payable and costs incurred jointly. Thus, if damages of £50,000 have

1 *Knight v Hosken* (1943) 75 Ll L Rep 74, CA.

to be paid to the third party claiming against the insured, and costs incurred with the insurer's consent amount to £5,000, the total claim for indemnity under the policy is £55,000, and from this figure will be deducted the Excess. If this is £7,500, the claim under the policy will be for £47,500, to which will be applied the policy limit (either for 'each and every claim' or for 'any claim' or the aggregate for the year of insurance).

It is to be noted that under the wording adopted in this 'basic' policy the exercise may result in the insured paying the whole expense of small claims. For instance, a small claim for professional negligence may be settled for £5,000, with total costs of £1,000. Applying the Excess in the example of £7,500, the insurer is under no liability to pay the insured anything under the terms of the indemnity policy. Variations of wording found in practice, however, *may* exclude the incurred costs and expenses from application of the Excess i.e. all costs and expenses authorised by the insurer will be paid, and only the damages awarded will be subject to the policy limit.

The second matter to be considered is the meaning of 'any one claim or number of claims arising out of the same occurrence'. What amounts to another 'negligent act, error or omission' under the terms of the policy will have an important bearing upon the amount recoverable from the insurer where there has been repeated negligence, either in respect of the same client or in respect of many clients. This aspect was brought before the court in a case concerning a solicitor's professional indemnity policy where there was an aggregate limit of £15,000 under the policy, but a limit of £3,000 'in respect of any claim or claims arising out of the same occurrence'.[2]

The facts were that the insured's employee advised the family of a deceased man that claims lay against his intestate estate for his negligence in causing a motor car accident killing himself and his father-in-law, and seriously injuring his mother-in-law, widow and infant son. No advice was given that a person other than the widow should be substituted to administer the estate, and no effective writ was issued against it within the required six months. The insured then notified his insurer of a likely claim because of an occurrence in connection with the handling of the matter. The mother-in-law sued on her own account and as administratrix of her deceased husband's estate, and the widow and son sued the insured for the assistant's negligence in depriving them of their right to be paid damages by the deceased's estate. The issue, then, was whether there was one or more occurrences of negligence under the terms of the insured's professional indemnity policy.

Donaldson J had this to say about the interpretation of 'occurrences' in negligence policies:[3]

2 *Forney v Dominion Insurance Co Ltd* [1969] 1 WLR 928.
3 Ibid at 934.

'Occurrences' like accidents can be looked at from the point of view of the tortfeasor or of the victim. [The son's] loss of his right to claim damages from [his father's] estate was from his point of view a different occurrence from the similar one by [the mother-in-law]. However, the provision of the policy which limits the indemnity contemplates the possibility that a number of claims may arise out of one occurrence. This seems to me to indicate that a number of persons may be injured by a single act of negligence by the insured − in other words that 'occurrence' in this context is looked at from the point of view of the insured. If this is right, I have to ask myself how often [the assistant's] negligence occurred. My answer to that question is 'twice', namely, when she allowed [the widow] to become administratrix of her late husband's estate and when she failed to issue writs within the six-month limitation period.

Exclusions

Exclusion clauses contained in the policy may be regarded as terms of definition of the contract of insurance, and thus matters within the exceptions are outside the scope of the policy. In certain circumstances, it may become necessary to determine whether a particular loss falls within an excepted risk in a policy, and, if it does, the indemnity under the policy will have no application. This will be so even though the loss may be proximately caused by some matter dealt with under the policy, e.g. professional negligence.[4] It is therefore very important to read and understand the exclusions laid out in the policy.

1 *'The Excess'*
This is to prevent any misunderstanding on the interpretation of the policy, and so avoid any construing of the policy as including the self-insured Excess that is to be borne by the insured in respect of each and every claim that he makes against the insurer under the policy.

2 *'Libel or Slander'*
No cover under the 'basic' policy is provided for defamatory remarks made by the insured partners or their employees, even if such statements were made negligently. The law relating to defamation is explained in the following chapter, where a possible extension of the 'basic' policy is considered.

3 *'Bodily Injury, Sickness, Disease or Death sustained by any person arising out of and in the course of his employment by the Insured under a contract of service or apprenticeship with the*

4 *Saqui and Lawrence v Stearns* [1911] 1 KB 426, CA.

*Insured or for any claim for any breach of any obligation owed by
the Insured as an employer to any employee'*
These risks are excluded from the ambit of the professional indemnity policy because they are risks that must be compulsorily insured
by the insuring partners under an Employers Liability Policy. The
Employers' Liability (Compulsory Insurance) Act 1969 requires
every employer carrying on business in this country to have
Employers Liability insurance as far as concerns the operation of his
business in Great Britain to cover his liability towards his employees,
whether they be manual workers, clerical workers, or other class of
worker.

4 *'Any claim directly or indirectly caused, or contributed to, by
any dishonest malicious fraudulent criminal or illegal act or
omission of the Insured partners or their predecessors or their
employees'*
This exclusion clause really adds nothing to the common law position relating to all insurance contracts, including professional
indemnity insurances, that an insured may not by his own deliberate
act cause the event upon which the insurance money is payable, and
this embraces criminal or dishonest acts or omissions on the part of
the insured,[5] or of his employee.[6]
   The wording of the clause is drafted in the widest possible terms to
avoid confusion as to its meaning in any particular set of circumstances. Losses arising to the insured due to any of these excluded
causes, either directly or indirectly, will thus not be recoverable
under the professional indemnity policy.

5 *Claims made upon the Insured prior to the inception of this
Policy*
This exclusion is, again, placed here really for the purpose of stating
the obvious, for the avoidance of doubt. The main operative clause,
of course, only refers to indemnifying the insured against damages
awarded 'as a result of any claim or claims made upon the insured
during the period of insurance'. Claims notified to the insured are
not intended to be covered by the policy unless they are first made
against the insured during the year of insurance.
   There is also the further matter that the proposal form will have
contained a question enquiring about claims notified to the insured
during the previous, say, five years. Not completing such a question
fully and accurately will amount to non-disclosure of a material fact,

5 *Beresford v Royal Insurance Co Ltd* [1938] AC 586, [1938] 2 All ER 602, HL;
   Haseldine v Hosken [1933] 1 KB 822, CA.
6 *Davies v Hosken* [1937] 3 All ER 192; *Goddard and Smith v Frew* [1939] 4 All ER
   358, CA.

and this will entitle the insurer to avoid the claim on that ground alone.[7]

6 'Any claim in respect of which the Insured are entitled to indemnity under any other insurance except in respect of any excess beyond the amount which would have been payable under such insurance had this Policy not been effected'

The purpose of this clause is to make this policy only operate to such extent that another professional indemnity policy held by the insured (if that be the case) does not cover the whole loss. In other words the insurer is seeking to create a situation where contribution between two policies covering the same risks does not come into operation, and this policy will only operate as an Excess policy, i.e. excess of loss policy (cf the self-insured 'Excess' borne by the insured upon each and every claim under the policy).

This clause will only be effective to exclude the equitable doctrine of contribution between two or more policies covering the same risks, if the other policies do not contain a similar exclusion clause. This point was recently considered in the Court of Appeal in a professional indemnity policy case, and it was said, obiter, that if both policies contain exclusion clauses which are indistinguishable in their effect, the court should invoke the equitable principle of contribution between co-insurers to avoid the absurdity and injustice of holding that a person who has paid premiums for cover by two insurers should be left without insurance cover because each insurer has excluded liability for the risk against which the other has indemnified him.[8] The two exclusions cancel each other out.

7 'Any claim arising out of the ownership, maintenance, operation or use of any aircraft, boats, automobiles or vehicles of any kind by or in the interest of the insured'

These risks are excluded from the policy because these risks are insurable under other insurances, and the policy is not intended to cover liability of the insured or his employee for, e.g. negligent driving of a motor car. Liability for such events must be insured under a Motor Insurance policy (under the Road Traffic Acts 1972–1974), or a Marine or Aviation policy.

8 The Insolvency of the Insured

Losses arising from the impecuniosity or bankruptcy of the insured are not covered by the indemnity, as is made clear in the operative

---

7 See ch 2, p. 83, above, heading 'Non-disclosure and misrepresentation'.
8 *National Employers Mutual General Insurance Assn Ltd v Haydon* [1980] 2 Lloyd's Rep 149 at 152, per Stephenson LJ; following *Gale v Motor Union Insurance Co Ltd* [1928] 1 KB 359, *Weddell v Road Transport and General Insurance Co Ltd* [1932] 2 KB 563, and *Austin v Zurich General Accident and Liability Insurance Co Ltd* (1944) 77 Ll L Rep 409.

clause's reference to claims arising from the insured's 'negligent act, error or omission'.

9 *'Any consequence of war invasion act of foreign enemy hostilities (whether war be declared or not) civil war rebellion revolution insurrection or military or usurped power'*
It is not easy to see how these events might give rise to a claim under a professional indemnity policy, but some insurers include this exclusion, as they do in Public Liability policies, pursuant to the War Risks Agreement between all insurers which has affected all such policies since 1 October 1937.

10 *'Loss or destruction of or damage to any property or any loss or expense whatsoever resulting or arising therefrom or any consequential loss or any legal liability of whatsoever nature directly or indirectly caused by or contributed to by or arising from*
(i) ionising radiations or contamination by radioactivity from any nuclear fuel or from any nuclear waste from the combustion of nuclear fuel
(ii) the radioactive toxic explosive or other hazardous properties of any explosive nuclear assembly or nuclear component thereof'
Again, this clause is really only inserted for the avoidance of doubt as to the extent of its cover. Private insurers have never intended to cover risks relating to nuclear assemblies, which are more properly borne by the government agencies and armed forces controlling the devices. Under the Nuclear Installations (Licensing and Insurance) Act 1959, it is the duty of the agencies licensed to operate with nuclear devices to insure through a single atomic energy insurance pool.

11 *'Any claims arising out of any defect in or use of any buildings, premises or land owned or occupied by the Insured'*
These liabilities in nuisance, under the Occupiers' Liability Act 1957, and under the Defective Premises Act 1972, are properly insured under a Public Liability policy, and are outside the scope of a professional negligence policy.

12 *'The cost of replacing documents which have been lost, mislaid or destroyed'*
Because of the nature of a professional man's business, he often has possession of various documents which belong to his client or otherwise entrusted to him for professional purposes. Therefore, an extension is often sought to include this risk, and this is dealt with in chapter 4.

13 *'Any claims in respect of any goods or products manu-
factured, constructed, altered, repaired, serviced, treated, sold,
supplied, or distributed by the Insured or from any other business
or occupation, even though the same may be carried on by the
Insured in conjunction with their practice or business described in
the Schedule hereto'*
This can be a very important exclusion for some particular professionals, for instance engineers, who may be responsible for advising
upon the use of particular materials, as may architects, and may
become involved in the supplying of particular construction
materials. These risks are insurable under what is known as Product
Liability insurance, and replacement of a defective product itself
may be covered by Product Guarantee insurance. The professional
negligence insurer aims only to insure against claims arising out of
the insured's advice, design, specification or omission to perform a
professional duty, and therefore excludes risks arising from products or goods rather than the act, error or omission of the insured in
the conduct of his practice or business.

14 *'Any claim arising out of a specific liability assumed under
contract which increases the Insured's measure of liability above
that normally assumed under the Insured's usual contractual or
implied conditions of engagement or service'*
This sort of exclusion clause has grown up because of the ever-
increasing demands placed upon professionals to somehow 'guarantee' their services to their clients. The professional's duty is to
exercise the normal degree of skill and care to be expected from a reasonably competent member of the profession of which he is a
member, and this is the risk as disclosed to the insurer, which he in
turn agrees to insure subject to the payment of the required premium. The insurer therefore, quite justifiably, excludes liabilities or
duties assumed by the insured that are over and above those normally incidental to the profession or business followed by the
insured, and the premium is requested and received on this basis.
   It is possible for the insured to submit a particular proposed contract to the insurer so that he may consider the effects of the contract
in relation to exposure to claims for breach of professional duties
accepted under the contract with the client. The insurer may then
inform the insured whether he is prepared to extend the policy by
endorsement, so as to cover these extra risks, and, if so, what additional premium will be required.

15 *'Any claim made upon the Insured for or in the name of a
consortium of professional men or firms or other association
formed of which all or any one of the Insured form part for the*

purpose of undertaking any joint venture or joint ventures'
This exclusion clause, like the one before, has grown up in response
to the practice of many engineers and/or architects to form loose
groups or joint ventures and so 'pool' their resources upon various
diverse projects, at home and abroad. In the vast majority of cases,
these joint venture groups or consortia are, in law, nothing more
than partnerships, with all the consequent responsibilities of joint
and several liability of the partners for each other's acts or omissions
committed for the purpose of the partnership.[9]

It is not the intention of an insurer to cover these partnership
liabilities. For instance, the engineer and architect of a consortium
may find themselves being pursued for the liabilities of their partner-
contractor who is now bankrupt and so cannot meet the claim
against him. This sort of liability is certainly not within the contemplation of the insurer during the negotiation of the policy, unless
specially alerted by the insured, and is therefore specifically excluded
from the policy. It is probable that such claims are outside the scope
of the 'basic' policy in any case, because of the wording of the operative clause which states that only the negligent act, error or omission
of the insured, committed in the course of the practice or business
described in the schedule to the policy, is covered.

Some insurers refuse under any circumstances to insure by extension of the policy, these extra consortium or joint venture risks, but
others will insure particular projects upon sight and approval of the
contractual documentation, together with an extra premium. Alternatively, the insured professionals may be as wise to accept the
exclusion under their professional indemnity policy, and arrange
instead, either a separate professional indemnity policy on behalf of
the consortium, or a 'project cover' insurance which will provide
insurance to all members of the joint venture upon a wide variety of
liabilities implicit in the particular project upon which they joined
resources.

16 *'Any claim or claims where the initial action and all subsequent actions and/or litigations are not brought in the Courts of
and subject to the laws of the United Kingdom*
The insurer will obviously judge the measure of risk to be insured
based upon his experience. This will be primarily gained within the
United Kingdom and the insurer will be familiar, it is assumed, with
the levels of awards in these courts and with the law relating to
breach of professional duty. Although the laws of other countries
may not be outside their cognisance, it is unreasonable to expect the
insurer to rate the risk in respect of all jurisdictions, and, indeed, this
would not be the wish of the majority seeking such insurance. It

9 See ch 1, above.

might also be said that that there is a risk of the insured being sued in another country is a material fact and should be disclosed to the insurer upon proposal.

It is because of these reasons that insurers will insert this type of exclusion clause, it being understood between the parties that there is a United Kingdom risk only. Insurers may well be prepared to extend the policy, however, upon full disclosure of all material facts relating to the foreign risk element, and consideration of the laws of the countries in which claims may be entertained by their courts.

Conditions

1 *'The Insured shall give immediate notice in writing to the Insurer of any claim made against them or any one of them, or of the receipt of notice from any person of any intention to hold any one or more of them responsible for the results of any breach of professional duty which may give rise to a claim under this policy and the Insured shall upon request give the Insurer all such information as the Insurer may reasonably require'*
The insurer obviously wishes to learn of claims or intimations that claims will be made against the insured at the earliest point in time reasonably possible. This is so that the full circumstances of the events giving rise to the claims may be investigated, which requires the cooperation of the insured, and, if it looks as though the claimant has a good case against the insured for breach of professional duty, the insurer may set aside a 'reserve' estimate in his funds for the settlement of the claim. It is here, though, that some conflict of interest may develop between the insured and the insurer, for the insurer may wish to settle the claim as quickly as possible to keep the expenses of the claim to the minimum, both in amount of damages and in costs, whereas the insured has his professional standing to consider and would rather fight the claim all the way through the courts in the hope that the courts would dismiss the claim on some ground, technical or otherwise. For this reason, the Q.C. clause (below) is inserted in most professional negligence policies.

Where the insured and the insurer are of one mind upon the defence or settlement of a claim, then obviously it is in both their interests to decide upon a course of action and carry it out with all due expedition.

It will be noticed that the insured must notify the insurer in writing of claims or potential claims − this is to prevent later argument as to whether the claim under the policy was made to the insurer within the period of insurance covered by the policy. Mere verbal or telephonic communications have the implicit unsatisfactory nature of leading to disputes as to the date of notification, and proof will only be possible upon the testing of each parties' word and memory of events against that of the other party.

The clause does, however, require the insured to notify the insurer of 'notice from any person of any intention to hold any one or more of them responsible'. These words are designed to embrace any verbal or informal intimation made to the insured by any potential claimant, and, to protect his position, the insured must give notice in writing to the insurer of this intimation of possible claim.

2 *'If during the subsistence of this Policy the Insured shall become aware of any occurrence which may subsequently give rise to a claim against any one or more of them for breach of professional duty in the conduct of their business or practice as described in the Schedule by reason of any negligent act, error or omission, the Insured shall immediately give notice in writing to the Insurer of such occurrence, and any claim which may subsequently be made against them arising out of that negligent act, error or omission shall for the purpose of this Policy be deemed to have been made during the subsistence hereof'*
Under this clause the insured will be covered under the policy for the year in which he first realised that a claim might arise from a negligent act, error or omission which he realises he has committed but, for which, he has not yet received any intimation of any potential claim. This enables the insurer to put aside a 'reserve' in his claims portfolio, but in these days of inflation it can work against the insured. This is because he will not benefit from later policies in which the limits will probably have increased, and this will be of especial importance in the case of policies with an 'aggregate' limit for claims made under the policy, but will also be important in 'each and every claim' policies, for when the claim is eventually settled the amount of the claim, because of inflation and an award of interest on the sum due, may well have increased beyond that amount provided for under the policy.

The clause can come to the aid of partners who retire, though, who have allowed their professional indemnity cover to lapse, but will be protected under the provisions of this clause against circumstances notified as an 'occurrence' to the insurer, which later culminate in a claim being made against them.

3 *'The Insured shall not, by himself or his agent, make any admission of liability nor make any offer promise or settlement nor incur costs or expenses relating to any claim made against him which forms a claim under this Policy without the written consent of the Insurer'*
The insurer, by this clause, ensures that he always is involved in matters concerning the defence or settlement of the claim. This

clause is a natural consequence of the principle of indemnity in insurance contracts, and an insured must not renounce or compromise the position of his insurer, so that the loss indemnified by the insurer is kept to a minimum.[10]

An admission of liability by an agent or employee of the insured to the claimant, which is made without authorisation of the insured, is apparently not a breach of this type of condition in a liability policy.[11]

4 *'The Insurer shall be entitled to take over and have the absolute control and conduct of any claim or proceeding using where necessary for its own benefit the name of the Insured. Save that the Insured shall not be required to allow their name to be used in the contesting of any proceeding unless a Queen's Counsel (to be mutually agreed upon by the Insured and the Insurer) shall advise that on the actual facts of the case such claim could be contested with a reasonable prospect of success'*

This clause is inserted firstly, to give the insurer his full rights of subrogation as soon as a claim is made under the policy (rather than after payment of moneys due under the policy which is the position at common law[12]), and so take complete control of the defence and/or settlement of the claim made against the insured.

The second purpose of this clause is to provide a procedure that may be adopted to settle the difficult position of the insured being unwilling to settle a claim which the insurer wishes to be settled. It has been held that where a claim is made against the insured alleging both negligence and another matter, e.g. fraud, the policy does not apply to indemnify the insured against the loss claimed, and, accordingly, the Queen's Counsel clause has no application.[13]

The clause will have equal application to the situation where the insured wishes the claim to be settled as quickly as possible, with as little consequent publicity as possible, but where the insurer wishes the claim to be contested. The insurer may not believe that the claim is being brought correctly against the insured, or that the particular point of professional negligence at issue is of such importance that he wants the question to be fully tested, i.e. he wants the case to be a 'test case' for the whole profession in the instance of an extension of that profession's duties to their clients as a whole.

---

10 This principle also applies to the compromise of subrogation rights, *Commercial Union Assurance Co v Lister* (1874) 9 Ch App 483; *Phoenix Assurance Co v Spooner* [1905] 2 KB 753.
11 *Tustin v Arnold & Sons* (1915) 84 LJKB 2214.
12 *Mason v Sainsbury* (1782) 3 Doug KB 61.
13 *West Wake Price & Co v Ching* [1956] 3 All ER 821, [1957] 1 WLR 45.

5 '*All differences arising out of this Policy shall be referred to the
arbitration of some person to be appointed by the Insurer and the
Insured, or, if they cannot agree upon such person, to the decision
of two arbitrators, one to be appointed by each party, and in case
of disagreement between the arbitrators to the decision of an
Umpire who shall be appointed in writing by the arbitrators. The
provisions of the Arbitration Acts shall apply to such arbitration
and the place of arbitration shall be London, England*'
This clause has the effect of requiring the insured to engage in the full
arbitration of disputes or differences arising between himself and his
insurer, prior to being able to institute proceedings in the courts
upon the issue.[14] The court will then only upset the award of the
arbitrator(s) if there has been an error in law in determining that
award, either upon the question of liability of the insurer under the
policy, or upon the issue of quantum due to the insured under the
policy.

If, however, the insurer repudiates the claim by the insured on
the ground, e.g. that non-disclosure by him of material facts,
had rendered the policy null and void, the issue is properly
brought before the court, and no stay in proceedings will be granted
to permit arbitration to take place, because the dispute cannot be
brought within the ambit of a repudiated contract's clause requiring
arbitration.[15]

It will be open to the insurer and insured to jointly agree that a
certain matter should be referred to the court rather than to arbitration, and so agree to vary the conditions of the insurance contract if
they so choose. This is perhaps more likely where a question of
liability of the insurer is in issue, rather than the extent or quantum
of his liability to pay under the policy.

6 '*This Policy may be cancelled at any time at the request of
either the Insured or the Insurer upon thirty days' notice of such
cancellation to the other party, the unearned portion of the paid
premium shall then be returned on surrender of the Policy, the
Insurer retaining the customary short rate premium unless the
Insurer has cancelled the Policy, in which case only the pro rata
premium shall be retained*'
This cancellation clause is inserted largely for the insurer's benefit,
but is generally only utilised in extreme cases where the insured is
either reporting an exceptionally large number of claims, such that
the insurer feels he must cancel the policy and not place an undue
burden on the joint pool of funds to meet the claims of other
insured under similar policies, or where the insured is proving most

---

14 *Stebbing v Liverpool and London and Globe Insurance Co Ltd* [1917] 2 KB 433.
15 *Furey v Eagle Star and British Dominions Insurance Co* (1922) 10 Ll L Rep 198.

unco-operative with respect to existing claims under the policy to the prejudice of the insurer.

The clause does enable the insured, however, to cancel the policy mid-term, and take his insurance elsewhere if he is not satisfied with the conduct of his existing insurer. He will have to pay the increased short term rate of premium for the period of risk prior to cancellation, though, which is a disincentive to such change of insurer prior to a renewal date.

7 *'The Insured shall declare to the Insurer within one month of the expiry of each period of insurance the total amount of gross fees received during the past financial year, and if the actual gross fees shall differ from the amount on which the provisional premium has been paid, the difference shall be met by a further payment to the Insurer or by a refund by the Insurer as the case may be. The records of the Insured may be inspected to verify the amount declared as gross fees by the Insurer or his duly authorised representative upon request'*

Many professional indemnity policies will be rated upon the gross fees earned by the practice or business of the insured, and this clause is inserted to ensure that the insurer receives the correctly adjusted premium for the period of insurance.

Those policies that are rated upon the number of partners and the number of assistants, will not contain this adjustment of fees clause, but may contain a clause requiring a year-end declaration of the number of partners and employees, with an appropriate adjustment of the premium provisionally received.

8 *'In the event of the death of the Insured or any one or more of them the Insurer will in respect of the liability incurred by such Insured indemnify the personal representatives of such Insured in the terms of and subject to the limitations of this Policy provided that such personal representatives shall as though they were the Insured observe, fulfil and be subject to the terms, exclusions and conditions of the Policy so far as they can apply'*

This clause is inserted to protect the estate of the deceased insured and his personal representatives against claims made for the negligent act, error or omission of the insured prior to his death. The old 'six-months rule' for making claims against a deceased's estate under the Law Reform (Miscellaneous Provisions) Act 1934[16] has now gone, and the Proceedings Against Estates Act 1970[17] has resulted in the normal periods of limitation being available to a claimant to pursue a claim against a deceased insured's estate.

16 S. 1(3) of the 1934 Act.
17 S. 1 of the 1970 Act.

Because, therefore, a claim may be made concerning the act or omission of someone who was once an insured under a previous policy, this clause makes it clear that his estate and personal representatives will be protected by the indemnity under the policy as though the insured, now deceased, were still alive.

9 *'The due observance and fulfilment of the terms and conditions of this Policy shall be a condition precedent to any liability of the Insurer to make any payment under this Policy'*
This clause makes compliance with the requirements of the Conditions listed a prior requirement before liability attaches to the insurer. Thus the insured must meet the notification of claims conditions, and co-operate with the insurer, otherwise the insurer will be entitled to avoid the claim for non-compliance with a condition precedent, although the period of insurance will continue to run and the policy will remain in force as regards other claims where the conditions are complied with exactly.[18] Equally, the Q.C. clause, and the arbitration clauses will have to be complied with to prevent the insurer avoiding the claim if these conditions are brought into play.

---

18 *Pawson v Watson* (1778) 2 Cowp 785, and see ch 2, p. 88, above, heading 'Warranties and conditions'.

Chapter 4

Extensions to the basic policy

Introduction

The purpose of this chapter is to present a discussion of the more commonly found extensions of cover, which extend the scope of the 'basic' policy as considered in the preceding chapter. Just as with the 'basic' policy, particular wordings will differ between the various insurers for these additional clauses, but the general purpose and effect can be studied by means of model examples.

Caution must always be exercised, for there are forms of wording that offer only a very restricted extension of cover to the main indemnity clauses of professional negligence policies, and policies must be read in full to gain an accurate measure of their worth.

The first three extensions considered − libel and slander, loss of documents, and fees recovery − are generally widely available, and will often form an essential part of a composite 'scheme' cover offered to the members of the various professions. Dishonesty, or 'fidelity', extensions for the acts of employees are also often available, as are the extensions relating to the several situations regarding the liabilities of partners not covered by the 'basic' policy, and these are also reviewed. Finally, rather less familiar, though not unusual, extensions to cater for more special circumstances are recited and their scope analysed. Chapter 6 will deal in more detail with the insurance covers catering for each profession on a more individual basis.

Libel and slander

There are two methods by which libel and slander cover may become included within the policy issued to the insured, namely, by deletion of the exclusion, or by the attaching of a special endorsement to the

135

policy. It will be seen that the latter method is more satisfactory for the insured.

An endorsement removing the exclusion for claims arising from libel and slander may read as follows:

> Subject otherwise to the limits exclusions terms and conditions of this Policy, Exclusion 2 — Libel or Slander — is deleted from this Policy.

This method of including libel and slander cover under the professional indemnity policy will not provide the insured with wide cover in respect of claims for these risks. This is because the deletion of the exclusion will not have any effect upon the all important main operative clause upon which the whole insurance is based. Therefore, the insured will only be indemnified against claims for libel or slander that are made against him or his firm which arise from a negligent act, error or omission of one of the insured, committed in the conduct of the specified business or practice. Unless the libel or slander arose from such a cause, the mere deletion of the exclusion will not be sufficient to include a libel or slander committed otherwise than by negligent act, error or omission.[1]

There has been one case that illustrates the limited ambit of the libel or slander committed in breach of a professional duty towards a client. This case concerned a solicitor acting for a client who was being sued for the negligent driving of a motor car. The client's motor insurers and his employers' insurers agreed between themselves to share the costs of meeting the claim against the client, and requested the solicitor to admit that his client had been driving negligently. Without taking his client's instructions upon this admission, the solicitor duly made the written admission requested. Upon learning of this admission, the client sued his solicitor for libel and received a large sum of damages for this breach of professional duty giving rise to the defamatory statement that he had driven negligently.[2]

It will be appreciated that, because of the need to first prove a breach of professional duty towards a client which gave rise to the libellous or slanderous statement, this is not the ideal way for a professional to insure himself against these risks of libel and slander.

The other method by which libel and slander can be included in the 'basic' policy is for an endorsement to be added which specifically includes libel and slander, rather than a mere deletion of the exclusion. It will be seen from the example of such an endorsement below, that the insurer will be careful not to include an indemnity for deliberate defamatory statements, in accordance with normal principles of insurance,[3] and will only provide insurance for defamatory statements made during the conduct of the notified business or practice.

1 The extent of the main operative clause is considered in ch 3, above.
2 *Groom v Crocker* [1939] 1 KB 194, [1938] 2 All ER 394, CA.
3 *Beresford v Royal Insurance Co Ltd* [1938] AC 586, [1938] 2 All ER 602, HL.

Notwithstanding Exclusion 2 herein, but subject otherwise to the limits exclusions terms and conditions of this Policy, the Insurer will indemnify the Insured in respect of claims made against the Insured during the period of insurance for libel or slander committed or alleged to have been committed in good faith by the Insured in the conduct of the practice or business provided that this indemnity shall not extend to any matter contained in a journal or publication or in any communication or contribution to the Press, Radio or Television.

Being otherwise subject to the normal terms of the policy, this extension will not include the amount of the Excess stated in the policy to be borne by the insured upon each and every claim under the policy.

The restrictive words of the last part of the endorsement are designed to emphasise to the insured that the insurer is not prepared to indemnify the insured for libels or slanders resulting from deliberate statements or articles submitted for publication by the insured.

Having discussed the inclusion of these risks into the 'basic' policy, it would perhaps be helpful to outline briefly the law relating to libel and slander, so that the cover can be more readily understood. Defamation consists of the publication to a third party of a false statement concerning another person without lawful justification. The tort of defamation is divided into two parts, namely libel and slander, and the action is regarded as of such a personal nature that the action will not survive either for the benefit of nor against the estate of a deceased person,[4] although it is also possible to defame a corporation.[5]

A defamatory statement is one which has a tendency to injure the reputation of the person to whom it refers. It has proved no easy task for the courts to provide a totally adequate definition of what is defamatory, but two of the more famous definitions are whether the words 'tend to lower the plaintiff in the estimation of right-thinking members of society generally',[6] or that convey 'an imputation on the plaintiffs, injurious to them in their trade, or holding them up to hatred, contempt, or ridicule'.[7] At trial, it is for the judge to rule whether the statement is *capable* of bearing such a meaning,[8] but it is for the jury to apply the objective test of whether a reasonable man *would* attach such a meaning to it.[9]

4 Law Reform (Miscellaneous Provisions) Act 1934, s. 1(1)
5 *Metropolitan Saloon Omnibus Co v Hawkins* (1859) 4 H & N 87; *South Hetton Coal Co v North-Eastern News Assn* [1894] 1 QB 133, CA.
6 *Sim v Stretch* [1936] 2 All ER 1237 at 1240, 52 TLR 669 at 67, HL, per Lord Atkin.
7 *Capital and Counties Bank Ltd v Henty* (1882) 7 App Cas 741 at 771, HL, per Lord Blackburn.
8 Ibid, *Henty's Case*; *Morris v Sanders Universal Products Ltd* [1954] 1 All ER 47, [1954] 1 WLR 67, CA.
9 *Broome v Agar* (1928) 138 LT 698, and generally since (Fox's) Libel Act 1792.

A *libel* is a defamatory statement made in some permanent and visible form, such as written words, printed words, a picture,[10] an effigy,[11] television or radio broadcasts,[12] and words and gestures performed in a play.[13]

A *slander* is a defamatory statement made in a transitory form, such as words spoken, audible sounds and visible gestures.

Perhaps of greatest relevance to the extension of cover for libel and slander under a professional negligence policy is to note that it is defamatory to impute to a trader or businessman or professional person a lack of skill, knowledge, qualification, capacity, judgment, or efficiency in the conduct of his trade or business or professional activity.[14] In this regard it is important to note that the person to whom the defamatory statement is made may 'not believe the imputation and may even know that it is untrue',[15] but that will not prevent a jury finding the statement defamatory.[16] Also, whilst it does not reflect on a trader's reputation to say that he has ceased in business,[17] it is defamatory to say that a trader or businessman or professional person is bankrupt or insolvent.[18] Equally, it is defamatory to impute that a corporation, e.g. limited company, is insolvent or is dishonest in the carrying on of its business or in the management of its property.[19]

Some statements will be prima facie defamatory, but others, although prima facie innocent in their natural and obvious sense, may become defamatory when uttered to a third party who has knowledge of some extrinsic fact which, when linked with the statement of gesture, imputes a defamatory meaning. Thus, to say that 'X is a good advertiser' is prima facie innocent, but if uttered to someone who knows that X is a member of a profession which forbids advertising, e.g. a practising barrister, then the *innuendo* renders the statement defamatory. This is called 'true' innuendo,[20] rather than 'false' or 'popular' innuendo which describes a situation where the statement is ambiguous in its meaning, and may or may

---

10 *Du Bost v Beresford* (1810) 2 Camp 511; *Garbett v Hazell, Watson and Viney Ltd* [1943] 2 All ER 359, CA.
11 *Monson v Tussauds Ltd* [1894] 1 QB 671, CA.
12 Defamation Act 1952, ss. 1 and 16(1).
13 Theatres Act 1968, s. 4.
14 *Drummond-Jackson v British Medical Assn* [1970] 1 All ER 1094, [1970] 1 WLR 688, CA.
15 *Hough v London Express Newspaper Ltd* [1940] 2 KB 507 at 515, CA, per Goddard LJ, and Defamation Act 1952, s. 2.
16 *Morgan v Odhams Press Ltd* [1971] 2 All ER 1156, [1971] 1 WLR 1239, HL.
17 *Ratcliffe v Evans* [1892] 2 QB 524, CA.
18 *Shepheard v Whitaker* (1875) LR 10 CP 502.
19 *English and Scottish Co-operative Properties, Mortgage and Investment Society Ltd v Odhams Press Ltd* [1940] 1 KB 440, [1940] 1 All ER 1.
20 *Slim v Daily Telegraph Ltd* [1968] 2 QB 157, [1968] 1 All ER 497, CA.

not reasonably be thought to be defamatory of the plaintiff, e.g. that he is 'bent'.[1]

One of the essential ingredients of an action for defamation, is that the plaintiff must prove that a reasonable person could conclude that he should be identified with the person named in the matter complained of as defamatory.[2] This identification need not be express, but may be latent, in which case it is sufficient for even one person to understand the identification.[3] It is completely irrelevant that the publisher of the defamatory matter was totally unaware that any such reference to the plaintiff would be attributed to his words, or even that the plaintiff existed at all. Thus in *Hulton & Co v Jones*[4] a newspaper article discussed life in Dieppe, and described one Artemus Jones as a churchwarden from Peckham and stated he was living with his mistress. The writer had, so far as he was concerned, invented the name, but, unfortunately, there was a real Artemus Jones. Although he was a barrister and journalist, those who knew him supposed the article to refer to him, and so the publishers had to pay damages to Mr Jones for their defamatory statement.

The question of reasonable reference to the plaintiff is more difficult where the plaintiff alleges that he is one of a group or a class referred to in the defamatory statement. This sort of instance was cited long ago, when it was said that 'if a man wrote that all lawyers were thieves, no particular lawyer could sue him unless there is something to point to the particular individual'.[5] The House of Lords has held that the fundamental approach in all 'class' libel or slander cases must be to see whether in all the circumstances the words were capable of referring to the plaintiff, whoever else they might or might not apply to.[6]

Libel is actionable per se, without proof of actual damage to the plaintiff's reputation, but slander must generally be proven by the plaintiff to have caused actual ('special') damage, that is capable of being estimated in money,[7] but is actionable per se in four cases:

1 *An imputation that the plaintiff has committed a criminal offence punishable by death or imprisonment*

For instance, that the plaintiff is a murderer,[8] a forger[9] or a blackmailer.[10]

---

1 *Allsop v Church of England Newspaper Ltd* [1972] 2 QB 161, [1972] 2 All ER 26, CA.
2 *Morgan v Odhams Press Ltd*, above.
3 *Le Fanu v Malcolmson* (1848) 1 HL Cas 637.
4 [1910] AC 20, HL.
5 *Eastwood v Holmes* (1858) 1 F & F 347 at 349, per Willes J.
6 *Knupffer v London Express Newspaper Ltd* [1944] AC 116, [1944] 1 All ER 493, HL. Also see *Orme v Associated Newspaper Group Ltd* (1981) Times 4 February.
7 *Chamberlain v Boyd* (1883) 11 QBD 407, CA.
8 *Oldham v Peake* (1774) 2 Wm Bl 959.
9 *Jones v Herne* (1759) 2 Wils 87.
10 *Marks v Samuel* [1904] 2 KB 287.

2 *An imputation that the plaintiff is suffering from a contagious or infectious disease*
Examples where it has been held that the disease would so cause other persons to shun the plaintiff are venereal disease,[11] leprosy[12] and plague. It is also probable that any contagious disease or complaint which is caused by personal uncleanliness would be included.[13]

3 *An imputation of unchastity in a female plaintiff*
The Slander of Women Act 1891 provides that words spoken or published which impute unchastity or adultery to any woman or girl shall not require damage to render them actionable. 'Unchastity' has been held to include lesbianism.[14]

4 *An imputation calculated to disparage the plaintiff in his profession or business*
Section 2 of the Defamation Act 1952 provides that:

> In any action for slander in respect of words[15] calculated to disparage the plaintiff in any office, profession, calling, trade or business held or carried on by him at the time of publication, it shall not be necessary to allege or prove special damage, whether or not the words are spoken of the plaintiff by way of his office, profession, calling, trade or business.

It is therefore actionable per se to impute that any person who is carrying on any trade or calling, however humble, is dishonest, immoral, lacks integrity, suffers from insobriety, or is ignorant or incompetent. Only in the case of honorary office holders is it necessary to prove that the charge is so serious as could lead to removal from that office, unless dishonesty is imputed.[16]

The tort of defamation is based upon the loss of reputation of the plaintiff by right-thinking members of society, and, accordingly, the tort requires proof of dissemination or 'publication' of the defamatory remarks, images or gestures, by the defendant to other members of society generally.

It is sufficient if the defamatory statement is made to one other person only, other than the plaintiff himself, although a defendant is not liable for an unsuspected overhearing of the words spoken by him to the plaintiff.[17] There is no 'publication' if the remarks are

---

11 *Houseman v Coulson* [1948] 2 DLR 62.
12 *Taylor v Perkins* (1607) Cro Jac 144.
13 See the Porter Committee Report on the Law of Defamation, para 45 (Cmnd 7536 (1948)).
14 *Kerr v Kennedy* [1942] 1 KB 409, [1942] 1 All ER 412.
15 As defined in s. 16(1) of the Defamation Act 1952, and so includes broadcast material.
16 *Robinson v Ward* (1958) 108 LJ 491.
17 *White v J and F Stone (Lighting and Radio) Ltd* [1939] 2 KB 827, [1939] 3 All ER 507, CA.

made only to the defendant's spouse,[18] but utterance to the spouse of the person defamed is publication.[19]

The law will presume that defamatory material openly sent, e.g. on postcards or in telegrams, will be read by those through whose hands it comes to pass, therefore the sending of the material by these modes will amount to publication of the libel.[20] This presumption does not apply, however, in the case of letters, even if the letter is unsealed,[1] unless the sender knows that it is likely that others may open the letter, for instance, the recipient's secretary or other staff where the letter is not marked 'personal', 'private' or the like.[2] Of interest also, is that the dictation of a letter containing defamatory statements to the defendant's secretary concerning the plaintiff, amounts to 'publication' of the defamation to the secretary, although it is not settled whether this amounts to libel or slander.[3]

The general rule is that anyone who publishes defamatory material is liable for each publication of the libel or slander;[4] it matters not that they might not be the originator of the defamation, for the mere repetition of the defamation will render the person the publisher of defamatory material.[5] Even upon repetition, the originator of the libel or slander will be liable for the repetitions where he either authorises, expressly or impliedly, the repetition,[6] or the person to whom he has published the defamation is under a legal or moral duty to communicate it and does so to that further person.[7] In the case of slanders that are only actionable upon proof of special damage, the originator may be able to avail himself of the defence that the repetition of the slander was too remote from the damage suffered by the plaintiff, whilst those who repeated the story to the plaintiff will be liable.[8]

A special common law defence is available to a limited class of disseminators of libels. Newsvendors, booksellers and librarians are permitted to plead 'innocent dissemination' as a defence to their prima facie liability. The defence will only be successful where they

18 *Wennhak v Morgan* (1888) 20 QBD 635.
19 *Wenman v Ash* (1853) 13 CB 836.
20 *Williamson v Freer* (1874) LR 9 CP 393.
1 *Powell v Gelston* [1916] 2 KB 615; *Huth v Huth* [1915] 3 KB 32, CA.
2 *Pullman v Hill & Co* [1891] 1 QB 524, CA.
3 See *Osborn v Thomas Boulter & Son* [1930] 2 KB 226, CA; and *Pullman v Hill & Co*, above.
4 *Duke of Brunswick v Harmer* (1849) 14 QB 185.
5 *M'Pherson v Daniels* (1829) 10 B & C 263; *Byrne v Deane* [1937] 1 KB 818, [1937] 2 All ER 204, CA.
6 E.g. makes a statement knowing it is likely to be reported and published by the Press, *Douglas v Tucker* [1952] 1 DLR 657.
7 *Derry v Handley* (1867) 16 LT 263; *Cutler v Mc Phail* [1962] 2 QB 292, [1962] 2 All ER 474.
8 *M'Gregor v Thwaites* (1824) 3 B & C 23; *Ward v Weeks* (1830) 7 Bing 211.

can prove on the balance of probabilities that they did not know, nor could reasonably be expected to have known, that they were circulating defamatory statements.[9]

There are some six defences available to those sued for libel or slander:

1 *Consent of the plaintiff*
The express or implied consent of the plaintiff for the defendant to make the libel or slander is a good defence to the action. It may not always be easy to decide the issue of consent to a repetition of the defamation, but it is submitted that a request of the plaintiff to utter the defamation in circumstances where the defendant would abandon the privilege attaching to the original publication, would not be a valid consent to the defamation.

2 *Justification*
Proof of the truth of what the defendant uttered is an absolute defence to the action,[10] but the burden of proof rests on the defendant.[11] It is sufficient to prove the *substantial* truth of the remarks, rather than truth in every detail,[12] and the Defamation Act 1952[13] makes it clear that the whole defence will not fail simply because every allegation is not proved to be true, provided that those remaining do not materially injure the plaintiff's reputation bearing in mind the truth of the other statements.

This is a dangerous defence to plead, though, because failure to prove the truth of the statements may lead to the result that the court must consider the attempt as an aggravation of the original injury to the plaintiff's reputation. The plaintiff may also put the defendant in a difficult position by only suing upon those defamatory statements which the defendant cannot prove to be true, and not suing upon those which he can prove to be true.[14]

3 *Absolute privilege*
Absolute privilege may be claimed in respect of:
(a)   Parliamentary proceedings[15] or published papers,[16] but this does not extend to a letter by a Member to a Minister;[17]

---

9 *Emmens v Pottle* (1885) 16 QBD 354; *Vizetelly v Mudie's Select Library Ltd* [1900] 2 QB 170, CA.
10 *M'Pherson v Daniels* (1829) 10 B & C 263.
11 *Beevis v Dawson* [1957] 1 QB 195, [1956] 3 All ER 837, CA.
12 *Alexander v North Eastern Rly Co* (1865) 6 B & S 340.
13 S. 5.
14 See *Plato Films Ltd v Speidel* [1961] AC 1090, [1961] 1 All ER 876, HL.
15 Bill of Rights 1688, art 9.
16 Parliamentary Papers Act 1840, s. 1.
17 591 H of C Official Report (5th Series) cols 207–346 (8 July 1958).

(b) Publication of reports of the Ombudsman;[18]
(c) State communications between Ministers of State, or reports to them from senior civil servants;[19]
(d) Judicial proceedings in all courts and similar tribunals.[20] It is settled that 'no action of libel or slander lies, whether against judges, counsel, witnesses, or parties, for words written or spoken in the course of any proceedings of any court recognised by law, and this though the words written or spoken were written or spoken maliciously, without any justification or excuse, and from ill-will and anger against the person defamed'.[1] Thus a professional called as a witness to testify against another professional in an action for breach of professional duty is protected from suit for his evidence about the propriety or competence of the defendant professional. It is also to be noted that fair and accurate reports of such proceedings in newspapers are protected if they are contemporaneous with those proceedings.[2] Absolute privilege does not attach to communications between solicitor and client unless litigation is pending;[3]

4 *Qualified privilege*

Statements that are made fairly by a person in the discharge of some public or private duty, whether legal or moral, or in the conduct of his own affairs where his interest is concerned, are protected.[4] The privilege is lost, though, if the defendant was actuated by malice or an improper motive.[5] The plaintiff must prove that the defendant was moved by malice either by intrinsic evidence about the contents of the statement itself,[6] or by extrinsic evidence of the circumstances in which the statement was made (e.g. that the defendant had no genuine belief in the truth of the statement[7]).

Two common examples of situations where a person who holds an extended professional negligence policy may find himself making possibly defamatory statements, but for which he will have this qualified privilege, are when he answers questions as to the character

18 Parliamentary Commissioner Act 1967, s. 10(5).
19 *Chatterton v Secretary of State for India in Council* [1895] 2 QB 189, CA.
20 *Addis v Crocker* [1961] 1 QB 11, [1960] 2 All ER 629, CA; cf *Lincoln v Daniels* [1962] 1 QB 237, [1961] 3 All ER 740, CA.
 1 *Royal Aquarium and Summer and Winter Garden Society Ltd v Parkinson* [1892] 1 QB 431 at 451, CA, per Lopes LJ.
 2 Law of Libel Act 1888, s. 3.
 3 Cf *More v Weaver* [1928] 2 KB 520, CA.
 4 *Toogood v Spyring* (1834) 1 Cr M & R 181; *London Assn for the Protection of Trade v Greenlands Ltd* [1916] 2 AC 15, HL.
 5 *Clark v Molyneux* (1877) 3 QBD 237, CA.
 6 *Turner v Metro-Goldwyn-Mayer Pictures* [1950] 1 All ER 449, HL.
 7 *Watt v Longsdon* [1930] 1 KB 130, CA.

of a former employee made by anyone proposing to engage him,[8] or in a reply to questions put by the police with a view to detecting an offender.[9]

5 *Fair comment*

Statements of opinion or comment, not statements of fact, which are made fairly on a matter of public interest are protected provided the defendant can prove the truth of the facts upon which the comments are based,[10] or a number of them,[11] or, if untrue, were published on a privileged occasion.[12] Malice or an improper motive will destroy the defence[13] for there will be no honesty in the criticism.

As regards matters of public concern or interest, the defendant must show that he made fair comment upon a matter of interest to the public at large.[14] For example, the public conduct of public office holders,[15] matters of government,[16] and books,[17] articles[18] or broadcasts,[19] are all matters of public interest. The works of an architect have also been held to be within the defence, being something submitted to the public for its appraisal.[20]

6 *Apology and amends*

Libels inserted in newspapers without malice or gross negligence are subject to a complicated defence if an apology is made with a payment into court by way of amends under the Libel Act 1843, section 2, but for other libels an apology and amends could only be considered by way of mitigation of damages.[1] Under section 4 of the Defamation Act 1952 a person who has published words[2] allegedly defamatory of another may make an offer of amends, which, if refused, shall be a defence to an action by a plaintiff innocently defamed, provided the defendant and his agents took all reasonable care. The ambit of section 4 is really rather limited.

---

8 *Jackson v Hopperton* (1864) 16 CBNS 829.
9 *Kine v Sewell* (1838) 3 M & W 297.
10 *Kemsley v Foot* [1952] AC 345, [1952] 1 All ER 501, HL.
11 See Defamation Act 1952, s. 6.
12 *Grech v Odhams Press Ltd* [1958] 1 QB 310, [1957] 3 All ER 556; affd [1958] 2 QB 275, [1958] 2 All ER 462, CA.
13 *Merivale v Carson* (1887) 20 QBD 275, CA.
14 *Sutherland v Stopes* [1925] AC 47, HL.
15 *Seymour v Butterworth* (1862) 3 F & F 372.
16 *Henwood v Harrison* (1872) LR 7 CP 606.
17 *Thomas v Bradbury, Agnew & Co Ltd* [1906] 2 KB 627, CA.
18 *Kemsley v Foot* [1952] AC 345, [1952] 1 All ER 501, HL.
19 *Turner v Metro-Goldwyn-Mayer Pictures Ltd* [1950] 1 All ER 449, HL.
20 *Soane v Knight* (1827) Mood & M 74.
1 Libel Act 1843, s. 1.
2 See the wide definition in Defamation Act 1952, s. 16(1).

Loss of documents

Some limited cover for loss of documents will be provided under Fire and Theft/Burglary policies held by professional persons in respect of their business premises, but the cover is very limited under these insurances, and only provide an indemnity in respect of the value of the documents lost, destroyed or stolen as stationery, together with the cost of the clerical labour expended in writing up the documents again. This cover is basically far too limited for the purposes of a person engaged in a professional business or practice, and, therefore, it has been found convenient to add an extension, when sought, to the 'basic' professional indemnity policy to cater for the special needs of this category of person, in the following form:

Subject otherwise to the limits exclusions terms and conditions of this Policy the Insurer shall indemnify the Insured in respect of

(a) any Legal Liability to third parties in consequence of the loss of or damage to Documents the property of or entrusted to the Insured which now or hereafter are or are by them supposed or believed to be in their hands or in the hands of any other party or parties to or with whom the Documents have been entrusted lodged or deposited by the Insured in the ordinary course of their business or practice

(b) all costs charges and expenses incurred by the Insured in replacing and/or restoring the Documents

PROVIDED ALWAYS THAT

(1) 'Documents' shall mean Deeds, Wills, Agreements, Maps, Plans, Records, written or printed Books, Letters, Certificates or written or printed Documents and/or Forms of any nature whatsoever used in connection with the Insured's business or practice, but excluding any Bearer Bonds or Coupons, Bank or Currency Notes or other negotiable paper, or any computer records.

(2) The Excess shall not apply to claims under paragraph (b) above.

(3) The amount of any claim for costs, charges and expenses under paragraph (b) above must be supported by bills and/or accounts which shall be subject to approval by some competent person to be nominated by the Insurer with the approval of the Insured.

(4) The Insured shall give written notice to the Insurer of any loss or damage to documents within seven days of the date of such discovery of loss or damage and within the Period of Insurance.

(5) The loss of damage shall have occurred within the United Kingdom.

The legal liability extension provides an indemnity against claims arising from actions for:

1 *Conversion*

A person (e.g. a client) who has an immediate right to the possession of some documents against a person who is in actual possession of them (e.g. the professional insured) may claim in conversion against him if he requests the return of the documents but is refused redelivery unreasonably.[3] It is also conversion to wrongfully take documents out of the possession of anyone else;[4] to wrongfully deliver documents to someone other than the owner;[5] to deal with them in a manner adverse to the title of the owner e.g. sell or pledge them;[6] or to destroy the documents[7] (not merely damage[8]) without lawful justification.

The related tort of detinue has been abolished by the Torts (Interference with Goods) Act 1977.[9]

2 *Trespass*

This tort is wider than conversion in that a mere act of interference is sufficient, it is actionable per se without any proof of actual damage,[10] and no denial of title is necessary; but it is narrower in that the act of interference must be direct.[11] Thus it is a trespass to erase a tape-recording,[12] or show a private letter to an unauthorised person.[13]

3 *Negligence*

The owner or person entitled to possession of the documents will be able to sue in negligence for wrongful interference with the documents in so far as the defendant's negligence results in damage to those documents.

The remaining parts of the extension endorsement relate to proof of replacement or repair costs, notification of claims condition, state that the Excess will only be applied to the legal liability section, and define a territorial limit for loss or damage which is in addition to the overall policy territorial limits.

Some such endorsements might include a special indemnity limit relating to claims under the extension, which will operate instead of the normal policy limits of indemnity.

Losses caused by dishonest, malicious, fraudulent, criminal or illegal acts of the insured, their employees, or predecessors, will continue to be excluded under Exclusion 4 of the 'basic' policy, as will war risks under Exclusion 9.[14] On the other hand, the endorsement

---

3   *Eason v Newman* (1596) Cro Eliz 495.
4   *Fouldes v Willoughby* (1841) 8 M & W 540.
5   *Consolidated Co v Curtis & Son* [1892] 1 QB 495.
6   *Syeds v Hay* (1791) 4 Term Rep 260.
7   *Hollins v Fowler* (1875) LR 7 HL 757.
8   *Simmons v Lillystone* (1853) 8 Exch 431.
9   S. 1.
10   *William Leitch & Co Ltd v Leydon* [1931] AC 90, HL.
11   *Kirk v Gregory* (1876) 1 Ex D 55.
12   *Flegon v Hayward* (1966) Times 1 October.
13   *Thurston v Charles* (1905) 21 TLR 659.
14   See ch 3, above.

will obviously override the content of Exclusion 12 (cost of replacing documents lost, mislaid or destroyed).

The extension provides cover for all the reasonable costs of the insured which he incurs in the replacing of lost or damaged documents, whether they be his or belong to someone else. It is therefore a useful extension where the costs of replacement are high e.g. where a fresh survey report on an extensive property has to be undertaken after loss or destruction of the original report by a surveyor, or an architect has to repeat weeks of work to reproduce destroyed plans.

Exclusion 6 (other insurances) will come into play in the case of the loss of or damage to documents where the risk is also covered by a Fire, Theft, or Combined Office insurance, so that first recovery will be made under those policies and any surplus of loss only will be recoverable under the professional negligence policy extension.

Fees recovery

In certain cases, a professional person may find himself in the position that he must sue a client for fees owed to him. Obviously, many will consider this a measure of last resort, but substantial sums may be at stake. Litigation can be an expensive venture and, for the benefit of themselves and the business or practice, some firms will seek insurance to indemnify the costs of bringing such proceedings, and attaching an extension to the professional indemnity policy is the popular course of the insurer rather than issue a separate policy.

An insurer will rarely be prepared to give a full indemnity for these costs, feeling that if the insured must bear a proportion of the costs he will not embark upon the litigation lightly. Furthermore, the extension is generally only granted upon terms that require the client to raise a breach of professional duty of the insured by way of a counter-claim to the action, in order to bring the indemnity into operation. This is because, in civil proceedings, costs generally 'follow the event', i.e. the party that loses the action must pay the costs of the successful party, and so upon a straightforward action for recovery of fees the insured will bear only a small amount of expense if successful. If the defendant client alleges some negligence of the insured, however, the action will become longer and more complicated, because the client will be seeking to prove some loss to him caused by the insured's neglect or breach of duty, which should be set off against the outstanding fees. At this stage, the integrity or competence of the insured will be called into question, and this may properly be considered as a risk that may be indemnified under an extension to the professional indemnity policy.

It should be noted that this clause only comes into operation where the insured commences proceedings for fees recovery, and does not operate as a further indemnity regarding actions initiated against the insured – that is solely the province of the main operative clause.

The extension also only applies for the recovery of professional fees which are based upon the insured's own professional body's scale of fees, and may not be used to pursue a recovery of extortionate fees even though previously agreed to by the client.

A feature that may be found in some extensions for this cover, is a requirement that the insurer's own legal advisers shall first approve the initiation of the proceedings for fees recovery. Many insured will consider that this requirement is unacceptable and would rather allow the general condition of the 'basic' policy to apply (Condition 4). This is the Queen's Counsel clause which operates to provide a means of settlement of the question of whether proceedings should be contested or settled (see chapter 3), when a 'claim' under the policy is made. A claim under this extension to the policy would constitute a 'claim' for the purposes of the general Conditions of the whole policy.

The fees recovery extension may be in the following form:

> Subject otherwise to the limits exclusions terms and conditions of this Policy the Insurer shall indemnify the Insured in respect of eighty per cent (80%) of all costs incurred by the Insured in recovering or attempting to recover any professional fees due to the Insured for professional work done in accordance with the scale of Professional Charges as sanctioned by the appropriate Professional Body of which the Insured is a Fellow, Member, Associate Member or Associate and that such fees are due under the terms of the contract for the work performed
> PROVIDED ALWAYS THAT
> no claim under this endorsement will attach until the Insured has instituted proceedings for recovery of fees and the party sued has intimated his intention to raise by way of answer a counter-claim as would be covered under main Operative Clause of this Policy.

Dishonesty of employees or partners

Claims made against the insured arising directly or indirectly from the dishonest or similar act of the insured partners or their predecessors or employees, are excluded from the policy under Exclusion 4 of the 'basic' policy. This exclusion is basically considered to be in the interests of public policy as applied by the courts, which will always presume that the insurer has not agreed to indemnify dishonest or similar acts or omissions of the insured.[15] An express inclusion of the indemnity will override this judicial presumption, which would not be achieved by a simple deletion of Exclusion 4. A mere deletion of the exclusion also suffers from the defect that if a claim is framed against the insured in the form of a 'mixed' claim e.g. of negligence and dishonesty, the 'basic' professional negligence

15 *Beresford v Royal Insurance Co Ltd* [1938] AC 586, [1938] 2 All ER 602, HL.

policy will not be held to apply to the claim,[16] and a claim based solely on dishonesty is certainly outside the scope of the 'basic' professional indemnity policy.[17]

The endorsement will read:

> Notwithstanding Exclusion 4 but subject otherwise to the limits exclusions terms and conditions of this Policy the Insurer will indemnify the Insured in respect of
> (a) any loss or losses sustained by the Insured during the Period of Insurance and
> (b) the legal liability of the Insured arising from any claim made against the Insured during the Period of Insurance
> by reason of any dishonest malicious fraudulent criminal or illegal act or omission of the Insured or their employees or their predecessors in the business or practice or their employees
> PROVIDED ALWAYS THAT
> no indemnity shall be afforded hereby to any person committing or condoning such act or omission, and at the request of the Insurer shall take all reasonable steps to recover the loss from any person committing or condoning such act or omission or from the personal representatives of such person, and any amount recovered (up to but not exceeding any amount paid by the Insurer) shall be paid to the Insurer.

Paragraph (b) of this endorsement, therefore, provides an indemnity against claims made by third parties and duly notified to the insurer during the currency of the policy.

Paragraph (a) is not always included in the 'dishonesty' extension in addition to paragraph (b). This is because it affords another limb of recovery by the insured, namely, for recovery of his own losses sustained by reason of the dishonest act or omission of his co-insured partner, or his employee. It is accordingly providing a measure of indemnity beyond cover for legal liability of the insured to third parties which is the fundamental intention of the 'basic' professional indemnity policy. More commonly, this risk of own loss is covered in a separate *fidelity guarantee* policy, which achieves the same object.

Both parts of the indemnity will be subject to the requirement that the dishonest act or omission, whether committed by an insured or an employee, must have been committed in the course of the business or practice, or in the course of the employee's duties thereat. In the case of an employee's dishonest act or omission, the employer will only be liable if such is the case in any event. The employer is *vicariously* liable for the acts of his employee if he has either permitted the employee's act,[18] or it is otherwise 'in the course of employment'. The mere fact that the employee was seeking to make a personal profit does not necessarily take his actions outside the

16 *West Wake Price & Co v Ching* [1956] 3 All ER 821, [1957] 1 WLR 45.
17 E.g. *Haseldine v Hosken* [1933] 1 KB 822, CA.
18 *Canadian Pacific Rly Co v Lockhart* [1942] AC 591, [1942] 2 All ER 464, PC.

course of his employment. In the leading case of *Lloyd v Grace, Smith & Co*,[19] a solicitor's clerk fraudulently induced a client to sign some documents which transferred the client's property to him. The firm was held liable to the client, for the clerk was performing that class of duties for which he was employed, albeit dishonestly. The employer will also be liable if his employee steals documents or goods that are in the hands of his employer from third parties.[20]

As regards the possibility of a request by the insurer that a recovery should be sought against the dishonest party or parties, it is submitted that in the case of reluctance of the insured so to do, the insurer would be entitled to rely on the provisions of the Queen's Counsel clause (Condition 4 of the 'basic' policy), and thus be entitled to avoid the claim completely if the insured refused to abide by the opinion of the appointed Queen's Counsel that a recovery had a reasonable prospect of success. This request for a recovery would not be affected by the inclusion of a 'waiver of subrogation against employees' clause (below) because the wording of that clause does not exclude subrogation for the dishonest, etc., acts or omissions of employees.

Waiver of subrogation against employees

This extension endorsement really adds nothing to the situation already achieved in law, that an employer, or insurer by subrogation, may not seek a recovery of a loss against an employee if the loss was caused by the negligent performance of his work by the employee. Such negligent performance of duties is technically a breach of the employee's duty of care to his employer, but public policy has rendered this breach unactionable.[1]

The endorsement is, however, often included by insurers, perhaps to appease the conscience of the insured. The extension reads:

> It is hereby agreed that if any payment is made under this Policy in respect of a claim and the Insurer is thereupon subrogated to all the Insured's rights of recovery in relation thereto, the Insurer shall not exercise any such rights against any employee of the Insured unless the claim has been brought about or contributed to by any dishonest malicious fraudulent criminal or illegal act or omission of the employee.

---

19 [1912] AC 716, HL; and see ch 1, p. 7, above.
20 *Morris v C W Martin & Sons Ltd* [1965] 1 QB 716, [1965] 2 All ER 725, CA; *Gilchrist Watt and Sanderson Pty Ltd v York Products Pty Ltd* [1970] 3 All ER 825, [1970] 1 WLR 1262, PC.
 1 *Lister v Romford Ice and Cold Storage Co Ltd* [1957] AC 555, [1957] 1 All ER 125, HL; *Morris v Ford Motor Co Ltd* [1973] 1 QB 792, [1973] 2 All ER 1084, CA.

Change of partners

The nature of the joint and several liabilities of partners has been discussed in chapter 1, to which reference should be made for clarification of the need for adequate indemnity cover at all times for all acts or omissions, whenever committed.

If a partner in a firm leaves and joins another firm, the new firm's professional indemnity policy in the 'basic' form, will not provide an indemnity to him if he is sued individually for a negligent act, error or omission committed in the course of his previous partnership's activities.[2] Nor will the new partnership's policy protect him from such claims, that policy will only provide an indemnity against claims made in respect of his negligent act, error or omission in the conduct of his practice or business with that insured partnership. The reference in the policy to 'predecessors in the practice or business' are not alone sufficient to include the activities of a new partner whilst he was with a completely different practice or business. The words are wide enough, though, to protect the change of partnership which technically takes place when any partner leaves the partnership, or a new partner is brought into the firm. Depending upon the circumstances of the case, the words may also provide an indemnity for past acts, error or omissions in the situation where a practice or business 'buys up' or amalgamates with another partnership or individual practice providing the same sort of professional services, e.g. a firm of accountants may expand by convincing a sole practitioner to join their partnership and so bring his existing clients' custom into the new, larger partnership.

There are two principal wordings that may be adopted to achieve the extension of liability of insurers to cover previous business liability of an insured partner: either

> The practice or business described in the Schedule is deemed to include any practice or business in the same profession in which any partner of the Insured has been previously engaged, subject otherwise to the limits exclusions terms and conditions of this Policy;

or

> Subject otherwise to the limits exclusions terms and conditions of this Policy, the Insurer agrees to indemnify (insert the name of the in-coming partner) in respect of claims made against him (or her) for a negligent act, error or omission committed in the conduct of the business or practice known as (insert the name of the firm he has left).

If the in-coming partner was not a partner in the previous practice, but merely an employee, the extension is not required.

---

2 The case of *Maxwell v Price* [1960] 2 Lloyd's Rep 155, Aust HC, does not run contrary to this submission due to the particular wording of the policy in that case.

The Recital clause makes it clear beyond doubt that any incoming partner is to be included within the definition of 'the Insured', and no specific endorsement is necessary simply to achieve that end.

When a partner leaves a practice or business, not to join another partnership, but to retire or otherwise to cease in that profession, or to join another firm or company as an employee, he will not have a new partnership policy which may be endorsed with an extension of indemnity in respect of claims arising from his activities with that practice or business which he is leaving. There are two possible solutions to the problem of indemnity cover.

The first is to seek an endorsement extension upon the leaving-firm's policy covering the retiring partner's liability specifically, this endorsement to be continued at each annual renewal. This will be the best solution from the retiring partner's point of view, but may not be so pleasing a prospect to the remaining partners who may be asked to pay any additional premium for the extension annually (although some insurers may only request a single, once-and-for-all premium — but what is the position if, subsequently, a new insurer issues a policy to the firm?). Some arrangement may, of course, be made between the firm and the retiring partner as regards the payment of those additional premiums. This type of out-going partner's extension endorsement will read:

> Subject otherwise to the limits exclusions terms and conditions of this Policy, the Insurer agrees to indemnify (insert name of out-going partner) in respect of claims made against him (or her) for a negligent act, error or omission committed whilst a partner in the business or practice of the Insured.

It should be remembered that all three of the above-mentioned extensions will be subject to Exclusion 6 of the 'basic' policy (above) which excludes liability of the insurer if the loss is covered by any other insurance, except in so far as that other insurance is insufficient to meet the whole loss.

The second course of action by the out-going partner is to arrange a separate 'run-off' liability policy from the insurer. This policy will be issued for a six year period for either a single premium, or annual premiums of decreasing amounts. The great drawback or limitation to this avenue of protection, is that insurers will not issue 'run-off' policies to provide a period of insurance of greater than six years. It will be noted from chapter 1 that the statutory periods of limitation do not prevent all claims being made after a period of six years from the commission of the tortious act or omission, and, therefore, a retired partner could find himself sued, but have no protection because the six year 'run-off' policy has expired.

Monies had and received

The 'basic' policy does not provide an indemnity against claims made against the insured for simple 'money had and received',[3] or a 'mixed' claim for negligence, and money had and received.[4] Insurers are usually prepared to extend the policy to cover claims based upon money had and received by the endorsement:

> Subject otherwise to the limits exclusions terms and conditions of this Policy, the Insurer agrees to indemnify the Insured in respect of their failure or alleged failure unintentionally and in good faith to account to clients for monies had and received in connection with the business or practice specified in the Schedule.

Breach of warranty of authority

In his role of providing professional services to a client, a professional man will often find himself acting as the agent of the client e.g. the engagement of an accountant to settle the annual accounts of his client with the Inland Revenue will have authority to deal with this matter. The authority to act as the client's agent may arise by express provision, or by implication from the very nature of the services to be performed, i.e. it is necessary for or reasonably incidental to the carrying out of the authority expressly given or is of a type that someone in the agent's profession usually does have authority to do or make. An example of implied authority of an agent is the case of an estate agent who is authorised to find a purchaser of property. In the absence of a contrary agreement with the client (the 'principal' in this agency relationship), the estate agent will have the implied authority to receive a deposit from a potential purchaser, for this is within the usual practice of an estate agent. An estate agent may well also have implied authority to make representations about the state of his client's property.[5]

Agency may also arise if someone by his words or conduct leads another to believe that he has appointed X to act as his agent, for he will generally be estopped from denying X's authority, even though no agency in fact existed.[6]

A person may also ratify and affirm the authority of someone to act as his agent after that person has led another to believe that he was acting as agent of that first person,[7] and that first person would have had full capacity to contract at the date of contract.[8]

3 *Goddard and Smith v Frew* [1939] 4 All ER 358, CA.
4 *West Wake Price & Co v Ching* [1956] 3 All ER 821, [1957] 1 WLR 45.
5 *Hill v Harris* [1965] 2 QB 601, [1965] 2 All ER 358, CA.
6 *Pole v Leask* (1863) 33 LJ Ch 155.
7 *Re Tiedemann and Ledermann Frères* [1899] 2 QB 66.
8 *Boston Deep Sea Fishing and Ice Co Ltd v Farnham* [1957] 3 All ER 204, [1957] 1 WLR 1051, and for a company's capacity to contract prior to formation see European Communities Act 1972, s. 9(2).

The principal is bound by every contract or disposition of property made by his agent with his express or implied authority, for the contract or disposition will, in law, have been made between the principal and the third party — the agent can look to his principal for indemnity in any action upon the contract or disposition. On the other hand, the principal incurs no liability where his agent acts completely without authority, and no liability for any action of his agent in excess of his authority (both subject to any ratification by the principal).

The burden in these latter instances, where the agent acts in breach of his warranty of authority to third parties, lies on the agent who may be sued upon such contracts or dispositions. This is obviously a matter of concern to professional persons who so often find themselves in the position of agent of their clients in so many matters. Wary of the liabilities that may be incurred for breach of warranty of authority, they wish to be insured against such liabilities.

Two examples may illustrate the problems. In *Yonge v Toynbee*[9] a solicitor was instructed by a client to defend some legal proceedings, and this the solicitor did, by subsequently issuing a defence to the writ and appearing upon several interlocutory matters. Unbeknown to the solicitor, however, his client had been certified insane by the time the writ had been issued, and the plaintiff in the action sued the solicitor for his costs in that action, the solicitor having defended the action with no authority from his client. This was the case, because insanity of a principal automatically terminates the authority of the agent. In *Cooper v Langdon*[10] the plaintiff principal succeeded in an action for breach of contract against a builder who had deviated from the plans, on instructions from the plaintiff's architect. The architect had no authority to order such deviations, and so the defendant builder had no defence to the action. In modern circumstances, the builder could sue the architect for his loss resulting from the architect's breach of warranty of authority.

The action arises for breach of a collateral contract with the third party that the agent has the authority he professes to have,[11] and no proof of dishonest or fraudulent intent (which would give rise to the tort of deceit) need be proved by the plaintiff third party. The doctrine of breach of warranty of authority has been explained as follows:

> If a person requests and, by asserting that he is clothed with the necessary authority induces another to enter into a negotiation with himself and into a transaction with the person whose authority he represents that he

---

9 [1910] 1 KB 215, CA.
10 (1841) 9 M & W 60, affd (1842) 10 M & W 785.
11 *Collen v Wright* (1857) 8 E & B 647.

has, in that case there is a contract by him that he has the authority of the person with whom he requests the other to enter into the transaction.[12]

The wording of the extension endorsement will be:

> Subject otherwise to the limits exclusions terms and conditions of this Policy, the Insurer agrees to indemnify the Insured in respect of claims made for breach of warranty of authority committed or alleged to have been committed in connection with the business or practice in good faith and in the belief that appropriate authority was held.

This extension does not provide an indemnity in respect of claims based on deceit, rather than breach of warranty of authority.

Consultants or other agents

The law relating to the liability of a principal for the acts of his agent that are within his authority has been outlined in the last heading.

When a professional person in the course of his business instructs other persons or firms in a similar profession to act for them (e.g. a firm of solicitors in other parts of England will commonly instruct a firm of London solicitors to act for them during an appeal hearing in London), the agent firm may ask specifically to be covered by the principal firm's policy. More usually, though, the principal firm, realising that they will be liable for their agent's acts of omissions if they are within the scope of their authority, and also appreciating that their agents will not be within the definition of 'the Insured' for the purposes of the professional indemnity policy, will seek an extension of their policy to cater for the situation. Insurers will generally oblige by including an extension:

> Subject otherwise to the limits exclusions terms and conditions of this Policy, the Insurer will indemnify the Insured in respect of claims made upon the Insured arising from any negligent act, error or omission committed by any agent or agents employed by the Insured in the conduct of the business or practice.

Similar considerations will apply regarding persons appearing on the firm's notepaper as 'Consultants'. This term can have a variety of meanings, but often a retired partner will be paid a retainer to provide the firm with the benefit of his experience. Such an arrangement may well lead to doubt as to the status of the consultant, he may be neither a partner nor an employee, and thus the firm will have no indemnity under the 'basic' policy for his acts or omissions. To ensure that both the insured and the insurer know who is in this category, and to include the firm's liability in this respect, an endorsement extending the policy will be required:

> Subject otherwise to the limits exclusions terms and conditions of this Policy, the Insurer agrees to indemnify the Insured and (insert the name

12 *Dickson v Reuter's Telegram Co* (1877) 3 CPD 1 at 5, per Bramwell LJ.

or names of the consultants) in respect of claims arising from any negligent act, error or omission of (insert name or names) whilst acting as Consultant to the Insured in the conduct of the business or practice.

Auctioneer's conversion

The elements of the tort of conversion, i.e. wrongful interference with goods of another, have already been mentioned under the loss of documents extension (above). Documents are just one type of 'goods' that can be wrongfully converted by another's refusal to surrender them to a person entitled to possession, or by wrongful delivery, or by otherwise dealing with the goods in a manner adverse to the title of the owner (e.g. to sell, pledge or destroy them). Only land and choses in action (negotiable instruments) cannot constitute 'goods' wrongfully converted.[13]

Whilst professionals will but rarely deal with goods that can be converted, other than documents, auctioneers are, in the very nature of their business, dealing with goods of all sorts, and will require a policy extension to indemnify themselves against accidentally giving the goods auctioned to the wrong person, or selling them without authority. Only negligence or similar breach of professional duty is embraced by the operative clause of the 'basic' policy, and, in point of fact, the tort of conversion cannot be committed with negligence as an element, for 'conversion consists in an act intentionally done inconsistent with the owner's right, though the doer may not know of, or intend to challenge, the property or possession of the true owner'.[14]

A recent illustration of the tort of conversion is *R H Willis & Son v British Car Auctions Ltd*.[15] The plaintiffs, car dealers providing hire-purchase facilities, let a car on hire-purchase terms which provided that the car would not become the property of the hirer until the price of £625 had been paid. The hirer paid the initial cash deposit of £350 and later took the car to the defendant car auctioneers for sale by auction. At the auction the car did not reach the reserve of £450. The highest bid was £410. The auctioneers applied their 'provisional bid' practice: they asked the highest bidder whether he would stand upon his bid of £410, and a sale was later agreed on the basis that the auctioneers had agreed to reduce their commission required from the hirer. Later, the hirer was made bankrupt and paid no hire instalments on the car, and the purchaser

---

13 Torts (Interference with Goods) Act 1977, s. 14(1).
14 *Caxton Publishing Co Ltd v Sutherland Publishing Co Ltd* [1939] AC 178 at 202, [1938] 4 All ER 389 at 404, HL, per Lord Porter.
15 [1978] 2 All ER 392, [1978] 1 WLR 438, CA.

of the car had disappeared. The plaintiffs claimed against the auctioneers for damages in conversion. The Court of Appeal upheld the award of damages, because the auctioneers had assisted in the sale of the car by private treaty to the bidder from the hirer who was not the true owner of the car.

The extension endorsement to be added therefore states:

> Subject otherwise to the limits exclusions terms and conditions of this Policy, the Insurer agrees to indemnify the Insured against claims for conversion of any goods submitted to the Insured for sale by auction provided the Insured shall have taken all reasonable steps to satisfy themselves that the person instructing them has the true and legal title to the goods or is the duly constituted agent of the lawful owner of the goods.

Surveys and valuations

Wherever the insured professionals are likely to undertake structural surveys, the insurer will exclude liability altogether in respect of such survey work, and will only be prepared to extend the policy to indemnify the insured against claims for negligent surveys or valuations upon the understanding that a disclaimer is inserted under each such report, and that only particularly qualified persons shall undertake surveying or valuing duties. The aim of the extension clause is protection of both the insured and the insurer from the pitfalls of insufficiently qualified staff undertaking such tasks, when the danger of a subsequent claim can be regarded as much apparent. Compliance with the requirements of the endorsement clause will be a condition precedent to the liability of the insurer to indemnify the insured in the event of a claim.

The extension will state:

> Subject otherwise to the limits exclusions terms and conditions of this Policy, the Insurer will indemnify the Insured in respect of claims arising from survey and/or valuation reports
> PROVIDED ALWAYS THAT
> (a) The following clause shall be inserted in all survey and valuation reports issued by or on behalf of the Insured, except in the case of
>   (i) reports undertaken for Building Socities, Life Assurance Companies or other Institutional Lenders, and
>   (ii) reports of pure valuation where no comment or advice is required or given on the structural or decorative conditions of the property:
>   We have not inspected woodwork or other parts of the structure which are covered unexposed or inaccessible and we are therefore unable to report that any such part of the property is free from defect.
> (b) Survey and/or valuation reports shall be made only by an Insured, or a member of the Insured's staff, who is a Fellow or Professional Associate of the Royal Institution of Chartered Surveyors, or a

Fellow or Associate of the Incorporated Society of Valuers and Auctioneers, or has not less than five years' experience of structural surveying and has been approved in writing by the Insurer.

(c) Notwithstanding Exclusion 1 (the Excess) the Insured shall bear an Excess of £100 in respect of each and every claim under this extension.

Special waiver clause

Some professional bodies when negotiating schemes of cover for their members with insurers, have been able to secure a special clause under which the insurers have agreed to waive their rights to avoid a claim on the grounds of non-disclosure,[16] misrepresentation,[17] or breach of warranty[18] regarding the answers in the proposal form being the basis of the contract, as contained in the Recital clause to the 'basic' policy in chapter 3.

The insurers will not go so far as to totally stultify their rights of avoidance of claims, and a rider is built into the clause to protect the insurers in the case of any fraudulently conceived claim. Additionally, the insurers will have a saving clause to permit adjustment of the claim innocently arising under a policy where there has been a non-disclosure of fact or a misrepresentation of fact.[19]

The clause will operate on both the initial proposal for insurance, and all subsequent renewals with the insurer.

The special waiver clause reads:

The Insurer agrees not to exercise the right to avoid this Policy where it is alleged that there has been non-disclosure or misrepresentation of facts or untrue statements at inception or at any subsequent renewal
PROVIDED ALWAYS THAT

(1) the Insured shall establish to the Insurer's satisfaction that such alleged non-disclosure, misrepresentation or untrue statement was innocent and free of any fraudulent conduct, dishonest motive, or intent to deceive;

(2) where the Insured's non-disclosure or misrepresentation or breach or non-compliance with any Condition of this Policy has prejudiced the handling or settlement of any claim the amount payable in respect of such claim (including costs and expenses) shall be reduced to such sum as would have been payable in the absence of such prejudice.

---

16 See e.g. *Dalglish v Jarvie* (1850) 2 Mac & G 231; *London General Omnibus Co Ltd v Holloway* [1912] 2 KB 72, CA; and ch 2, above.
17 *Graham v Western Australian Insurance Co Ltd* (1931) 40 Ll L Rep 64.
18 *Pawson v Watson* (1778) 2 Cowp 785; Marine Insurance Act 1906, s. 33(3); and see ch 2, above.
19 But see the views of the Law Commission concerning the practicality of such provisions in paras 4.98–4.108 of their Report: Insurance Law: Non-Disclosure and Breach of Warranty (Cmnd 8064 (1980)).

Condition 5 of the 'basic' policy (above) will govern any dispute under this clause, as any other, and require the matter to go to arbitration, e.g. a dispute concerning the insurer's view that there was non-disclosure or misrepresentation.

Legal defence clause

A feature of some policies is an extension that will provide for an indemnity in respect of the costs incurred by the insured at legal proceedings that do not directly arise from a claim, but at which a matter touching upon a claim or a possible breach of professional duty by the insured professional will be examined. It is in both the insured's interest, and in the insurer's interest for the insured to be properly represented at such hearings where such questions of competence are considered.

The clause will read:

Subject otherwise to the limits exclusions terms and conditions of this Policy, the Insurer will indemnify the Insured in respect of eighty per cent (80%) of the costs, charges and expenses of legal representation, not otherwise covered by this Policy, of the Insured at any proceedings before any duly constituted court or tribunal (but not any hearing before any domestic or disciplinary body of the Insured's professional association) at which, in the opinion of the Insurer, the Insured should be represented by reason of any conduct of the Insured which might be relevant to an existing or possible claim under the main operative clause hereof, or by reason of likely prejudice to the Insured's professional reputation

PROVIDED ALWAYS THAT

(a) No indemnity shall be provided for any penalty, fine, or award of costs made against the Insured;

(b) The written consent of the Insurer must be obtained before any costs, charges or expenses are incurred; and

(c) The Insurer shall be entitled to nominate a solicitor, and, if appropriate, a barrister, to represent the Insured.

Chapter 5

Underwriting the risk

Introduction

The first comment is an obvious one. No insurer, be it an insurance company or Lloyd's underwriter, will intentionally underwrite risks so as to produce a loss, the insurer's aim is the same as the professionals insured – to make a profit. The basic principle of underwriting is simple, by collecting numerous premiums, the insurer agrees to indemnify the insured against a particular risk, which the insurer has researched and considers will only occur at a particular frequency so that all claims may be met from the pool of insurance premiums, leaving a final layer of profit for the insurer. Generally, it can be said that insurers will grow wiser about the nature of the risk, and its frequency of arising, from their analysis of each year's claims experience.

This simple principle still applies to professional negligence insurance, but its application is found to be much more difficult than in most other fields of insurance. One reason is the variance in the insured that can be found, thus the insurer will wish to know the precise qualifications and experience of each insured practitioner. Secondly, the numbers that may seek a particular class of insurance are limited to very small groups, e.g. there are only some 4,500 practising barristers, comparative to the numbers of people that may seek household insurance (perhaps some 20 million households). Thirdly, claims experience for all the professions has revealed that the amount of a settlement arising from a claim can vary enormously which leads to difficulties in forcasting the amounts required to be set aside by the insurer to meet claims arising under the issued policies (i.e. the 'reserves'). A further aspect of this is the 'claims arising in the year of insurance' basis of most professional negligence policies, so that insurers will be covering past negligence with very little knowledge of what was undertaken by the insured in those previous years, or, indeed, who were the responsible partners at the relevant time.

These difficulties have led to the fact that only a handful of insurance companies and a small number of Lloyd's syndicates will underwrite professional risks. Insurers will also make the point that they feel there may well be an amount of selection against the insurer with this type of insurance – those that are most worried about their competence will seek insurance more readily than those practices or businesses which feel secure from claims. There may well be an element of truth in this, but it may be countered by saying that the most prudent professionals will also be the sort of people that will pursue their prudence through to insuring themselves against claims for negligence. Further, of course, the insurers' argument loses its veracity in the case of those professions that require their members to insure against professional negligence risks under their rules. Whilst some insurers have dropped out of the market, those remaining have been able to gain more experience in assessing the level of premium required to meet the claims encountered each year, but even these specialists still find it difficult to obtain a normal pattern of claims experience because of the wide variation in the costs of claims within each professional grouping.

The first step, then, will be for an insurer to estimate the probable number of persons who will take the insurance offered as available. This necessarily requires the insurer to consider the level of indemnity that will be made available e.g. £10,000, £50,000, or some larger sum. Also, it must be considered whether the cover will be on an aggregate basis or an each and every basis, the breadth of cover under the policy wording, and costs of administering the claims process from the insurer's point of view, together with the total claims liability to be anticipated and catered for.

Having taken these matters into consideration, the insurer will arrive at a figure of total premiums that will be necessary to achieve full claims settlement and also provide the broker's commission, the expenses of the insurer, and profit for the insurer. It is also usual for the insurer to err on the pessimistic side as regards claims, and any surplus left from each year's pool will be applied to future insurance pools so that those who have paid the premiums do not lose the benefit of those premiums. This total premium figure assessed as necessary will then have to be divided in some manner between those likely to take out the insurance to arrive at a rating structure that may be quoted to the insured.

The insurer will have to decide whether to charge premiums according to a per capita charge, or a fees earned basis, in order to arrive at a framework of rating scales to cope with differing limits of indemnity, unless only one limit of indemnity is to be offered. This will be the case under a compulsory insurance requirement of a professional body, e.g. each member to have £250,000 aggregate cover each year, but even in this case many will seek additional cover to 'top-up' the minimum compulsory layer.

The insurer will go through this exercise each year to arrive at new rates of premium if necessary, or to justify the maintenance of existing levels of premium. Claims experience of the past insurance year, and the levels of indemnity sought by the professionals, will be very important considerations. It will readily be appreciated that this sort of insurance cannot be underwritten with the precision of e.g. life assurance, where actuaries will be constantly working over new life-expectancy data, and will be a matter of judgment for each insurer. No doubt some insurers are better than others in correctly predicting the level of claims.

The proposal form

Insurers will generally only insure members of recognised professions or businesses in respect of their liability incidental to the skill in carrying out their work. For this reason, among others, defective workmanship is excluded from the normal public liability policy which otherwise provides the general protection to businessmen, tradesmen, and professionals against liabilities to third parties. This ambiguity as to the nature and skill of a particular trade, business or profession leads those few insurers that are prepared to insure the competence of their insured, to only do so where the members of the business or profession must obtain their qualifications by examination, and where there is a recognisable body which is responsible for prescribing professional standards of competence and professional rules of conduct and discipline.

This information will not be sufficient from the insurer's viewpoint when an actual policy is sought by an individual or partnership, and the insurer will require a proposal form to be completed by all who seek an insurance to cover professional negligence. The insurer may possess some general knowledge of the business or profession, but will require specific information from each proposer upon many matters, for it will be the experience and competence of each insured practitioner that concerns the insurer who will bear the liability for negligence of each of his insured. One matter of particular concern will be the level of specialisation of the insured within his chosen business or profession, because it is the variation in specialisms that prevents the insurer from obtaining the normal pattern of claims experience that may be assessed to gauge future premium requirements.

In chapter 2, the elements of insurance law relevant to professional negligence risks were outlined. At this point it is as well to remember that the offer for insurance may be made by either the proposer or the insurer − all will depend on the particular circumstances. Further, the fundamental principle of indemnity pervades through all insurance law, with all its ramifications of the principle of good faith between insurer and insured; of full disclosure of all material facts known by the insured to the insurer; of the true representation of facts to the insurer; and of the strict and binding nature of conditions or warranties in insurance contracts. Accordingly, the insurer will prepare a questionnaire called a proposal form to be completed by the proposer to the utmost of the proposer's knowledge, and this will be stated to form the basis of the contract of insurance between them if such insurance is finalised. The mere fact that the insurer has not requested information about a matter does not mean that the insured need not disclose that matter, if it is a fact material to the risk to be insured, and this is tested by the standard of the reasonably prudent insurer concerned with that type of insurance, not the view of the proposer as to its materiality to the risk insured.

In this chapter, the normal questions that appear on a proposal form for professional indemnity insurance will be considered, with the underwriting reason for the inclusion of the question about a matter which the insurer regards as material to the risk, and then some aspects of each business or profession that may be either expensive or difficult to insure will be examined.

It must also not be forgotten that the duty of disclosure arises upon every renewal of the policy, and not merely upon the initial inception of the policy. Thus any material change in circumstances, e.g. reduction of the number of principals in the insured firm, must be reported to the insurer during renewal negotiations. Nonnotification of a claim under a previous policy period would therefore not only remove cover under that previous policy in respect of that claim, but also technically invalidate the whole policy of insurance for the new period, even in the absence of fraud or any dishonest intent on the part of the insured. It is accordingly in the interests of both insurer and insured alike that there should be full disclosure of all material facts at inception and upon renewal each year. The insurer will thus be able to charge an appropriate premium, and will have no fear of his claim being avoided by the insurer on the grounds of non-disclosure or misrepresentation of material facts.

Question 1
Full names of all partners/principals, with full details of qualifications, date obtained, and period of time each has been a partner/principal
This question when answered will provide the underwriter with the facts concerning the number of partners or principals in the firm

proposing insurance, together with a breakdown of their respective qualifications. These will enable the insurer to gauge the acceptability of the firm as a whole. It may be that not all proposers will possess any qualifications pertinent to the business or profession, and the insurer will then have to consider that individual's experience in the firm, and may even request further information about such persons, e.g. number of years experience in that profession or business, and what other qualifications or experience is possessed by them that may suggest skill or competence in the insured practice. Certainly, the number of years experience as a partner or principal will be a relevant consideration as well.

The information provided will also be required for preparation of the policy schedule, and for the maintenance of the insurer's record of individuals insured under the policy for that practice. The insurer will also be able to follow through the career of individuals who leave one practice and join another, if it so happens that the insurer also insures that second practice.

Question 2
Style or title of the business or practice
In many cases the title of the practice does not contain the name of any living partner or principal, or is otherwise not identifiable with any of the insured individuals. The policy schedule will have to be prepared by the insurer with this information, and the insurer will also need to know the practice's name in order that any writ arriving with the practice's name on it, rather than the names of the partners or principals, will be accepted as covered by the negligence policy without any dispute from the insurer. Previous practices can be named here also if cover is required.

Question 3
Business or profession of the practice
This is a very important question, because the operative clause of the policy is in terms that only the activities of the specified business or profession will be covered by the indemnity under the policy. The answer to this question will be copied on to the policy schedule, therefore the proposer must ensure that full disclosure of all activities is disclosed. For instance, an engineering practice that also undertakes architectural work must state this when answering this question, otherwise claims arising from architectural work will not be covered. The insurer will wish to consider the partners' or principals' qualifications in relation to the notified business or profession, and will also consider whether it is a suitable practice to insure. It may be that the insurer will require an additional premium to cover ancilliary activities to the main practice, or may even specifically exclude those claims that do not arise from the primary

activities of the notified primary business or profession.

The insurer will also be concerned with the nature of the business or profession for rating methods will vary between the professions, and the risks incidental to each also vary to an extent that the insurer may not feel he can ignore them – indeed, what claims experience that insurers have been able to gather is naturally divided between the professions, and a composite picture would be distorted when applied to any one business or profession. Certain insurers will only insure particular professions, so in these circumstances also the insurer will be very interested in the reply to the question.

Question 4
Date practice established
An insurer will be more ready to insure a long-established practice with a claims-free experience, than a recently formed practice which is claims-free to date. This stands to reason on grounds of common sense alone, but can be justified in that the insurer will have evidence of the practice being well-directed with a good standard of competence among the partners and the staff. With a more recently formed practice, the insurer will scrutinise the experience and qualifications of the principals with more care in order to evaluate the level of risk that he will attach in underwriting the professional negligence risk.

If more than one practice is to be covered by the policy, the proposer will have already mentioned the others in answer to Question 2, and will here have to respond with their respective dates of opening (and closing, in the case of previous practices) of each. The underwriter will be very wary of covering other existing practices without the completion of individual proposal forms in respect of each, unless the partners or principals are substantially the same in each, and the business or profession is the same. In the case of previous practices, the insurer will also need to make further enquiries to ascertain the claims experience of that practice, which may not be disclosed under subsequent replies which the proposer may consider only apply to the existing practice.

Question 5
Addresses of all offices from which the practice operates
Many practices have expanded and it is no longer the case that professionals operate only from one address. The insurer will wish to know the location of each office, and will also wish to know which partner or principal is in charge of each brance office. It will do neither the insured nor the insurer any good service to operate branches without competent staff and proper supervision, and the question will alert the insured to the need for precautions should he need any reminding.

One of the most important aspects of this question is whether it reveals that the insured has one or more offices in foreign jurisdictions. It has already been mentioned that many insurers will not indemnify any insured against claims brought in jurisdictions other than the United Kingdom. Other insurers may be prepared to cover those foreign claims, but in order to assess the additional premium will need to know all locations so that the legal liability laws in each relevant country may be considered. As a general rule, it can be said that insurers will not cover liabilities attaching in the United States of America — any offices located there will have to be insured in the American insurance market. Obviously, the proposer must make sure he is aware of the policy cover in this regard, he should not merely presume that non-UK liabilities will be covered simply because he has given the addresses of foreign offices in answer to the question on the proposal form; often a specific extension would be required which will name the foreign offices for which the indemnity is extended.

In the case of an office functioning without the full-time attendance of a partner or principal, many underwriters will not be prepared to accept the risk on the grounds that employees may be tempted to cover up mistakes, but, of course, it will be the partners who are liable in the event of the mistake giving rise to a claim against the practice from a third party e.g. a client. There is the further point that, if there is a dishonesty extension under the policy, the chances of employees having the opportunity to embezzle clients' funds or otherwise defraud clients, will be greatly increased. It is understandable that insurers should not wish to insure such inadequately supervised branch offices, although the proposer will often be given the opportunity of seeking to persuade the insurer that such an office is suitably supervised by the partners, and is in the control of a particularly well-experienced, well-qualified and absolutely trustworthy employee.

Occasionally, the insurer of a particular practice will add a special condition where he is not satisfied as to the level of competence of the staff generally, that all incoming mail must be seen by a partner or principal, and that all outgoing correspondence is signed by them also. An endorsement attached to the policy would usually be necessary to effect this sort of requirement.

Question 6
Have any principals or employees been required to leave the practice in the last five years because of errors committed?
If the answer is yes, the insurer will wish to know the full circumstances. Whilst such dismissal may show the degree of supervision is good, i.e. the error was detected, it might also indicate that the level of training and supervision is inadequate in that the error may have

arisen due to these factors. Obviously, however, the insurer will not be an expert in the needs for supervision and adequacy of training in professions in which he, the insurer, has no training. He can add this information on dismissals to his general knowledge about the practice, though, and can ascertain from other questions on the ,proposal form whether that error actually gave rise to a claim, and, if so, whether it was a serious or small claim.

A practice with a bad claims record, but with no corresponding record of dismissals, will put the insurer on alert, for it can suggest the practice as a whole is not a good risk, or one that can only be accepted with a higher premium, or a particularly large Excess to be borne by the insured practice on each and every claim.

Question 7
Have any claims for professional negligence or the like ever been made against the practice or any of the partners or principals? If yes, give full details
This question is one of the most important on the proposal form, and it must be answered in the fullest detail before an insurer will be prepared to consider insuring the proposer firm. The question is designed so that the claims experience of each individual will be disclosed to the insurer. Small, isolated claims against an individual will not be a matter of great concern to the insurer, because the element of human error is precisely the risk being insured and is to be expected, but only to an extent. The insurer will be on the look out for a particularly bad claims record of the firm as a whole, or of a particular partner or principal, who may have a record of claims against him both in past practices as well as the practice he is currently with. Such a circumstance will severely prejudice the proposer firm's chances of insuring the negligence risk either at a reasonable premium, or even at all.

Non-disclosure of claims known to the proposing partners or principals will, of course, be a very serious matter, and may severely endanger the protection granted by the policy obtained without revealing the claims. The insured might well be faced with the insurer's repudiation of liability for a claim due to non-disclosure and breach of good faith, not to mention breach of the warranty certifying the truth of all answers on the proposal form. Even in the case of the 'special waiver clause' inserted in some professional scheme policies a proposer who has deliberately concealed claims from his insurer will not be protected. The duty of disclosure arises at each renewal, which must also be remembered.

Upon any disclosure of a claims record, the insurer will obviously wish to consider whether there is one particular underlying cause of the majority of claims, e.g. a particular individual, or a particular aspect of the professional services provided by the proposer, and discuss with the proposer the possibilities of eradicating that weakness. Such an exercise will be in the interests of both parties, for no practice wishes to be continually caught up in claims, even if insured, because of the Excess under the policy provisions and because of the injury to the professional standing of the practice.

A reduction over the years in the number of claims made against a proposer practice will have the reverse effect upon the insurer, and suggest a more attractive risk, and perhaps suggest to the insurer that there is an increasing standard of competence and supervision within that practice. The result may be the removal of a prejudicial loading that had been placed on the practice in previous years, by that insurer or another insurer.

It goes without saying, however, that just as it will please the proposer to have a claims-free record, so it will please the insurer to receive such a proposal. In these circumstances the insurer may well be prepared to accept the risk at a premium that is substantially below the standard rate for that business or profession. Such reductions in premium will be harder to obtain, though, in the case of scheme insurances, because the insurer will have specifically determined his rating structure bearing in mind that many of those seeking the insurance will have a claims-free history, and will have allowed for this factor throughout his analysis of required premium.

Question 8
Are any of the partners/principals aware of any claim pending or of any circumstance likely to give rise to a claim?
The insurer is not asking if the proposer is blissfully unaware of any pending claims or probable claims, but is asking the proposer to answer this question after making enquiries throughout the practice to ascertain the true facts.

It is an unfortunate truth that the honest of the proposer in a sense will often work to his detriment, for some insurers, when approached by a proposer who has not previously been insured with him, will exclude claims notified under this question by endorsement. This would be on the principle that the occurrence was before they became interested in the proposer, but this argument may be countered by the fact that the proposer's record system is shown to be good enough to disclose errors or omissions prior to receipt of claims. This suggests a good administration system, and, because of early warning, the insurer can set aside a 'reserve' to meet the claim at an early stage.

Question 9
Have the partners/principals held a Professional Indemnity policy prior to this date or presently hold such a policy?
The insurer will want to know about existing and previous policies of

all the partners or principals, with either the present practice, or when with a different practice. The insurer will want to know the indemnity limit of the other policies, the identity of those other insurers, the periods of the other insurances, the Excesses under those policies, and the period of continual insurance.

One of the main questions in the insurer's mind will be why the proposer wishes to be insured by him rather than the other insurer(s). This may be a simple matter of a more competitive premium, and/or better cover under the policy. Other factors might be that the insurer has become the leading insurer to the profession, or that the insurer has gained a reputation of prompt and efficient claims settlement. The answer may lie, however, in the answer to the next question (below).

If the proposer has not been continuously insured since the first policy was taken out, why does the proposer now seek insurance? Could it be that the proposer ceased taking out insurance for a number of years because no claims arose, in which case does the request for insurance come about because of the proposer's fear of claims being made in the near future? This sort of question will always be in the mind of the insurer in this type of insurance, for there is a constant fear of selection against the insurer i.e. only the poor risk practices will seek to insure themselves against professional negligence. This factor is obviously less prominent in the case of a profession where the taking out of professional indemnity insurance is compulsory.

Question 10
Has any insurer—
(a) *declined a proposal for this practice or any partner or principal?*
(b) *declined to offer renewal terms?*
(c) *cancelled or voided a policy?*
(d) *required a special premium increase or special terms?*

If the answer to any of these questions is in the affirmative, the insurer will be put on enquiry and will require full details from the proposer. The insurer will most probably check the information given with the previous insurer to gain the benefit of his explanation of the request, decline, or insistence on special provisions. The insurer will wish to know whether the previous insurer has some information about the proposer which is not in his possession from the proposal form. There may be quite a harmless explanation for some events, though, for instance, the previous insurer may have declined to renew the proposer's policy for the simple reason that he no longer wishes to insure any member of the proposer's profession and is concentrating on insuring one profession only.

The cancellation or voiding of a policy will particularly require the eliciting of the circumstances from the other insurer.

It must be mentioned that all sorts of insurance proposal forms will contain questions about previous insurances, and there is nothing unusual in this sort of question. Insurers will generally always co-operate with each other when one insurer requests information about an insured from another, for it is in the general interest of the insurance industry as a whole. As regards professional indemnity insurance, however, one can expect higher standards of discretion between insurers concerning their insured.

Question 11
State amount of indemnity required and amount of Excess to be borne by the insured. State whether the indemnity sought is aggregate, or is for each and every claim

The three factors of indemnity limit, Excess, and the basis of the indemnity are three of the most important rating factors to the insurer. If the insured is seeking a very large indemnity limit, the insurer will wish to know why it is sought. It may that the insured does not fully understand the aggregate basis of the indemnity provisions, as against the 'each and every claim' basis, and this may lead to an incorrect or inappropriate level of indemnity being sought. For instance, whereas a proposer may require a limit of indemnity of £750,000 aggregate in any one year of insurance, it may be that the maximum to be expected on any one claim is £400,000. Even though the rating structure will generally provide for a higher rate where the 'each and every' claim basis is sought, the premium may be less expensive for cover of £400,000 'each and every claim' rather than £750,000 on the aggregate claims basis. It will obviously be finally up to the proposer to choose which indemnity limit to seek, assuming the insurer is prepared to offer both covers, but the proposer is well advised to give a great deal of consideration to the basis of indemnity he will seek. Another factor that the insured must bear in mind at each renewal, is the effect of inflation upon the level of claim settlement to be expected, and it will be prudent to reconsider the adequacy of the indemnity limit, comparative to the cost of increasing it, each renewal.

Related to the question of the indemnity, and the basis of the indemnity, is the question of the amount of the Excess to be borne by the insured. It stands to reason that the higher the Excess that the proposer is prepared to bear, the lower the premium will be. The proposer must, however, not end up in the situation that he has such a high level of Excess under the policy that the majority of claims that may arise will be within the Excess, for he will be paying a large amount of premium for very little effective protection. One factor to bear in mind here is the effect upon the proposer's cash flow to have to meet this Excess once, or even more, during any one financial year, if claims arise. Certainly, the respective premiums required for the various optional levels of Excess will have to be evaluated by the proposer in the consideration of his needs, and, as has been mentioned earlier, no insurer will give professional indemnity insurance which bears no Excess under its terms, and most insurers will require a significant Excess to be borne e.g. representing 5 per cent to 10 per cent of the insured sum in many cases.

Another matter in regard to the Excess, is for the proposer to be aware of the operation of the policy and the application of the Excess. Some policies will apply the Excess to the whole claim, i.e. settlement cost plus legal costs, whereas other policies only apply the Excess to the claim settlement figure. This will have important repercussions where a claim is made that later fails, thus the proposer would be left with only legal costs of his own (there having been no payment in settlement) and if the Excess is applied to the legal costs, this figure may well be below the Excess so that the insured would have to pay all the costs of the abortive claim. If the policy only provides for application of the Excess to payments in settlement of claims, the insured will be indemnified in full by the insurer for all legal costs and expenses incurred in resisting the claim with the written consent of the insurer.

Question 12
Does the proposer undertake any work for clients outside the United Kingdom? Does the proposer wish to include liability in respect of this work?
It has already been mentioned that most professional indemnity policies only provide an indemnity in respect of liability for claims brought in the courts of the United Kingdom (see chapter 3). If some work is either carried out abroad, or is carried out for foreign clients, this is a matter of which the insurer will want full details. The insurer may require a full list of the contracts with a foreign element undertaken by the practice in the past ten years, so that the insurer can gauge the nature and value of this work. He will also wish to know the proportion of the total work of the practice that has a foreign element.

The insurer will generally expressly exclude these named contracts from the policy unless he is prepared to cover them, most probably for an additional premium. The insurer will also look back to Question 5 to see the location of foreign branch offices of the practice, and to consider the relation between the foreign contracts and the foreign branches. If these foreign liabilities are to be included under the policy, the insurer will draw up an endorsement naming either the particular contracts or the relevant countries for which indemnity is expressly extended.

If the proposer practice wishes to have the foreign element included, it will obviously be in its own interests to maintain accurate and complete records of the nature, location, and value of work with a foreign element, to avoid the situation of finding itself uninsured in respect of these services.

Question 13
Does the proposer require any extensions to the policy?
Under this sort of question each insurer will usually give a list of those extensions he will normally be prepared to consider, and the proposer is able to merely answer 'yes' or 'no' against each item. Such extensions were considered in the last chapter, and will be extensions relating to libel and slander, loss of documents, past partners, dishonesty, fees recovery, change of partners, conversion, money received, and the like.

The cost of these various extensions will vary between insurer and insurer, as will the extent of the cover under the extension. Furthermore, different underwriting considerations will apply to the different professions in every case, which will affect the additional premium required.

Under scheme insurances with a master policy, the scope for special extensions may be rather limited, although one or more extensions may be included automatically under the scheme cover.

Question 14
State numbers of—
(a) *partners/principals*
(b) *qualified staff*
(c) *unqualified staff*
(d) *all other staff e.g. typists*
Just as some insurers will give a loading on the premium required from a practice that has many offices, so may some insurers analyse the structure of the proposer practice. The insurer will generally only do this where the rating structure is geared towards the variation of the premium with this factor, as well as indemnity limit and basis of indemnity. The insurer may even have a guideline as to the maximum number of employees that may be supervised effectively by each partner, e.g. one partner for fifteen staff, and this figure may well vary between the different professions. Such a rule of thumb will be largely guesswork on the part of the insurer, and is rarely applied as a consideration in the rating of scheme insurance cover.

The insurer may also wish to have details of the qualifications of staff that are qualified as far as the proposer is concerned, and may also be wary of a practice where there are large numbers of unqualified staff tackling the everyday work of the practice. In this circumstance, the insurer will reconsider the aspects of adequacy of supervision and training of these staff.

The number of other office staff, such as typists, receptionists, and office boys, will give the insurer the total size of the practice, from which he may choose to make a number of observations which might affect his individual assessment of the level of risk presented by the proposer practice.

For those insurers that rate the risk upon the per capita basis, this question will also give the figures required for the calculation of the premium, taking into consideration the other underwriting features e.g. limit of indemnity.

Question 15

Please state gross fee income over each of the previous five years, and the anticipated fee income for the year of insurance
This information will be required where the insurer rates the premium required upon the fees-earned basis. The proposer, if his insurance proposal is accepted, will have to undertake to keep proper records and declare the gross fee income of the practice at the year end, in order that the premium may be adjusted, either up or down, according to whether the provisional fee estimate was either too low or too high.

The insurer will be interested in the figures for the previous five years or so for two main reasons. First, it helps him to gauge whether the proposer's provisional fee estimate is realistic (it may be set low deliberately, so that the initial premium payment is less). Secondly, an increase in fees received after accounting for inflation, would suggest that the volume of work undertaken by the practice is increasing, and the insurer has his other information to consider whether there has been a similar enlargement of the complement of partners/principals and qualified staff. If this is not the case, the insurer may think that the level of supervision may be becoming inadequate.

Special underwriting features of professions

Accountants
Insurers will generally rate accountancy firms on a fees earned basis, but will apply special rating considerations to international firms, most notably where some work is performed in the USA. Figures of £20 million indemnity are not unheard of for these multinational conglomerates, and it is quite understandable that the insurer must apply particular care when insuring such a high sum on indemnity.

Generally, for United Kingdom risks, the insurer when underwriting an accountancy risk will bear in mind that there is no legal requirement that a person practising as an accountant shall be a member of any of the accountancy professional bodies. The main consideration will therefore be the qualifications of those under-taking the practice's work. Experience has revealed that the majority of claims arise from two main activities, namely, tax work and auditing work. The experience of unqualified staff, together with the claims record of the firm will be further important factors influencing the insurer, especially in relation to these two areas of activity. Policies will be issued only to qualified accountants, or to proposers of long experience and with exceptionally good claims' records.

The policy will normally be extended to cover the accountant in respect of certain common appointments e.g. company secretary or executor, but it will only provide cover in regard to claims for negligent acts, errors, or omissions in that capacity. In this regard, an insurer will not insure the accountant for certain liabilities attach-ing to these appointments. The risks that are uninsurable relate, for instance, to the personal liability of the accountant, not arising from professional negligence, but from the personal liabilities flowing from the establishment of personal overdrafts or borrowings or guarantees to loans. The accountant will often have to accept these liabilities when appointed as a liquidator or a receiver to a company, but can only protect himself by carefully keeping an eye on the company's portfolio of standard covers e.g. interruption of business insurance, public liability insurance, product liability insurance, and employers liability insurance.

Architects
Architectural practices will generally be rated on a fees earned basis, rather than numbers of offices and/or qualified staff. Two features of the normal policy will be a United Kingdom jurisdiction clause, and a requirement for immediate notification of claims. Insurers underwriting professional indemnity insurance for architects have discovered over the years that claims arise from a lack of administra-tion in the practice apart from the obvious design fault claims. Such claims can emanate from over-certification on projects; failure to check planning permissions; delays in preparation of plans or drawings; and failure to notify the client that variations will increase the project cost.

Difficulty will be encountered by the architect who wishes to insure against liability for projects in the USA or France. In the former case, the insurer will be worried about the high awards of damages often granted, and in the latter case, there are special problems relating to what is known as 'decennial liability', for French law imposes certain strict liabilities upon persons who build structures for a period of ten years from completion. Certain Middle Eastern Countries have adopted similar provisions into their Consti-tutions. In other countries, however, the insurer will normally be prepared to extend the policy to include coverage for liability under local laws.

Most policies will include the following extensions free of additional premium:

(a) infringement of copyright;
(b) libel and slander; and
(c) costs relating to legal representation at any enquiry or proceeding not otherwise covered by the policy.

Extensions for loss of documents and fees recovery will be readily obtainable, but for an additional premium.

The other main area of anxiety for the insurer, other than work abroad, is that of the architect being involved in a 'design group', 'consortium', 'joint venture' or 'partnership', for, be the project at home or abroad, the architect often does not realise the full ramifications of these arrangements. More often than not, the effect of the agreement will be a partnership between all parties, with all the consequent joint and several liabilities. For this reason it is prudent to seek both legal assistance and the assistance of the insurer *prior* to the agreement being finalised – otherwise the architect may find himself with an uninsurable risk, or at least one that is very expensive to cover. The insurer will, of course, need to see copies of all contract documents in order to consider the risk and a suitable premium.

Similar wariness is found on the part of the insurer where the architect is appointed 'design team co-ordinator' or 'project leader'. Unless each member of the project team is appointed directly by the client, e.g. the structural engineer, the quantity surveyors, and the architect, then there is a danger that the architect will either be involved in an unacceptable design partnership, or be the employer of the other professionals and so be vicariously liable for their errors.

Auctioneers
Professional negligence policies for auctioneers will be rated on a combination of factors, namely fees earned, turnover, and class of business.

The policy will normally include the conversion extension to protect the auctioneer from claims based in tort for the wrongful taking of goods from the true owner; for the wrongful detention of goods despite a request by the person entitled to possession of them for their handing over (which might occur where there is some mistake or confusion as to the identity of the purchaser upon collection of the goods); for wrongful destruction of the goods; or for wrongful delivery of the goods i.e. the handing over of goods to someone other than the purchaser or his authorised agent.

No special underwriting considerations arise other than to note that some insurers will exclude cover as regards motor vehicle auctions. This may result from a fear on the part of the insurer that he would be accepting an onerous liability comparative to the premium, due to the larger number of claims arising from the auction of motor vehicles because of defective title of many persons purporting to the auctioneer that they are the owner of the vehicle.

Barristers

Barristers differ from other professionals in that not only are they forbidden to practice behind the veil of a company, they are also prevented by their professional rules to practice in partnership with any other barrister. Each barrister is a sole practioner, but a number of barristers will share accommodation ('chambers') and the services of a clerk and office staff. The professional indemnity policy, therefore, is rated for each set of chambers upon a per capita basis, and the cover is automatically extended to include the clerk and his staff under the chambers single policy. Furthermore, cover will also be provided free of charge for 'pupils' i.e. barristers who are serving their year under a practising barrister prior to being permitted to practice on their own account. It will be incumbent upon the head of the chambers, the senior barrister, to notify the insurer of the names of pupils in chambers each year.

Insurers may apply a varying scale of per capita rating which will provide for younger members of chambers being rated more cheaply than more senior members, to reflect the probable lower level of advisory work. Other insurers may prefer to rate the premium upon a percentage of fees received during the year.

The majority of barristers practice in London, and the specialist chambers are also located there, but, for various reasons, insurers will offer a discount on the normal rates of premium if the chambers are located in the provinces of England and Wales, rather than the metropolis. Moreover, insurers will offer a substantially lower rating for those barristers who certify that a high proportion of their work involves criminal matters rather than civil litigation and advisory work. This is to recognise the lower risks attaching to criminal work of the barrister being sued for damages for breach of professional duty to his client.

Company directors and officers

Basically premiums demanded will depend on the size and the type of the company, the number of directors and officers involved, and, of course, the level of indemnity required. Insurers will look for evidence of stability in the history of the company, and will hesitate to accept proposals from companies and directors where there have been previous proceedings taken against them. The insurer will also be wary if there is a probability of an imminent take-over or merger of the company, for this might prompt a disgruntled shareholder to consider action against the company's directors and officers.

Usually, the insurer will wish to see the previous three years' audited annual accounts of the company, and will also require such normal information as the names and qualifications of the directors and officers who are sought to be covered, together with their individual claims experience. The insurer will consider other matters over a longer period, e.g. the previous five years, such as details of all mergers, acquisitions, takeovers, and sale of associated companies, and also disclosure of changes in the capital structure of the holding, parent or associated companies. Obviously, the question of insuring the directors and officers in companies outside the United Kingdom will require special attention.

The levels of indemnity sought are often high, and there will be a correspondingly high rate of premium.

In the case of recent acquisitions by the company of other companies, the insurer will be wary of the risk of picking up the claims that might arise against the acquired company for past events.

Estate agents

Professional indemnity cover for estate agents will be rated on a combination of factors, namely, fees earned, annual turnover, and class of property handled.

Estate agency is not a 'closed' profession, and anyone can establish himself as a house-selling agent. Insurers, however, will enquire of the proposer of his recognised qualifications in this occupation. Moreover, because unqualified persons may well be in positions of responsibility, albeit supervised by a qualified principal, insurers will require full information about the qualifications and experience of employees in key positions in the practice.

The main area of risk to an estate agent is being accused by his client of not acting timeously in the sale or purchase, or, alternatively, of suggesting a sale price that is so high as to render the property difficult to sell. There is also the risk of the theft by staff of deposit moneys by prospective purchasers, and for this reason, the policy granted to estate agents will normally automatically include this aspect of liability cover, and the premium rating will be assessed accordingly.

Engineers

Professional engineers tend to specialise and this is a factor that cannot be ignored. There is, of course, virtually no possibility of a person being accepted for indemnity insurance in this category unless he has passed the necessary examinations to become a member of one of the many recognised engineering institutes. These institutions will cater variously for structural engineers, civil engineers, mechanical engineers, chemical engineers, mining engineers, and several other disciplines.

The insurer will need to know in which spheres of expertise the proposer practices, and these will be incorporated into the schedule of the policy, with the consequence that if the engineer undertakes duties in respect of an undisclosed expertise, different to those notified to his insurer, the engineer may find that the insurer will repudiate liability for claims arising from such undisclosed activities.

The normal basis for assessment of the premium will be the fees earned basis, with an adjustment clause for end of year premium adjustment, the rate varying with the level of indemnity and the basis of indemnity limit (i.e. aggregate or 'each and every' basis).

Many insurers will only offer UK cover at the basic premium rates, and will only insure the engineer in respect of work abroad upon special application, and for an additional premium. Extensions will be difficult to obtain for work undertaken in the USA because of the large damages awards often encountered, and the basic professional negligence policy will not cover all the liabilities of engineers operating in France or other countries that have laws of strict liability, without proof of fault, binding those responsible for constructing a building.

The fact that in recent years more and more engineers have had to seek work abroad also has another repercussion, in that the engineer will often become involved in some international 'partnership', 'consortium', 'joint venture', or 'design group', rather than establish a properly constituted subsidiary activity (a company based abroad will generally not be against the engineering institutions' rules) in that foreign country. Sometimes the arrangements are evolved simply because there is only one project in that country and the joint project arrangement will suffice. The prudent insurer, however, will realise that these arrangements will usually render the engineer a partner with all the consequent partnership liabilities of accounting for the defalcations of partners committed in the course of the partnership's activities. Insurers will, therefore, refuse to cover these partnership liabilities that extend the liabilities of the engineer beyond those of a direct appointment by the client. Exceptionally, an insurer may extend the policy for such consortium arrangements, if satisfied that the consortium is really only a guise over a direct appointment by the client of the various professional firms involved, rather than an appointment of the consortium or joint venture, to undertake the project.

On no account will an insurer undertake to indemnify an engineer in respect of claims resulting from any express warranty of fitness or other guarantee of work performed given to a client or other third party. The policy is maintained as a 'negligent act, error or omission' policy, rather than a version of product guarantee or product liability policy.

Solicitors

The Council of the Law Society, under section 37 of the Solicitors Act 1974, has made it a rule that all solicitors, and former solicitors, shall hold professional indemnity insurance under the Law Society's Master Policy Scheme. These rules have been in operation since 1976, and are currently cited as the Solicitors' Indemnity Rules 1975–81.

Cover is provided to all solicitors at basic premium rates, varying only upon the location of the practice. Partners within the Inner London area are required to pay an additional £250 per partner to that payable by partners of practices elsewhere. Low earning sole practitioners have a special scale applicable to them, dependent upon their gross fee income in the financial year prior to commencement of the period of insurance.

Within the rating system to be applied under the Master Policy Scheme is the provision of four scales of loading that are to be applied to practices with poor claims experience, these loadings are 20 per cent, 30 per cent, 40 per cent, and 50 per cent, and vary with the extent to which the practice has received insurance moneys comparative to its aggregate premium payments.

The limit of the indemnity is on an 'each and every claim' basis, not an aggregate of claims made in the year of insurance, and is £100,000 in the case of a sole practitioner, but in the case of a partnership, will be £50,000 multiplied by the number of rateable partners, e.g. in the case of a firm with five partners, each partner will pay a full premium, and each will thereby be indemnified to a limit of 5 × £50,000 (£250,000) per each and every claim. The Excess applicable to each claim is £500 multiplied by the number of partners (e.g. in the last example would be £2,500 per claim).

These indemnity rules only apply to solicitors practising in England and Wales, and the Law Society of Scotland has its own special scheme of professional indemnity insurance.

If a solicitors' practice wishes to supplement the limit of indemnity provided by the Law Society Scheme, it will be at perfect liberty to seek additional cover from the general insurance market. In these circumstances the insurer will wish to know why the solicitors feel that additional cover is necessary, e.g. does it arise from specialist tax advisory work or other specialist area from which very large claims might arise? A variety of factors will be weighed by the insurer to determine the applicable premium for such risks, but in a straightforward case an additional premium per partner will be applied.

Stockbrokers

Stockbrokers will normally be rated upon the level of indemnity, the number of operational staff, and the annual turnover of the business.

The most important aspect for the insurer is whether the stockbroker is recognised as a member of one of the world's reputable stockmarkets. If this is the case, the insurer will rely upon the adequacy of the regulatory standards of competence and integrity of these stockmarkets to prevent brokers of inadequate experience operating in those markets. An insurer will not generally be prepared to insure a stockbroker who is not a member of a recognised Stock Exchange.

Many staff within a stockbrokers will deal with the sale or purchase of stocks and shares, not merely the principals, and it is for this reason that an assessment of the level of staff responsibility and numbers will be taken into account by the insurer when rating the risk. The factor of turnover will permit the insurer to gauge the level of activity of the brokerage activities, and, perhaps, to consider the possibilities of a very large claim being made.

Surveyors and valuers

These professionals are usually rated on a combination of fees or turnover, limit of indemnity, and class of business. The insurer must consider the different risks attaching to surveying industrial properties as against small houses, and equally the difference between valuing fine art and antiques, and country properties.

Insurers will generally insist upon surveys and valuations of buildings only being undertaken by chartered surveyors, qualified members of the ISVA, or other suitably qualified and experienced staff. A special clause will be inserted into the policy, and this has been considered in chapter 4 (above), which also discusses the special clause that must be inserted by the surveyor or valuer in his contract with his client. The ISVA now requires its members to hold professional indemnity insurance in the sum of £250,000 for each and every claim.

The extensions relating to breach of warranty of authority, and dishonest acts or omissions (see chapter 4) are also included in the basic policy free of additional charge.

The Excess to be applied upon a claim is often not a very large figure, comparative to other professional indemnity policies, but will always be a feature of the policy.

Chapter 6

Special schemes

Introduction

As has been discussed in the preceding chapter, each profession has factors that are unique to the mind of the insurer who may be considering a proposal for the insurance of professional negligence risks. It is also true that each profession will have slightly different needs or objects to achieve through the professional indemnity policy, and, generally, a differing pattern of extensions of the 'basic' policy will be both offered by the insurer and pursued by the professional. Accordingly, it has become a popular practice for insurers to offer special 'schemes' of insurance that are, to some extent, tailor-made for the various professions' requirements.

The purpose of this chapter is to discuss these special schemes of professional indemnity insurance that are commonly encountered. No particular special scheme cited can be regarded as necessarily the one that will be encountered by the professional seeking insurance, save the exceptional case of the solicitors' compulsory scheme, and the intention is not to proffer these special schemes considered as necessarily the 'best' available for each profession. Rather, there will be a sample of the special schemes offering composite cover for the professional practice, there being other permutations of extensions of cover to the 'basic' underlying negligence cover.

One other matter to be mentioned, is that further extensions of cover for various risks not embraced by the special scheme will generally be available upon a proposal being put before the underwriter concerned; the mere exclusion of cover for a particular risk, e.g. breach of warranty of authority, does not mean it cannot be obtained for an additional premium.

Reference should be made to chapter 4 for more detailed explanation of the various extensions of indemnity included in the special schemes and the basis of their application. Obviously, the particular wording in each extension clause must be considered on its own merits, and the model clauses in chapter 4 are for guidance purposes and not definitive versions.

Accountants

The main insuring clause will indemnify the insured accountant against any claims made against him during the period of insurance arising from:
(a) Any negligent act, error or omission;
(b) Breach of contract;
(c) Breach of warranty of authority;
(d) Breach of trust that was committed in good faith;
(e) Libel or slander.

The cover is fully retrospective, but must have a direct bearing upon the conduct of the professional business of the insured accountant. This is defined as any advice given or services performed by the accountant for which the fee has been included in the computation of the income of the accountant (or of the firm where there are a number of accountants in partnership). Furthermore, the cover extends to the accountant whilst holding any appointment of receiver, liquidator, executor, trustee, company secretary, registrar or arbitrator, without the need for special endorsement of the policy.

As accountants so often find themselves appointed company directors, the policy confers an indemnity, covering the same risks as are contained in the main operative clause, for breach of professional duty as a company director in the provision of defined services to the company. These 'services' include such matters as tax advice, share registration, financial advice, investment advice, insurance advice, and company formations (with legal assistance).

Both a 'moneys had and received' extension, and a 'loss of documents' extension are included, as is an indemnity against claims arising from the dishonest or fraudulent act or omission by any past or present partner or employee. This fidelity cover also extends to a fidelity guarantee clause to indemnify the insured against his own losses, apart from claims from others, arising from the dishonesty of his partners or employees.

The accountant is also provided with a generous clause covering liability that may arise directly or indirectly from joint appointments.

Finally, extensive cover to the insured accountant personally is provided in respect of losses directly sustained by reason of forged or stolen documents (e.g. receipts, call letters, powers of attorney, marriage certificates), or by erroneous or fraudulent entry upon a share or debenture register. These losses must have been sustained in the ordinary course of business, in good faith, and without the insured accountant having notice of any defect or error.

The policy provides for the payment of all costs and expenses incurred by the accountant with the written consent of the insurer, without the application of the Excess, unless the claim settlement exceeds the policy limit of indemnity, in which case the authorised legal costs and expenses are only reimbursed in proportion to the settlement as compared to the limit. Thus, if the limit is £100,000, and the settlement £200,000, the insurer only pays half of the legal costs and expenses incurred.

The Excess is also not applied to the costs of replacing or restoring documents under the 'loss of documents' clause.

The 'insured' under the policy includes all those named in the proposal form, their employees, their personal representatives and any person who becomes a partner in the insured practice during the currency of the policy.

Two benefits are found:
(a) up to 30 per cent discount on the premium for no claims in preceding years;
(b) the special condition of waiver is included, whereby the insurer agrees to waive avoidance rights for innocent non-disclosure, misrepresentation, or untrue statement, but allowance will be made for prejudice suffered by the insurer in the handling or settlement of the claim, and the insured will not be afforded any wider indemnity than contained in a previous policy under which a claim should have been made rather than the current policy (e.g. there might have been a lower limit of indemnity).

Exclusions
(1) All claims alleging death, personal injuries, or physical loss of or damage to any property;
(2) Claims covered by another policy, except for the uninsured amount of loss;
(3) Claims notified under any previous policy;
(4) Claims subsequent to reasonable suspicion of dishonesty of a person otherwise covered by the policy;
(5) All claims before judgment is obtained that arise out of the insured's activities as an insurance agent if the claim is made by an insurer;
(6) Claims arising out of advice rendered concerning investment in publicly quoted companies, unless tendered upon the written recommendation of a member of a recognised Stock Exchange;
(7) Claims arising out of trading losses or liabilities;
(8) Most claims arising from loss, damage, distortion or erasure of computer systems records;
(9) Radiation, war and kindred risks.

General Conditions
(1) Non-admission of liability clause, including the Q.C. clause;
(2) Notice of claims or intimations of claims, and any discovery of dishonesty or fraud on the part of any partner, past partner, or employee, must be made 'as soon as practicable';
(3) Notice as soon as practicable to insurers of circumstances which may give rise to a claim under the policy;
(4) All possible action must be taken to seek reimbursement of losses caused by dishonesty or fraud against those responsible;
(5) All fraudulent claims shall be void.

Architects

The policy will indemnify the insured architect, or architectural practice, against sums that the insured becomes legally liable to pay to persons claiming to have suffered loss or damage directly arising from any negligent act, error or omission of the insured. Such must have arisen during the conduct or execution of the insured's professional activities and duties, which are defined as being those normally undertaken by architects. In this regard, it should be noted that all supervision of construction work will be excluded from the ambit of the policy unless an extra premium is paid to include responsibility for the interpretation of construction plans, but the normal responsibilities of building contractors will not be embraced by the policy even under the extension.

The policy Excess will be applied to the sum of the costs of the claim plus the insurer's costs of investigating and defending the claim, but will not be applied to legal costs and expenses incurred by the insured with the written consent of the insurer – unless the settlement cost exceeds the limit of indemnity, in which instance, only proportional costs will be paid to the insured in correlation with the settlement cost and the indemnity limit. The limit of indemnity under the policy may be expressed as a figure for 'each and every claim', with an overriding aggregate maximum limit of indemnity for the year of insurance.

The insurer extends the basic policy to include, by a special clause, the liability of the insured architect(s) for any negligent act, error or omission arising out of their responsibilities for the design of a building or other structure, notwithstanding that the insured was undertaking other duties or activities concerned with any particular project. A special clause adds provisions forbidding the insured prejudicing the insurer's rights of subrogation against any specialist consultants, sub-contractors, or designers who might be in some way responsible for the design error indemnified under the special extension. Furthermore, the insured would be required to render the insurer with every assistance in any subrogated action.

Exclusions
 (1) Claims covered by an Employers Liability policy, Public Liability policy, or Motor policy, whether or not such a policy was actually maintained by the insured;
 (2) All claims for death, bodily injury, disease or sickness;
 (3) Any liability for any work undertaken outside the United Kingdom, unless the policy is specifically extended to include such liability;
 (4) Libel and slander;
 (5) Loss of documents;
 (6) Claims arising from any dishonest or malicious acts of any of the insured;
 (7) Radiation risks;
 (8) The insolvency of the insured;
 (9) Claims covered by any other professional indemnity policy of the insured;
 (10) Any claim arising from any express warranty or guarantee given by the insured insofar as that warranty or guarantee extends the insured's liability to others beyond their normal measure of liability, in contract or in tort, for breach of professional duty.

General Conditions
 (1) Immediate written notice must be given to the insurer of any claim, or receipt of notice of an intention to pursue a claim, covered by the indemnity granted in the policy; or of the discovery of any circumstance that the insured believes may give rise to a claim against him (or them).
 (2) Non-admission of liability to claimant or promise of settlement to be made, nor the incursion of any legal costs without the prior written consent of the insurer;
 (3) The Queen's Counsel clause;
 (4) Waiver of subrogation against employees unless dishonest or malicious conduct gave rise to the claim on the part of such employees;
 (5) All fraudulent claims to be void.

Auctioneers

The policy indemnifies the insured auctioneer against legal liability for breach of professional duty upon claims made against the insured during the period of insurance covered by the policy. Such breach of professional duty must arise from the conduct of the business or practice described in the policy schedule, but full retrospective cover is granted to indemnify the present practice from claims arising from the actions of the predecessors in the business or practice (this does not extend to a partner's previous other business activities unless specifically endorsed on the policy).

Also, an indemnity is provided in respect of liability for breaches of professional duty arising from any dishonest or malicious act or omission of an insured partner or employee, provided always that the errant party may not be indemnified under the policy, nor anyone condoning such conduct. The insured must take all reasonable steps to recover the amount of the loss prior to seeking recovery of the loss under the policy, and any money owed by the insured to the errant party must be set off against the insured loss if it would be payable but for the dishonest or malicious conduct.

Cover is extended in the following manner:

(a) failure to account for moneys had and received;
(b) liability for breach of warranty of authority;
(c) full loss of documents cover within United Kingdom, including cost of replacing or restoring such documents (excluding any negotiable instruments);
(d) for libels written or slanders spoken;
(e) full cover for employees where the practice could have been sued.

All claims attributable to the same act, neglect, error or omission, will be regarded as one claim only.

The Excess does not apply to claims covered by extensions (c) (that is, to the costs of replacement or restoration), and (d) above, nor to any costs and expenses incurred with the written consent of the insurer in resisting or settling a claim covered by the policy. The usual rider applies to this last provision that in the case of the claim exceeding the insurer's liability under the policy, the insurer will only be liable for proportional costs and expenses in relation to the settlement cost and indemnity limit.

The normal auctioneers' conversion clause (see chapter 4) regarding the auctioneer's legal liability for tortious conversion in connection with any property committed for sale will be included so far as such liability was incurred in good faith on the part of the auctioneer (not motor vehicles).

The limit of indemnity is on an 'each and every claim' basis.

Exclusions
(1) Any action not commenced in the United Kingdom, unless commenced in a foreign country where the insured has no company, firm, branch, or domiciled representative;
(2) Nuclear radiation risks;
(3) Sonic bang pressure waves;
(4) War and kindred risks;
(5) Death or bodily injury, and loss of or damage to any property, unless arising directly out of the breach of professional duty;

(6) Claims arising from dishonest or fraudulent acts or omissions after reasonable cause for suspicion of such has been discovered by the insured.

General Conditions

(1) The insured must give written notice to the insurer as soon as possible of any claim or circumstance that may result in a claim covered by the policy, even if the claim may fall below the Excess;

(2) No admission of liability or promise of settlement must be made by the insured without the written consent of the insurer, who shall have the right to full control and conduct of the claim. All correspondence and legal documents must be forwarded by the insured to the insurer immediately upon receipt thereof;

(3) The Queen's Counsel clause;

(4) The insurer shall be entitled at any stage to pay the full indemnity limit under the policy to the insured, or any lesser amount for which the claim could be settled, and thereby relinquish all further liability in the matter. Costs and expenses incurred with the insurer's written consent to that date would be paid;

(5) The special waiver clause is included, with its usual provision for deduction of an amount for any prejudice suffered by the insurer consequent to the innocent non-disclosure, misrepresentation, or untrue statement in the proposal or upon renewal; also, claims that should have been reported under a prior policy will only be indemnified to the extent that such indemnity was provided under that earlier policy;

(6) All fraudulent claims shall be void;

(7) Any other policy indemnifying the insured for the claim shall be applied in full before this policy is applied to the excess of loss (this is the 'non-contribution' clause);

(8) The insurer alone is entitled to cancel the policy, on thirty days notice, the insured thereupon being entitled to a proportionate return of premium for the unexpired period of insurance.

Barristers

The policy may be in the name of the head of the set of chambers, but will insure each member of chambers named on the proposal form, together with any other barristers that may become members of the set of chambers, or a pupil within it, during the currency of the policy. Also, the policy will indemnify the barristers, or any one or more of them, against liability arising from the conduct of their employees, which for the purposes of the policy means all clerks who are working, or who have worked, in the set of chambers.

The liability must arise by reason of a negligent act, error or omission committed, or alleged to have been committed, in the conduct of the insured barristers' professional practice either by themselves or on their behalf by their clerks.

The limit of the policy indemnity may be expressed as an aggregate figure for the total of claims notified during the policy period, or on the 'each and every claim' basis. In the latter instance, it will be provided that all claims consequent upon or attributable to one original insured cause, shall be deemed to be one claim, so limiting the insurer's liability. In the former instance, the aggregate sum insured may be maintained after a claim is paid by the insurer, upon payment by the insured of an additional premium (thus the insured need not be caught out by the declining balance of indemnity under the policy, provided the additional premium is paid).

The normal waiver of subrogation against employees is provided, with the saving that the waiver will not apply if a claim was brought about by, or contributed to by, any dishonest, fraudulent, criminal or malicious act or omission of the employee concerned.

Exclusions

(1) Any claim made against a barrister after he has joined another set of chambers, unless the intention to claim was notified to the insurer prior to the barrister leaving the insured set of chambers;

(2) Any claim where an indemnity is provided under any other policy (the exclusion of contribution clause);

(3) Nuclear radiation risks;

(4) Libel and slander;

(5) Claims arising from the dishonest, fraudulent, criminal or malicious act or omission of the barrister against whom the claim is made, or any employee employed in the professional practice.

General Conditions

(1) The Excess shall be applied to the cost of the claim, but not to the costs and expenses incurred in the defence or settlement of a claim. Proportionate costs and expenses only will be paid where the settlement of the claim exceeds the limit of indemnity under the policy;

(2) Non-admission of liability or promise to settle are conditions precedent to the liability of the insurer, and once the insurer has been duly notified of a claim, the insurer shall be entitled to take over and conduct the defence or settlement of the claim. The barrister shall be entitled to settle the claim at any time, but if he does so, the insurer will only be liable for costs and expenses incurred with his written consent up to the date of settlement;

(3) The Queen's Counsel clause to resolve disputes between insured and insurer upon the defence of any claim;
(4) If the barrister refuses to consent to the settlement of any claim, or to admit liability for a claim, the insured shall be entitled to a sum of indemnity no greater than the amount for which the claim could have been settled, but the insurer will pay authorised costs and expenses in defence of the claim until the final outcome of the claim;
(5) It is a condition precedent that the barristers give immediate written notice to the insurer of any claim, or written notice of intention to claim, covered by the policy. Thereupon, the insured barristers must give the insurer all information reasonably required relating to that claim or intimation of a claim;
(6) The barristers must notify the insurer if they become aware of any circumstance that may give rise to a claim for breach of professional duty covered by the policy. If this is done within fifteen days of expiry of the policy, any claim that subsequently arises from the notified circumstance will be dealt with as though the claim was made at that early date;
(7) All false and fraudulent claims upon the policy will be void.

Company directors and officers

The policy will indemnify the insured directors and executive officers as notified to the insurer on the proposal form, and upon their demise, will indemnify their personal representatives in like manner. The insurer will include in his definition of the insured, any other person who becomes a director or executive officer of the notified company or subsidiary company, in a capacity that has already been described to the insurer (e.g. the position of marketing director), during the period of insurance prior to renewal.

The indemnity under the policy applies to the legal liability of any one or more of the insured incurred by reason of claims against the insured, either jointly or severally, arising from:
(a) breach of trust;
(b) breach of duty;
(c) neglect, error, omission, misstatement or misleading statement; committed by the insured in their respective capacities as directors or officers of the notified company or companies.

The limit of indemnity is often on the aggregate of claims notified in the period of insurance, but the Excess to be borne by the insured will always be on an 'each and every claim' basis. It may be that under a particular policy the limit of indemnity applies to the sum of the claim settlement plus the authorised legal costs and expenses, rather than merely to the claim settlement figure. The Excess will also be applied to the combination of claims cost plus legal costs incurred, therefore, if a claim is made and costs are incurred, but the claim is subsequently withdrawn, the insured may find themselves bearing all the legal costs and expenses because of the application of the Excess.

Exclusions
(1) The liability of any director or officer arising from his own dishonest, fraudulent, criminal or malicious act or omission (others not colluding in or condoning such act or omission will remain indemnified);
(2) Libel or slander;
(3) Any claim brought outside the United Kingdom;
(4) Claims in respect of death or bodily injury, or loss of or damage to any property (this will embrace the exclusion of the insurer's liability under the policy in respect of claims following pollution, seepage, contamination, emissions into the atmosphere or land or water);
(5) Nuclear radiation risks;
(6) Any claim in respect of which the insured director(s) or executive officer(s) are legally entitled to an indemnity from the notified company or companies;
(7) Any fines or penalties (the policy does not indemnify the insured in respect of their criminal liability generally or under the Companies Act 1980).

General Conditions
(1) Written notice of a claim or intimation of a claim must be given as soon as possible, and such notice will render the claim as notified to be dealt with under that policy in force at the time of notification;
(2) The insured must not make any admission of liability or promise of settlement to the claimant without the written consent of the insurer;
(3) The insured must give every assistance to the insurer;
(4) The Queen's Counsel clause where the insurer wishes the insured to contest a claim;
(5) The insurer shall have full rights of control over the conduct of the defence or settlement of the claim, and shall be forwarded every letter, writ or process received by the insured immediately upon receipt;
(6) The insurer shall be at liberty at any time to pay the insured the full limit of indemnity, or lesser amount if the claim could be settled for such smaller sum, and the insurer will only be liable for legal costs and expenses incurred with its written consent up to that time;

(7) The normal non-contribution clause is inserted in an attempt to render this policy an excess of loss policy, operating only to supplement other policies covering the same risks;
(8) Fraudulent claims under the policy are void;
(9) Thirty days' notice may be given by the insurer to the insured to cancel the policy, whereupon the insured shall receive a proportionate return of premium.

Estate agents

The insured practices of estate agents are indemnified against claims made against them in respect of the following:
(a) Any neglect, error or omission of the insured, their predecessors, their employees or agents or any other firm acting jointly with the insured in their business or practice of estate agents, or that of their predecessors;
(b) Any dishonest, fraudulent, criminal, or malicious act or omission of the insured or any employee, except that the errant person may not be indemnified under the policy, nor may anyone condoning those acts or omissions. Liability of insurers under this clause only comes into operation after the insured have failed to recover the extent of the loss from the responsible person;
(c) Any other breach of professional duty for which they are held legally liable;
(d) Failure in good faith to account to clients for monies had and received;
(e) Breach of warranty of authority committed in good faith;
(f) Loss of documents (excluding negotiable instruments). The insurer will also indemnify the insured in respect of all costs and expenses relating to the replacement or restoration of such documents, and the Excess will not be applied to these costs and expenses;
(g) Libels written and slanders spoken in good faith by the insured – the Excess is not applied to this clause's cover.

The insurer will also indemnify any employee in respect of claims that would be covered under the policy if made against the insured, subject to the terms and conditions of the policy, if the insured so requests.

The limit of indemnity is on an 'each and every claim' basis, as is the Excess, but there is the normal rider that all claims emanating from the insured cause, shall be regarded as one claim only. In addition, the insurer will pay the costs and expenses incurred with its written consent in the defence or settlement of the claim, save that where the settlement exceeds the limit of indemnity under the policy, the insurer will only be responsible for a proportion of those costs and expenses to reflect the deficiency of the indemnity to cover the whole loss settlement. The Excess will not be applied to these costs and expenses.

Exclusions
(1) Death, bodily injury and loss of or damage to property, and any consequential losses relating thereto;
(2) Actions brought in countries other than the United Kingdom where the insured has a branch office, firm, company or domiciled representative;
(3) Nuclear radiation risks;
(4) War and kindred risks;
(5) Loss caused by pressure waves from supersonic aircraft;
(6) Claims for events subsequent to the suspicion of any person being dishonest or fraudulent, which in fact arise from the dishonesty or fraud of that suspected person.

General Conditions
(1) Written notice shall be given as soon as possible to the insurer once the insured has become aware of any claim, intimation of intended claim, or circumstance that might give rise to a claim.
(2) No admission of liability or promise of settlement shall be made by the insured without the written consent of the insurer, who shall have control and conduct of the proceedings in full, except that the insured has the benefit of the Queen's Counsel clause if required to contest any claim;
(3) All letters, writs and the like are to be forwarded immediately to the insurer, and the insured estate agents must give the insurer every assistance in the defence or settlement of a claim — if the insured is unwilling to settle any claim, the insurer is entitled to pay the insured the costs and expenses to date together with either the full limit of indemnity or such lesser amount for which the claim could have been settled, and thereafter the insurer is relieved of any further liability under the policy;
(4) If the insurer becomes entitled to avoid the policy for breach of a condition, it will not do so but will reduce the claim to such amount as reflects the prejudice to the insurer caused by the breach of condition in the handling or settlement of the claim made upon the insured;
(5) The special clause waiving avoidance of the policy for non-disclosure or misrepresentation made innocently by the insured appears, with the usual accompanying provision that where a claim should have been made under a previous policy, the insurer will not indemnify the insured to any greater extent than that previous policy would have indemnified them;

(6) The non-contribution clause also is present which seeks to make this policy an excess of loss policy, only applying over and above any other policy indemnifying the insured;

(7) All fraudulent claims for indemnity under the policy shall be void;

(8) The insurer, but not the insured, may cancel the policy upon thirty days' written notice to the insured's last known address. Should this be done, the insured is entitled to a return of premium proportionate to the unexpired period of the insurance.

Engineers

The policy provides the insured engineer with an indemnity against claims arising from the following causes:

(i)   Any neglect, omission or error whenever committed or alleged to have been committed by the insured or their predecessors;

(ii) Libel and slander, but excluding any publication of such in any journal, magazine or newspaper, or by means of radio or television;

(iii) Loss of documents (excluding negotiable instruments and any computer records). The insured is also indemnified against the costs and expenses of replacing and restoring such douments.

All claims must emanate from the insured's conduct of the engineering practice or business, as notified to the insurer on the proposal form.

The insured will also be indemnified in respect of three matters:

(a) Costs incurred in prosecuting any claim for an injunction and/or damages for infringement of any copyright vested in the insured;

(b) Costs incurred in litigation to recover fees that accord with the insured's professional body's scale of fees (the fees recovery extension);

(c) Costs of the legal representation of the insured at proceedings not directly concerned with a claim, but not wholly unrelated to an issue of the insured's breach of professional duty (the legal defence extension).

The policy will specify different limits of indemnity in respect of the indemnities (i), (ii) and (iii) above, and will express yet another limit of indemnity for the legal defence clause (c), above. The limit for the main indemnity clause for allegations of breach of professional duty will be on an 'each and every claim' basis rather than an aggregate basis.

Exclusions
(1) The indemnity only extends to apply to work done or commissions carried out or connected with any country outside the United Kingdom under the main professional indemnity clause, and not to the extensions relating to libel and slander, etc.;
(2) Any liability arising out of work carried out by the insured for and in the name of a consortium of professional men or firms or other association formed which all or any one of the insured form part for the purpose of undertaking any joint venture or joint ventures;
(3) Any liability arising from the dishonesty of the insured;
(4) Any liability in relation to the insured's use of any vehicle, aircraft or watercraft;
(5) Nuclear radiation risks.

General Conditions
(1) The insured must give immediate notice in writing to the insurer of any claim made or of the receipt of notice from any person of an intention to make a claim against the insured;
(2) The insured must not disclose the nature or terms of the policy to any person without the written consent of the insurer if a claim has been made or is likely to be made;
(3) There is a special waiver clause of a type that gives the insurer the option not to avoid the whole policy in the case of non-disclosure in the proposal form, but may merely refuse to deal with a particular claim, the circumstances of which should have been disclosed to the insurer (this clause appears to offer no material benefit to the insured, for the insurer could always choose to deal with the matter in this way);
(4) There is a waiver of subrogation against employees clause;
(5) All disputes and differences arising under the policy must be referred to a Queen's Counsel of the English Bar (arbitration clause);
(6) There is no liability hereunder in respect of any claim for which the insured are entitled to indemnity under any other policy;
(7) All fraudulent claims shall be void.

Solicitors

The solicitors' Master Policy Scheme is wide in that the insurers agree to indemnify the insured solicitors against all loss to the insured (subject to the Excess, of course,) arising during the period of insurance in respect of any description of civil liability whatsoever incurred in connection with the practice of the insured solicitor. The policy does have its limitations, however, which are described in the main indemnity clause as not indemnifying the insured solicitor in respect of:

any undertaking given by or on behalf of the insured to any person in connection with the provision of finance, property, assistance or other advantage whatsoever to or for the benefit of
(a) the solicitor;
(b) any partner of the solicitor;
(c) any partner's spouse or children; or
(d) any business, firm, company, enterprise, association or venture owned or controlled by the solicitor or any partner, whether alone or in concert with others.

The limit of indemnity is on an 'each and every claim' basis, and, therefore, the usual provision appears that all claims against the insured, or any one or more of them, arising from the same act or omission shall be regarded as one claim.

Costs and expenses incurred in the defence or settlement of any claim indemnified under the policy with the written consent of the insurer, are paid in addition to the limit of indemnity, which only applies to the amount of the claim and claimant's costs.

Exclusions
(1) The Excess upon each claim;
(2) Death, bodily injury, physical loss or physical damage to property of any kind whatsoever (but always including property in the care, custody and control of the insured so that liability for e.g. loss or theft of documents, is included in the indemnity);
(3) Any trading loss of the solicitor or his firm;
(4) Any loss arising from an occurrence or circumstance notified under any other policy attaching prior to the period of insurance;
(5) In respect of the insured's own dishonest or fraudulent act or omission (the liability for such events incurred by innocent partners is covered);
(6) Any liability arising from nuclear radiation risks or war risks;
(7) Any liability arising from a practice conducted wholly outside England and Wales.

Conditions
(1) A special waiver of avoidance of the insurance for non-disclosure or any other ground appears, but there is the usual provision that where substantial prejudice in the handling or settlement of any claim occurs because of the insured's non-disclosure, or other breach of condition, the insurer will only be liable under the policy for such amount as would have been payable without such prejudice. It is provided, however, that the

insurer must first indemnify the insured in full, and then must seek reimbursement of any sum for prejudice suffered;

(2) Special conditions apply to the calculation of the limit of indemnity and Excess, which depend on the number practising in partnership on the defined 'relevant date';

(3) Where the insurers indemnify the solicitor(s) in respect of claims arising from a dishonest or fraudulent act or omission of a past or present partner, the insurer is entitled to request the solicitor(s) to take all reasonable steps, at the insurer's expense, to recover sums from such partner or former partner, or their personal representatives, for those acts or omissions;

(4) The usual form of waiver of subrogation against employees is included;

(5) The normal Queen's Counsel clause covers reluctance of the insured to contest any claim upon the insurer's request;

(6) No admission of liability must be made, nor promise of settlement, without the insurer's written consent. The insurer shall have full rights to be subrogated to the position of the insured once a claim has been made, subject only to Condition 5 above;

(7) Written notice of claims, or of any person's intention to make a claim covered under the policy, must be made 'as soon as practicable' to the insurer. Notice is deemed to have been duly given to the insurer if the notice is sent to the Scheme brokers;

(8) An arbitration clause provides that all disputes or disagreements, other than those covered by Condition 5 above, shall be referred to the decision of a sole arbitrator, chosen by mutual agreement, or, failing this, by the President of the Law Society;

(9) All fraudulent claims shall be void and will result in all such claims under the insurance covering the period of insurance being forfeited.

Stockbrokers

By the rules of the Stock Exchange, every stockbroker or stockbroking firm must insure against losses caused by the dishonest acts of employees, but, apart from this, many will seek to have cover included in their policy for an indemnity in respect of negligence. The 'insured' is defined as being not only the current partners and those who become a partner, but also any former partner is protected, and past and present employees, as well as the legal representatives and/or the personal estates of such insured persons.

The prescribed business activities will be broad, e.g. mentioning stockbroking, moneybroking, and associated business activities.

The limit of indemnity will be of an aggregate limit, but the limit will be reinstated, if the insured desires, by the payment of an additional premium subsequent to the payment of a loss during the period of insurance. Thus, the full limit of indemnity may be obtained throughout the whole period of insurance – provided additional premiums are paid after a loss is settled under the policy.

As is common, the policy will indemnify the insured stockbroker against all costs and expenses incurred in the defence or settlement of any loss covered by the policy, provided the written consent of the insurer has been obtained. Where the insured loss exceeds the limit of indemnity, then costs and expenses will only be paid in proportion to the loss and the policy indemnity limit.

The main indemnity clause will provide an indemnity in respect of:
(a) neglect, error or omission of the insured (as defined);
(b) fraud, dishonesty or forgery; and
(c) physical loss, destruction, theft or damage of 'Securities' and 'Cash'.

Losses must arise from the above causes, and within any territorial limit specified in the schedule. Cover is also provided in respect of items in transit until delivery to the addressee.

To be an insured loss, the loss must be one which the insured becomes legally liable to pay or liable to pay under the rules of any Stock Exchange of which the insured is a member. It will be seen that the insured's own losses sustained through events (b) and (c) above, will also be covered.

'Securities' are broadly defined to include all documents of value or of a negotiable value, and 'Cash' covers bank notes, gold, silver, and other coins of all descriptions and cheques.

Optional extensions will be available in respect of auditors' fees; the cost of replacing lost securities; and a run-off facility is possible for an eighteen-month period in the event of non-renewal of the policy.

Exclusions
(1) The Excess;
(2) Any event prior to inception of the policy which results in a claim upon the insured before operation of the policy;
(3) Loss of market or delay;
(4) War and civil disturbance risks;
(5) Nuclear radiation risks;
(6) Losses covered by any other insurance;
(7) Loss sustained by any person as a result of his own fraudulent, dishonest, criminal or malicious acts or omissions.

General Conditions
(1) Non-admission of liability and non-settlement of claims without the written consent of the insurer, including the incurring of costs and expenses;
(2) Queen's Counsel clause effective upon either the insured or the insurer not wishing to contest a claim upon the insured;
(3) As a condition precedent to the liability of the insurer, the insured must give written notice to the insurer as soon as practicable of any claim, any loss sustained, any circumstances that may give rise to a claim or loss, or the discovery of dishonest acts or omissions on the part of any insured person;
(4) Full rights of subrogation are reserved by the insurer;
(5) False or fraudulent claims shall be void and all claims in respect thereof under the policy shall be forfeited.

Surveyors and valuers

The policy will indemnify the 'insured' against a number of different claims. The 'insured' is defined so as to mean not only the partners named in the proposal form, but also any former partner of the firm, any past or present employee of the firm, and all their personal representatives after their deaths. The 'firm' is defined as including the predecessors in business of the insured partnership. The claim against the insured must arise in the conduct of their professional business which will be defined very broadly as any advice given or services performed, provided that the fees for that business is taken into account in ascertaining the income of that firm.

The main indemnity clause and subsidiary indemnity clauses will provide the insured surveyors and valuers with cover for claims arising from:
(a) Any negligent act, error or omission;
(b) Breach of contract;
(c) Breach of warranty of authority;
(d) Breach of trust (committed in good faith);
(e) Libel or slander;
(f) Conversion of any property submitted to the insured;
(g) All claims and the insured's own losses arising from any dishonest or fraudulent act or omission of any past or present partner or employee, but only to the extent that the insured has been unable to recover from those parties responsible or their personal representatives;
(h) Liability arising from loss of documents (excluding negotiable instruments), including the costs of replacing or restoring such documents;
(i) Failure unintentionally and in good faith to account for monies had and received;

(j) Liability arising directly or indirectly from a joint appointment with other firms or individuals;

(k) Eighty per cent (80%) of costs incurred in seeking legal recovery of professional fees owed.

The limit of liability will be on an 'each and every claim' basis, with the usual rider that all claims attributable to one source or original cause shall be regarded as one claim only.

The policy Excess is applicable to all claims under the policy, excepting (e), (h) (in relation to the restoration or replacement costs), and (k) above, nor is the Excess applied to costs and expenses incurred with the insurer's consent, and the latter element is paid in addition to any limit upon the claim and claimant's costs.

A 'no claims bonus' will be granted to the insured who, upon renewal have three, five or ten years claims-free experience, at 5 per cent, 10 per cent and 20 per cent respectively.

Exclusions

(1) Liability arising which would fall to be covered by a Motor insurance policy;

(2) Matters covered by Public Liability insurance;

(3) Claims where the insured is entitled to indemnity under any other policy (the non-contribution clause);

(4) Claims arising from circumstances notified under a previous policy;

(5) Liability arising from surveys or valuations unless carried out by a suitably qualified person as defined;

(6) Trading losses;

(7) Liability for dishonest or fraudulent acts or omissions after such person has been suspected of such acts or omissions;

(8) Nuclear radiation risks, and war and related risks.

General Conditions

(1) The insurer shall have full rights over the defence or settlement of any notified claim under the policy, and, accordingly, the insured must not admit liability or settle any claim, nor incur costs and expenses, without the written consent of the insurer. The Queen's Counsel clause will apply where the insured does not wish to contest a claim but is requested to do so by the insurer;

(2) Written notice must be given to the insurer 'as soon as practicable' of:
   (i) any claim;
   (ii) any intimation that a claim will be made;
   (iii) any circumstance which the insured feels may give rise to a claim;

     (iv) any discovery of a past or present fraud or dishonest act or omission of any of the insured or their predecessors;

(3) Waiver of subrogation against employees unless their conduct was dishonest, fraudulent, criminal or malicious;

(4) Any claims under heading (g) above shall only be met once the insured has taken all possible action to sue for and obtain reimbursement from the dishonest or fraudulent partner or employee, or their personal representatives;

(5) All fraudulent claims shall be void, and all such claims under the policy shall be forfeited;

(6) The special waiver clause appears, whereby the insurer agrees not to avoid the policy for innocent non-disclosure, misrepresentation, or the making of an untrue statement, provided that the insurer is entitled to deduct from the sum otherwise payable under the policy, an amount representing the prejudice suffered by the insurer by virtue of the non-disclosure, etc., in the handling or settlement of a claim. Moreover, where a matter should have been reported under a previous policy, the insurer will only indemnify the insured to like extent, and no more, as the previous policy would have indemnified the insured.

Chapter 7

The practice and procedure of claims

Introduction

The purpose of this chapter is to explain the requirements of the policy conditions in greater detail, and to discuss the practical steps followed by the insurer in the defence and settlement of claims made against the insured covered by the policy. Thus, the full range of topics, from initial notification of the claim to the insurer, through the assessment of the claim and disputes between the insurer and the insured, culminating in the settlement of the claim, subject to the limits and Excess of the policy, are discussed.

After settlement of a claim by the insurers, the insured may still be under certain obligations, for instance, to reimburse the insurer should recovery be made against a responsible party, or if the insured obtains payment for the loss from an extraneous source.

Finally, there is a consideration of the operation of 'excess' or 'topping-up' policies (and also the role of the 'lead' insurer on such policies) and, not to be forgotten, are the 'ex gratia' payments sometimes made by insurers to their insured.

Notice of claims

Most professional indemnity policies will require prompt written notification of any of several happenings, namely:
(a) of claims made against the insured;
(b) of circumstances or occurrences that become known to the insured and which may give rise to a claim;
(c) of any intimation, verbal or written, that some person may make a claim against the insured; or
(d) of suspicion of any partner or employee, be he past or present, having committed any dishonest, fraudulent, malicious or

criminal act or omission, which may give rise to a claim against the insured firm, or any one or more of the named insured professionals.

The policy conditions will variously require 'immediate' notification, notification 'as soon as possible', or notification 'as soon as practicable'. In case of ambiguity, the words will be construed against the insurer who has inserted the words in accordance with the *contra proferentem* rule of construction. Such phrases as quoted will obviously have to be interpreted in all the circumstances of the case,[1] but if more specific time periods are laid down, then they must be complied with, e.g. within fourteen days.[2]

The compliance with the requirement for prompt notification will almost always be expressly or impliedly a condition precedent to the liability of the insurer to meet a claim under the policy, and failure on the part of the insured to comply with the condition, which is a matter of fact in each case,[3] renders the insurer entitled to avoid the claim.[4] The fact that the insured was unable to comply with the condition due to circumstances beyond his control will be irrelevant, even if notice was given at the earliest feasible time,[5] but it has been held that, for liability insurances, time does not begin to run until it is clear that the insurer may become involved.[6] Where the stipulation for prompt notification is not a condition precedent upon its true construction, the insurer will be liable to meet the claim once notice is given,[7] but the indemnity may be reduced by the amount of damages sustained by the insurer by reason of the late notification.[8]

It is always possible for the insurer to waive compliance with the stipulation for prompt notification, and this will be judged on the particular circumstances e.g. the insurer dealing with the claim despite late notification.[9] Where the special waiver clause appears in the policy, it will, generally, provide that the insurer will not be able

1 See e.g. *Verelst's Administratrix v Motor Union Insurance Co Ltd* [1925] 2 KB 137.

2 *Cassel v Lancashire and Yorkshire Accident Insurance Co Ltd* (1885) 1 TLR 495; *T H Adamson & Son v Liverpool and London and Globe Insurance Co Ltd* [1953] 2 Lloyd's Rep 355.

3 *Re Williams and Lancashire and Yorkshire Accident Insurance Co's Arbitration* (1902) 19 TLR 82; *Monksfield v Vehicle and General Insurance Co Ltd* [1971] 1 Lloyd's Rep 139.

4 *Cawley v National Employers' Accident and General Assurance Assn Ltd* (1885) 1 TLR 255; *Elliott v Royal Exchange Assurance Co Ltd* (1867) LR 2 Exch 237.

5 *Gamble v Accident Assurance Co Ltd* (1869) IR 4 CL 204.

6 *Smellie v British General Insurance Co* [1918] WC & Ins Rep 233; *General Motors Ltd v Crowder* (1931) 40 Ll L Rep 87.

7 *Stoneham v Ocean Railway and General Accident Insurance Co* (1887) 19 QBD 237.

8 *Re Coleman's Depositories Ltd and Life and Health Assurance Assn* [1907] 2 KB 798, CA.

9 *Webster v General Accident Fire and Life Assurance Corpn Ltd* [1953] 1 QB 520, [1953] 1 All ER 663.

to repudiate a claim for breach of policy conditions (of which prompt notification will be one), subject to the prejudice to the insurer in defending or settling the claim against the insured being accounted for when the insured is indemnified by the insurer.

The notification condition will invariably specify that notice must be in writing, but without such express provision a verbal notification would suffice.[10] As regards who should receive the written notice of the claim or occurrence, most policies provide that it must be sent to the insurer and in such cases notice to the insured's broker will not suffice[11] for the broker is his agent, and is not the insurer's agent. In the case of Master Policy Scheme insurances, where the specialist broker is authorised under the Master Policy to issue the proposers with certificates of insurance, the broker may reasonably be regarded as the agent of the insurer, not only for the issuing of insurance cover, but also as agent of the insurer for receipt of notification of claims or occurrences. However, to avoid any ambiguity, certificates of insurance issued under a Master Policy Scheme of professional indemnity insurance will usually specify in the Schedule, or elsewhere, that written notice should be given to the broker named therein. Most Lloyd's policies will also specify that claims should be notified to a named Lloyd's broker, usually the one through which the insurance was obtained.

The purpose of the condition is to prevent the insurer being prejudiced by undue delay in notification of the claim or occurrence, for without notice, the insurer is not to know that measures must be taken to defend and settle an indemnified claim, and vital time may be lost when memories of events may fade, or records be destroyed, to the prejudice of the insured's defence (and hence the increased liability of the insurer to indemnify the insured). A prompt offer of settlement will often prove more acceptable to a claimant, than a long legal battle, and the facts of a culpable error are usually more readily ascertainable when the events are recent. The movements of partners or staff from the firm can also lead to difficulties in accurately tracing the events resulting in the negligent act, error or omission.

Assistance to the insurer

The insurer is usually bound by the conditions of his contract of insurance to render the insurer all reasonable assistance (or some such similar phrase) in the ascertaining of the extent and cause of the act, error or omission which has given rise to a claim against the insured and, for which, the insured is seeking an indemnity from the

10 *Re Solvency Mutual Guarantee Society, Hawthorn's Case* (1862) 31 LJ Ch 625.
11 *Roche v Roberts* (1921) 9 Ll L Rep 59.

insurer under the terms of the professional indemnity policy. Some insurers go further, and expressly require the insured to forward to them, immediately upon receipt, any letter, writ, process or document received by them in connection with the claim against them. These provisions emphasise the fact that the insurer is the financially interested party in the resisting or settling of claims against the insured. The insured is, of course, financially interested in the claim also, under the Excess provisions, but will also probably be deeply involved in the claim for the insured's professional standing will suffer. Indeed, often the insured professional will resent the control of the insurer because he is so deeply worried about the claim being undetermined for a protracted period. The insured may prefer to have all claims settled promptly, irrespective of their merits, merely to avoid the tarnishing of his professional reputation. Others may wish that all claims be resisted uncompromisingly, for the admission of their having committed an error, or having been negligent, would be a difficult matter for them to digest.

The importance of assistance being readily given by the insured to the insurer cannot be overemphasised, both from the insurer's point of view (and it should not be forgotten that it may be open to the insurer to cancel the insurance if the insured proves awkward, or may choose to decline to accept renewal from the insured if the insured is not proving very co-operative), and, it is submitted, from the insured's point of view, for no reputable insurer will wish to resist a valid claim indefinitely, not least because of the effects of inflation and escalating legal costs, nor will the insurer wish to settle claims merely to avoid the nuisance of dealing with their defence. The insurers who have entered into the professional indemnity market will not have entered it lightly, and will presumably wish to retain the confidence of their clientele – they will not retain their share of the market if they handle claims with a total disregard of the feelings of the insured.

Of great assistance to the process of investigating the circumstances of events giving rise to claims, will be the keeping of accurate and detailed professional work records, together with an efficient structure of accountability within the insured firm. No policy will require this of their insured as a condition, but in the event of a claim, the insured may well save themselves many long hours of searching for records, or contract papers, or trying to find out which of the partners and staff were involved in the relevant work alleged to be wrong, if proper records are continuously maintained.

In the case of engineering, surveying, valuing, or architectural claims, the insurers will often engage independent professionals to investigate the damage for which the insured are allegedly responsible, and the requirement for assistance to the insurer will extend to the rendering of assistance to these investigators by, e.g. allowing their inspection of the relevant plans and documents. Sometimes the insurer will engage loss adjusters to report on the circumstances and estimated value of the claim, and co-operation will also be required with these persons.

Compliance with a term of the insurance that the insured should take every possible measure against partners or employees who have caused a claim to be made because of their dishonest or fraudulent act or omission, is really a separate requirement of the insurance prior to indemnification, but may also be mentioned under this general heading of rendering assistance to the insurer so that the loss to be indemnified may be kept to its minimum.

Non-admission of liability

A condition in the policy that the insured shall not admit liability to the person claiming against him, nor make any settlement or compromise, nor any promise thereof, will be a binding condition upon the insured.[12] If not expressed as a condition precedent to the liability of the insurer to meet the insured's claim under the policy, it will be a matter of construction whether it is an implied condition precedent, or merely a condition subsequent. The insurer is perfectly entitled to lay down contractual stipulations as to the future conduct of the insured in so far as it relates to the claim under the policy,[13] and it is not uncommon for an insurer to insert a general condition to the effect that no claim shall be payable unless all conditions have been complied with,[14] thus making all conditions in the policy conditions precedent to the liability of the insurer to meet the claim.

The insurer will be indemnifying the insured against any claim covered by the policy, it is therefore quite understandable that the insurer will not wish the insured to settle a claim against himself, and then seek an indemnity of the settlement from the insurer. The insurer wants to be involved at every stage of the defence and negotiation of any settlement, and can be regarded as under a moral duty, if no more, so to do, in the sense that the insurer is the guardian of the pool of funds received in premiums from the insured's fellow professionals. Moreover, the insurer will want to be fully engaged in the investigation of the claim against the professional, so as to be able to increase his own knowledge of the underwriting risks relevant to the insurance of that profession's negligence risks. The insurer needs to know the nature of the cause of each claim, as well as the cost of meeting such claim, to ensure that he may continue to insure those risks in future years, and this can only be accomplished by his

12 See *Tustin v Arnold & Sons* (1915) 84 LJ KB 2214.
13 *Woolfall and Rimmer Ltd v Moyle* [1942] 1 KB 66, [1941] 3 All ER 304, CA.
14 *Welch v Royal Exchange Assurance* [1938] 1 KB 757, [1938] 1 All ER 451.

ability to charge the correct level of premium. The requirement that the insured shall not admit liability nor settle any claim is a natural consequence of the foregoing.

Insurer's control of proceedings

The insurer is entitled to be placed in the position of the insured, and succeed to all the insured's rights and remedies against third parties in respect of the subject matter of the insurance, once the insurer has indemnified the insured for his loss under the terms of the policy. This is a principle of common law, called the doctrine of subrogation, and has grown out of the general law that aims to prevent the insured from recovering more than a full indemnity for his loss.[15]

In modern circumstances, the insurer will prefer to have conduct and control of the third party claim against his insured, for in this type of liability insurance, the insurer wishes to assure himself that the settlement, if any is made, is at the minimum, and to simply have subrogation rights against other third parties once the claim under the policy has been met, will not be adequate to attain this goal. Therefore, this form of condition whereby the insured agrees that the insurer shall have full rights over the conduct of any proceedings and negotiations, has been developed.

Problems were found to arise where an insurer wished his insured to resist a claim for professional negligence, but the insured wanted the matter settled as soon as possible. Due to these divergencies of opinion between the insured and the insurer, the Queen's Counsel clause has been developed to provide a machinery whereby these differences, when they arise, may be reconciled. This provision is discussed in the succeeding heading.

Other differences may arise, for instance, the insured may wish to fight a claim, and yet the insurer, upon legal advice, wishes the claim to be settled as soon as can be so that no additional expenses are incurred through a prolonged, yet fated, defence. To cater for such differences, some professional indemnity policies will have inserted a special clause, under which, the insurer may at any time pay the insured the full limit of indemnity under the policy, or such lesser amount as would be sufficient to meet a compromise of the insured claim, and will, in addition, pay all legal costs and expenses to date, incurred with their written consent, but thereafter will be relieved of any further liability under the terms of the policy. It is submitted that where such a condition appears, and in a particular case is acted upon, if the insured is eventually successful in defeating the claim, either in whole or in part, the insured will have to account to the insurer for such sum as the insurer has overpaid under the condition,

---

15 *Castellain v Preston* (1883) 11 QBD 380 at 387, CA, per Brett LJ.

for it will be money had and received recoverable at common law by the insurer.[16] The insured would be entitled, however, to deduct the reasonable expenses of recovery from the amount he hands over to the insurers.[17] These are consequences, it is submitted, that will be natural derivations of the fundamental principle of indemnity applicable to all insurance contracts – the insured must not profit from his loss by means of insurance.[18]

The Queen's Counsel clause

The insurer has the conduct and control of the defence and settlement of claims against the insured under the conditions of most professional indemnity policies. This entitlement to what may be regarded as advanced subrogation rights, is subject, however, to a proviso that will be regarded as essential by the insured professional. It is the insured professionals' reputations that are at stake when claims for negligence or other error are made, and they would be most reluctant to resign their powers of control of the proceedings entirely. The insured professionals naturally wish to be involved in the decisions made to defend or settle, and at what cost, claims that are, after all, made against them. The mere rendering of assistance to the insurer in his investigation and defence of the claim will not be sufficient, for instance, where the insured would much rather meet a claim because the negligence is accepted, or because it is felt that professional reputation is better served by prompt payment of claims for errors. The insurer, who is indemnifying the insured for all settlements, may well have a rather different view of the matter.

The Queen's Counsel clause will provide those insured under a professional indemnity policy with a form of arbitration of the question of the contesting of a claim where the insured wishes the claim to be settled. Such clauses are perfectly valid[19] and are now commonplace. The clause will provide that a Queen's Counsel shall be appointed by mutual agreement to determine the prospects of a successful defence of the claim against the insured. Should the Queen's Counsel consider that the claim could be contested with a reasonable prospect of success, then the insured must consent to the claim being defended if the loss (i.e. the costs of the claim and legal costs) is to be recovered under the policy. The insured will, however,

16 See *Law Fire Assurance Co v Oakley* (1888) 4 TLR 309; *Horse, Carriage and General Insurance Co Ltd v Petch* (1916) 33 TLR 131; and *Yorkshire Insurance Co Ltd v Nisbet Shipping Co Ltd* [1962] 2 QB 330, [1961] 2 All ER 487.
17 See *Assicurazioni Generali de Trieste v Empress Assurance Corpn Ltd* [1907] 2 KB 814.
18 *Castellain v Preston* (1883) 11 QBD 380, CA.
19 *Knight v Hosken* (1943) 75 Ll L Rep 74, CA; *West Wake Price & Co v Ching* [1956] 3 All ER 821, [1957] 1 WLR 45.

still have the option of settling the claim, despite the advice, but he will not be entitled to recover the cost of the settlement from the insurer for he will not have complied with the condition precedent in the policy. Some policies will name a person, e.g. the Chairman for the time being of the Bar Council, to appoint a Queen's Counsel to decide the merits of the case to cater for the event of the insured and insurer being unable to agree on a particular Queen's Counsel.

The costs of any reference under this clause will be met by the insurer as a normal cost or expense incurred with its consent.

Action by the insurer

After receipt of the written notice of the claim from the insured, the insurer will, via its claims department, gather details of the circumstances of the claim, with the assistance of the insured. Sometimes, the insurer will engage a firm of loss adjusters to investigate and report upon the substance of a claim e.g. in the case of a structural defect which was not noticed upon a structural survey, the loss adjusters would report upon the extent of the damage, the cost of repairs, and make observations upon the merits of the case as known to them.

Once the claimant has issued and served a writ upon the insured claiming damages for breach of professional duty, the insurer must then, if it has not been done before, appoint solicitors to enter an appearance to the writ, and, at a later date, a formal defence after the receipt of advice from counsel. Once solicitors have been appointed to act, it is normal for all negotiations between the claimant and the insured (and insurer) to be conducted through their respective solicitors. As regards the claim generally, many policies will have an express provision requiring the insured to forward all relevant correspondence and legal documents received by them on to the insurer (which will be the solicitors to all intents and purposes, once the proceedings have been commenced).

The clause giving the insurer the full conduct and control of the claim against the insured has been discussed above, and under this clause the insurer will be entitled to act in any way that is seen fit, and may select the tactics to be adopted in the defence or settlement of the claim. All decisions, however, must be made in the bona fide interests of both the insurer and the insured − the insurer cannot ignore the fact that it is the insured who is the person against whom the claim is made, and, as such, the insured's interests must be considered in all decisions upon the handling of the claim.[20]

Although the solicitors are appointed by the insurer, and it is the insurer who will pay their costs and expenses relating to the insured

20 *Groom v Crocker* [1939] 1 KB 194 at 203, CA, per Lord Greene MR.

claim, the solicitors appointed are the solicitors of the insured. Accordingly, the insured is entitled to inspect all the document in his solicitors' possession that relate to the claim.[1] The solicitors appointed will owe the same duty to the insured as any other client, and must conduct the proceedings with a corresponding regard to the insured's interests. Failure so to do will render the solicitor liable to the insured for breach of that duty.[2]

Where the insurer makes a bona fide settlement with those claiming damages from the insured, under the power of conduct and control given in a policy condition, the insured will be bound by that settlement, even if the insured will have to pay some part of the damages agreed as payable.[3] The insured will always in professional indemnity policies have to pay an amount towards any settlement or judgment under the Excess provisions of the policy. The insured would likewise be bound if the insurer settled a claim for an amount in excess of the indemnity limit if the insurer was acting in the bona fide interests of them both.

One last comment in this regard is that the insurer, even though he may have conduct and control of the claim against the insured, will not be able to prevent the insured himself pursuing another third party, whom he holds responsible for the loss resulting from the claim;[4] but where an insured does this, if he pursues the third party for an amount greater than the Excess borne by himself, he must not compromise that action except in good faith.[5]

Disputes and arbitration

Most professional indemnity policies contain a clause stating that all disputes and differences arising under the policy shall be referred to the arbitration of some person or persons. The clause may state expressly that compliance with this clause is a condition precedent to the liability of the insurer; others, by the inclusion of a clause stating that compliance with all conditions on the face of the policy are conditions precedent to the insurer's liability, also achieve that result. Generally, the arbitration will take place in London, and will thus, either expressly or impliedly, be subject to the Arbitration Acts 1950–1979.

The provisions of the clause only, of course, operate between the insurer and the insured, and do not affect the dispute between the

1 *Re Crocker* [1936] Ch 696, [1936] 2 All ER 899.
2 As in *Groom v Crocker* [1939] 1 KB 194, [1938] 2 All ER 394, CA.
3 *Beacon Insurance Co Ltd v Langdale* [1939] 4 All ER 204, CA.
4 *Moorley v Moore* [1936] 2 KB 359, [1936] 2 All ER 79, CA; *Bourne v Stanbridge* [1965] 1 All ER 241, [1965] 1 WLR 189, CA.
5 *Commercial Union Assurance Co v Lister* (1874) 9 Ch App 483.

claimant and the insured. There is a long tradition in this country for commercial disputes, such as these, to be referred to arbitration on the basis that the process of arbitration will be quicker and less expensive than litigation.[6] Further, quarrels on policies of insurance, or other commercial matters, would be less prone to publicity if discussed in a private arbitration rather than open court where the process might be painful and injurious even to a successful litigant.[7] Since 1956, however, the insurance companies that are members of the British Insurance Association, and all Lloyd's underwriters, will not insist on arbitration of, inter alia, professional indemnity policies, where the dispute relates to the liability of the insurer under the policy, rather than the amount or *quantum* of a certain liability, and the insured prefers to have the matter decided by a court in the United Kingdom. Such waiver will not apply to specially negotiated policies, though, where the arbitration clause has been included by express agreement between the insured and the insurer.[8]

A condition requiring the arbitration of disputes between the parties to an insurance contract is valid and enforceable, provided that it is not intended to oust the jurisdiction of the courts after due determination of the arbitration award,[9] e.g. by declaring that the award shall be final and no appeal on a point of law may be made to any court. If a dispute should be referred to arbitration under the policy clause, yet one party brings legal proceedings concerning that dispute, the other party may make an application to the court to stay those proceedings[10] until the arbitration award is made. The court's power to grant a stay of proceedings is purely discretionary,[11] but the court will normally refuse a stay where either only questions of law are in dispute,[12] or where difficult questions of law are entwined with questions of fact.[13]

The insurer may not rely on an arbitration clause in a contract that he seeks to avoid for non-disclosure or misrepresentation,[14] or for fraud,[15] or where he alleges no binding contract of insurance came

---

6 *Piercy v Young* (1879) 14 Ch D 200 at 208, per Jessel MR.
7 *Russell v Russell* (1880) 14 Ch D 471 at 477, per Jessel MR.
8 See Law Reform Committee Fifth Report, Conditions and Exceptions in Insurance Policies (Cmnd 62 (1957)), para 13.
9 *Scott v Avery* (1856) 5 HL Cas 811.
10 Arbitration Act 1950, s. 4(1).
11 *Lock v Army, Navy and General Insurance Assn Ltd* (1915) 31 TLR 297.
12 *Re Carlisle* (1890) 44 Ch D 200; *Montagu v Provident Accident and White Cross Insurance Co Ltd* (1935) 51 Ll L Rep 153.
13 *Clough v County Live Stock Insurance Assn Ltd* (1916) 85 LJ KB 1185.
14 E.g. *Stebbing v Liverpool and London and Globe Insurance Co Ltd* [1917] 2 KB 433.
15 Per Ridley J in *Stebbing's* case, above, at 438; and see the power of the court under Arbitration Act 1950, s. 24(2).

into being.[16] Disputes relating to the insurer's entitlement to rescind the contract of insurance for breach of condition by the insured, may be referred under an arbitration clause using such expressions as differences which have arisen 'in respect' of, or 'with regard to', or 'under' the contract, or similar expressions.[17] As a result, insurers often will rely on breach of the warranty as to the truth of all answers in the proposal form, rather than seek to avoid the policy entirely.

Settlements greater than the indemnity limit

All professional indemnity policies will have limits of indemnity expressed in the Schedule to the policy, and where there are extensions to the 'basic' negligence indemnity, other limits applicable to those extensions will also be specified. These limits define the extent of the indemnity provided by the contract of insurance, and, therefore, limit the scope of the policy. The courts will always be prepared to uphold such contractual definitions of the extent of indemnity and prevent the insured claiming a greater indemnity than stipulated in the policy Schedule.[18]

Policies with an *aggregate* limit applicable to all claims will operate in the following way: if the limit is £100,000 aggregate in the Schedule, the policy will be exhausted when claims costs total £100,000. Of course, because of the 'claims notified in the period of insurance' basis of professional indemnity policies, it may be many years before an insured will be told by his insurer that settlements have reached the limit attaching to the policy in force at the time the claim was duly notified. If the policy period were July 1982 to June 1983, it may be that claim A is settled in May 1983 for £15,000; that claim B is settled in December 1985 for £65,000; and that claim C is settled in August 1987 for £50,000. The insured will find himself in August 1987 without an indemnity in respect of £30,000 worth of that settlement on claim C. Understandably, a prudent insured may wish to seek cover on the 'each and every claim' basis as an alternative, in order to protect himself against the possible situation of some claims being settled for which he has little, or no measure of indemnity under his professional indemnity policy.

If the above example is worked through for a policy with an *each and every claim* limit of £50,000 for July 1982 to June 1983, the insured would only have a deficit of £15,000 to meet the three claims (ignoring Excesses) even though the limit is half the indemnity limit

---

16 *Toller v Law Accident Insurance Society Ltd* [1936] 2 All ER 952, CA; *Woodall v Pearl Assurance Co* [1919] 1 KB 593, CA.

17 *Heyman v Darwins* [1942] AC 356 at 336, HL, per Viscount Simon.

18 *Allen v London Guarantee and Accident Co Ltd* (1912) 28 TLR 254; *Forney v Dominion Insurance Co Ltd* [1969] 3 All ER 831, [1969] 1 WLR 928.

under the aggregate policy should only one large claim be made in the period of insurance, e.g. one claim costing £100,000. An each and every claim limit of £70,000 would, in the example, have provided the insured with complete, or full, indemnity of the three claims.

It is important to note the effect of the operative clause regarding the indemnity, without specific limit, of the costs and expenses incurred in the defence or settlement of a claim against the insured. Only such costs and expenses for which the insurer has given his consent (which must usually be in writing) to be incurred, may be recovered – such costs as are awarded to a claimant will form part of the main indemnity, and be subject to the limit thereto. In the case of settlements which exceed the policy limit, be it in the aggregate or for each and every claim, the clause will provide that only proportional costs may be recovered, to reflect the liability of the insurer and insured respectively. For example, taking the circumstances of claim C, above, the insured can only recover £20,000 of the £50,000 settlement under the aggregate policy given, thus, if legal costs and expenses of the defence were £5,000, the insurer would only be liable for £2,000 of those costs i.e.

$$£5,000 \ \times \ \frac{£20,000}{£50,000}$$

The same principles apply to claims where there is a deficiency in the 'each and every claim' indemnity in meeting the settlement.

Application of the Excess

It will be an express condition or exclusion in every professional indemnity policy, that the insured is to bear some amount of each claim made against him. This self-insured amount will be specified in the policy schedule, and is termed the 'Excess'. It will be expressed as a figure (e.g. £500), as a proportion (e.g. 5%), or as a combination (e.g. '£1000 or 5%, whichever be the greater'). This first part of every claim against the insured will thus not be covered in the stated amount (which is often variable at commencement of the period of insurance, subject to a varying premium). The courts will uphold these Excess provisions,[19] for they represent the bargain struck between the parties to the insurance contract and define the scope of the indemnity granted under the policy.

Most professional indemnity policies will provide that the Excess is not to apply to any amount claimed under the policy for costs and expenses incurred with the insurer's written consent, which

19 As in *Beacon Insurance Co Ltd v Langdale* [1939] 4 All ER 204, CA.

obviously provides a larger measure of protection to the insured than a policy where the Excess can be applied to the sum of the claim plus costs and expenses incurred. In the latter instance, if a claim is made against the insured, but is subsequently withdrawn by the claimant, the Excess will be taken away from the sum otherwise payable for the insured's legal costs and expenses incurred in defeating that claim, and, because of the comparatively large amount of Excesses in professional indemnity policies, the insured may find that he can make no recovery from the insurer, the costs incurred being a lesser amount than the Excess.

Fraudulent claims

It is a fundamental rule of insurance law that both the insurer and the insured observe the strictest good faith (*uberrima fides*), and it is a natural corollary of this principle that the insured must only put forward honest claims under the policy, otherwise the duty is breached and the insurer may avoid the claim.[20] An express clause in the policy, stating that all fraudulent claims shall be void, in fact adds nothing to the position at common law.[1]

Whether a claim is fraudulent or not is a matter of fact for the jury, if there is one, or for the judge if sitting alone. There is no exhaustive list of matters that constitute fraud, for the issue will have to be tried upon all the circumstances, for example did the insured intend to defraud the insurer,[2] or did he connive at causing the loss,[3] or could fraud be inferred by the insured's gross negligence to prevent the occurrence of the risk insured?[4]

Due to the nature of insurances indemnifying an insured against claims brought against them by third parties, and because of the control of the proceedings exercised by the insurers, the opportunities for fraud are very few − virtually the only scope being the connivance at bringing about the error or 'negligence' deliberately, but there is little to be gained by the insured in the vast majority of claims. Insurers will not have suspicion of fraud on the insured's part on the top of their list when investigating and settling claims against the insured.

---

20 *Goulstone v Royal Insurance Co* (1858) 1 F & F 276 at 279, per Pollock CB.
1 *Britton v Royal Insurance Co* (1866) 4 F & F 905 at 909, per Willis J.
2 In relation to examples of fraud upon fire insurance claims, see *S and M Carpets (London) Ltd v Cornhill Insurance Co Ltd* [1981] 1 Lloyd's Rep 667; *Watkin and Davis Ltd v Legal and General Assurance Co Ltd* [1981] 1 Lloyd's Rep 674.
3 *Slattery v Mance* [1962] 1 QB 676, [1962] 1 All ER 525.
4 *Goodman v Harvey* (1836) 4 Ad & El 870.

Indemnification 'aliunde'

Indemnification of a loss suffered by an insured, by a person other than the insurer, is referred to as indemnification 'aliunde' ('by another'), and if allowed to retain both the insurance monies and any other amounts reducing his loss, the insured would be able to make a profit from his loss. This, the law will not let happen, and only the true loss suffered by the insured may be recovered under the insurance policy. It was said long ago in the House of Lords that:[5]

> The general rule of law is that where there is a contract of indemnity . . . and a loss happens, anything which reduces or diminishes that loss reduces or diminishes the amount which the indemnifier is bound to pay; and if the indemnifier [the insurer] has already paid it, then, if anything which diminishes the loss comes into the hands of the person to whom he has paid it, it becomes an equity that the person who has already paid the full indemnity is entitled to be recouped by having that amount back.

Thus, the insured may not recover under the policy in respect of amounts in fact already received by him from another source, but, rather, any such amounts must be applied to reduce or extinguish the loss (i.e. the cost of the settlement of the claim against the insured). If the insurer has already paid over insurance monies to the insured, then the insured will have to account for any amounts received and repay the insurer, otherwise he would recover twice over.[6]

In circumstances where the full costs of the claim against the insured are not covered by the insurer, e.g. because of the policy limits, then the insured is under no duty to account for any monies received from third parties in respect of the loss, except in so far as his actual loss is exceeded. Thus, if a claim against the insured is settled for £100,000, and the professional indemnity policy has a limit of £80,000 and an Excess of £1,000, the insured may receive up to £20,000 from a third party without any duty to account to the insurer arising. It follows that the insured will always be entitled to recover the amount of the Excess without having to account for it to the insurer.

Third parties from whom amounts may be received to offset the cost of a claim (the insured loss) may be other parties liable to the insured for their share in the negligent act; a party who has contractually agreed to indemnify the insured for any loss (or portion thereof) arising out of a particular contract; or by a third party who makes a gift to the insured because of the loss. Under this last instance, a gift, the insured will not have to account for any sum

---

5 *Burnand v Rodocanachi, Sons & Co* (1882) 7 App Cas 333 at 339, HL, per Lord Blackburn.
6 *Darrell v Tibbetts* (1880) 5 QBD 560, CA.

received where the donor's intention was that only the insured, and not the insurer, should benefit.[7]

Excess policies

Excess policies should not be confused with the 'Excess' under a particular policy; the term refers to policies that provide an additional layer of indemnity, i.e. a layer in excess of the primary insurance. Where, for instance, a Master Policy Scheme insurance only provides an indemnity limit of e.g. £250,000, the insured professional firm may decide that they wish to have an indemnity limit of £500,000, and another policy, possibly with different insurers, will have to be arranged for the £250,000 to £500,000 layer of indemnity. The 'excess insurer' will obviously be aware of the nature of the 'primary layer' insurance in all its aspects, and will agree to provide insurance in the same terms, but with a special provision that they will only be liable for costs and expenses where they are called upon to indemnify the insured above the primary layer's limit of indemnity. When this does occur, they will be liable under the excess policy to pay only the costs and expenses that are proportional to their indemnification of the loss.[8]

It would be most unusual for an excess insurer to disagree with the conduct and control of the claim being in the hands of the primary insurer, and he will abide by settlements made by that insurer, although will generally liase closely with the primary insurer upon claims in which they may become interested under their excess policy.

Ex gratia payments

The legal entitlement of the insurer to pay only those claims that are within the scope of the policy issued to the insured has been discussed in much of this book. The right to avoid the contract of insurance for breach of the duty of good faith (*uberrima fides*) on the part of the insured, by non-disclosure, misrepresentation, or untrue statement of fact in the proposal form, has also been the subject of discussion. An insurer cannot forget that he lives in a commercial world, however, and this can lead an insurer to meet particular claims in circumstances when the claim could be avoided under the terms and conditions of the policy. The insurer may have an important connection which he wishes to retain with the insured concerned,

7 *Burnand v Rodocanachi, Sons & Co* (1882) 7 App Cas 333, HL; and *Castellain v Preston* (1883) 11 QBD 380 at 404, CA, per Bowen LJ.
8 Cf *Greyhound Corpn and Greyhound Lines Inc v Chester and Orion Insurance Co Ltd* [1975] 1 Lloyd's Rep 677, NY Sup Ct.

and the insurer may therefore decide to voluntarily pay the whole of a small claim, or, perhaps, part of a large claim, in order to protect that valuable relationship. Alternatively, an insurer may choose to make voluntary (ex gratia) payments to one insured so that his prestige among many insured may be enhanced e.g. meeting a claim to one architectural practice might maintain that insurer's reputation at a time when a new insurer enters the professional indemnity market and is endeavouring to persuade other architectural practices to change insurer.

It is really a matter of conjecture why insurers make ex gratia payments when there is no legal liability upon them to meet a particular claim under the policy, but the fact remains that this occasionally happens. The vital point to grasp, however, is that the payment of an ex gratia sum to an insured is voluntary, and, therefore, does not estop or preclude the same insurer from avoiding a subsequent claim, even in identical circumstances.[9] It might be wondered whether such payments were *intra vires* the insurance companies' constitutions – being merely voluntary, would not such ex gratia payments be *ultra vires* the companies? The Court of Appeal has held that ex gratia payments of claims are not *ultra vires* the company insurer, for such payments are made in the ordinary course of insurance business,[10] provided the policy has been validly issued by the insurance company concerned.[11]

9 *London and Manchester Plate Glass Co Ltd v Heath* [1913] 3 KB 411, CA.
10 *Breay v Royal British Nurses' Assn* [1897] 2 Ch 272, CA.
11 See *Evanson v Crooks* (1911) 28 TLR 123.

Chapter 8

Duties of the broker

Introduction

Professional negligence policies are always negotiated by professional people through the agency of an insurance broker, or other intermediary, who may, or may not, specialise in the procurement of such policies. If a scheme policy of a recognised insurer is sought, there may be rather little negotiating to be done, but in the case of more individually-tailored indemnity policies, the professional person will trust in his insurance broker to obtain a suitable policy in accordance with the instructions given to him. In short, the insurance broker is a professional agent, akin to those professionals seeking professional negligence cover. Unlike his clients, though, the insurance broker or intermediary is not paid directly by his client, but indirectly, by the insurer paying him a percentage commission on the premium obtained on the policy that he has procured for his client. For professional indemnity insurance policies this commission can be in the region of 12 per cent to 20 per cent, which is a similar rate of commission to many other types of insurance policy, but the large premiums required for many professionals' indemnities where cover is provided in millions of pounds, will result in a correspondingly large commission being earned by the broker or intermediary. Broking such policies can therefore be a relatively high commission-earning activity.

The purpose of this chapter is to discuss the duties of the insurance broker to his client when arranging insurances; the effect of the broker's knowledge of his client's affairs upon submission of a proposal to an insurer; the extent of the liability the broker faces for breach of duty to his client; and the circumstances when an insurance broker may also be acting as agent of an insurer. Lastly, an explanation of the professional organisation of insurance brokers in England and Wales will be given, for this may well be of interest to the professional persons to whom this book is directed.

The obligation to effect insurance

A broker may undertake to procure an insurance policy for somebody either for reward or gratuitously, and once the broker takes any steps to achieve that purpose, he will owe his client a duty of care. Even where no consideration is given for his efforts, he will be liable if he is negligent so that the other party cannot recover under the policy effected.[1] The insurance effected by the broker must be with responsible and solvent underwriters, otherwise there is a breach of the duty of care owed to the client,[2] should the client be unable to recover from the insurer for an insured loss.

It has been held that there is no general legal obligation upon a broker to reveal to his client, immediately, the full terms of the insurance policy that he has effected on his client's behalf, though, in practice, this is usually done.[3] It is open to the client to expressly require such information to be passed on to him immediately, or, indeed, to specify that the insurer must be approved by himself prior to the insurance being effected.[4]

In the same way as other professionals do not usually guarantee to bring about a particular result, insurance brokers are under a general legal obligation to take all reasonable steps to procure an effective insurance of the type suitable for their client's needs. Insurance brokers do not normally undertake, without reservation, to procure an effective insurance at all events, although such an absolute undertaking can be given.[5] The general liability of an insurance broker upon agreeing to act for his client in the procurement of an insurance policy in the desired terms, has been expressed in these terms:

> When a person is instructed to procure an insurance he is bound to use reasonable care and skill to effect the policy. If he is unable to procure the policy, he must at once inform his principal (i.e. his client) of his inability to do so.[6]

Moreover, when engaging the services of an insurance broker, the client is entitled to put his faith in the competence of that insurance broker in the same way that clients of solicitors, architects, and other professionals, trust in their skills. It was said, long ago, that:

---

1   *Wilkinson v Coverdale* (1793) 1 Esp 74; *Bromley London Borough v Ellis* [1971] 1 Lloyd's Rep 97, CA.
2   *Hurrell v Bullard* (1863) 3 F & F 445; *Osman v J Ralph Moss Ltd* [1970] 1 Lloyd's Rep 313, CA.
3   *United Mills Agencies Ltd v R E Harvey Bray & Co* [1952] 1 All ER 225n.
4   See *Dixon v Hovill* (1828) 4 Bing 665.
5   *Hood v West End Motor Packing Co* [1917] 2 KB 38, CA.
6   Ibid at 47, per Scrutton LJ, the policy must be effected by the broker within a reasonable time of receipt of instructions, *Turpin v Bilton* (1843) 5 Man & G 455; *Bromley London Borough v Ellis* [1971] 1 Lloyd's Rep 97, CA; *Cock, Russell & Co v Bray, Gibb & Co Ltd* (1920) 3 Ll L Rep 71.

When a broker is engaged to effect an insurance, especially when the broker employed is a broker of repute and experience, the client is entitled to rely upon the broker to carry out his instructions, and is not bound to examine the documents drawn up in performance of those instructions and see whether his instructions have, in fact, been carried out by the broker. In many cases the principal (i.e. the client) would not understand the matter, and would not know whether the document did in fact carry out his instructions. Business could not be carried on if, when a person has been employed to use care and skill with regard to a matter, the employer is bound to use his own care and skill to see whether the person employed has done what he was employed to do. I think the principal is entitled to rely upon the reputation of the person whom he employs.[7]

Compliance with instructions

The exact scope of the insurance broker's authority to effect a contract of insurance on behalf of his client is to be determined from the client's instructions to the broker. The broker must comply with his instructions, in the same way that all agents must carry out their instructions, otherwise the broker will be liable to make good any loss suffered by his client in consequence of his non-compliance. If the client does not specify which insurer is to be approached, then it is perfectly proper for the broker to exercise his bona fide discretion as between different insurers offering the requisite insurance[8] – such will not be outside his directions.

Should the broker depart from his instructions, and effect an insurance other than that which he was engaged to effect, the law will not permit him to excuse himself by merely stating that the client should have checked the insurance.[9] On the other hand, a broker is entitled to effect an insurance on terms which are strictly outside his instructions, but are as close to them as can be obtained. For instance, if a client instructs his broker to obtain a particular scheme of professional indemnity insurance with an indemnity limit of £500,000, yet knows that the scheme only provides a maximum of £400,000, the client cannot protest if the broker effects that maximum level and hands the client the policy with that limit specified upon it. It might be otherwise, though, if the client had stated that if a £500,000 limit could not be obtained, then no insurance was to be effected at all.[10] This is because the client may be taken to have acquiesced in the variation of the initial instructions,

---

7 *Dickson & Co v Devitt* (1916) 86 LJ KB 315, per Atkin J.
8 *Moore v Mourgue* (1776) 2 Cowp 479.
9 *Dickson & Co v Devitt*, above; see also *Strong and Pearl v S Allison & Co Ltd* (1926) 25 Ll L Rep 504.
10 See *King v Chambers & Newman (Insurance Brokers) Ltd* [1963] 2 Lloyd's Rep 130.

or the initial instructions were ambiguous and a reasonable interpretation was permissible.[11]

It should be mentioned that it is wise to seek the advice of the broker being instructed upon the suitability of the policy sought, for in the absence of a specific request for such assistance, the broker is not obliged to do anything other than effect the desired insurance – he need make no mention of the fact that the insurance is unsuitable for his client's needs unless asked.[12]

Skill of the broker

When advice is sought by a client from his broker, the client is entitled to except that that advice is correct, unless the broker informs him to the contrary. For instance, a client may seek the broker's advice on a question of law relevant to the risk that he wishes to have insured. As far as professional indemnity insurance is concerned, the professional client may seek the broker's advice upon whether a particular consultant of the client firm should be named as an insured upon the negligence policy that is to be effected. Whilst the broker may not hold himself out to be a lawyer, he should do all he can to ascertain the correct answer to his client's query, otherwise he exposes himself to a possible claim for the negligent giving of advice. This very issue of the giving of advice upon legal matters, was considered in *Sarginson Brothers v Keith Moulton & Co Ltd* where Hallett J said:[13]

> In my view, if people occupying a professional position take it upon themselves to give advice upon a matter directly connected with their own profession, then they are responsible for seeing that they are equipped with a reasonable degree of skill and a reasonable stock of information so as to render it reasonably safe for them to give that particular piece of advice . . . I do not for one moment say that they are bound to be acquainted with everything. I think it is open to them always to say: 'Well, this is a difficult matter; I shall have to make inquiries.' They can say, if they like: 'This is a matter for a solicitor, not for me'; and if they went to a solicitor he very likely would say: 'You had better consult Counsel.' No one is under obligation to give advice on those difficult matters. If they are going to give advice, they can always qualify their advice and make it plain that it is a matter which is doubtful or upon which further investigation is desirable; but if they take it upon themselves to express a definite and final opinion, knowing, as they must . . . that their clients would act upon

---

11 *Ireland v Livingston* (1872) LR 5 HL 395; *James Vale & Co v Van Oppen & Co Ltd* (1921) 37 TLR 367; *Dixon v Hovill* (1828) 4 Bing 665.
12 *Waterkoyn v Eagle Star and British Dominions Insurance Co Ltd and Price, Forbes & Co Ltd* (1920) 5 Ll L Rep 42.
13 (1943) 73 Ll L Rep 104 at 107.

that, then I do think they are responsible if they give that information without having taken reasonable care to furnish themselves with such information, of whatever kind it be, as will render it reasonably safe, in the view of a reasonably prudent man, to express that opinion.

It will be appreciated that the principle being enunciated by Hallett J is not limited to the giving of legal advice, but applies to the giving of any advice relevant to insurance by a broker. A little later in his judgment, Hallett J also pointed out that when asked by a client whether it is possible to insure a particular risk, the broker can simply put up any proposed risk to whatever insurer he thinks proper, and thus find out whether the risk would or would not be accepted by that insurer. Merely to tell a client that the risk is uninsurable, on the experience of a different client's similar risk being declined in the past, may well not be enough to discharge the duty of care.

Particular care is to be expected from an insurance broker when advising his client upon which insurer to effect insurance. If, for instance, a client comes to his broker and states that he feels that his present insurer is charging excessive premiums, and would the broker find him another insurer offering lower premiums, the broker must exercise care in recommending another insurer. If the broker advises his client to remove his insurance to the X and Y Insurance Company, who offer lower premiums, but are under much attack in the financial press with regard to their financial stability, the broker will not be discharging his duty of care to his client.[14] The broker is expected to keep a watch on the financial position of insurers with whom he may place insurance.

Moreover, if an insurance broker advises his client to insure with a particular insurer, for whatever reason, in preference to others, then the broker is expected to know the full details and exclusions of that policy he recommends, which must insure his client for the risk he wishes to insure. A failure by the broker to ensure that all features of the policy suit his client's needs may well render him liable to his client in the circumstance of the client being unable to recover insurance moneys, because of the non-compliance with a condition or exclusion of which he had not been appraised by his broker.[15]

Duty of disclosure to insurer

As agent of the proposer, the insurance broker is under an obligation to disclose all material facts concerning the risk, made known to him

14 *Osman v J Ralph Moss Ltd* [1970] 1 Lloyd's Rep 313, CA.
15 *McNealy v Pennine Insurance Co Ltd* [1978] RTR 285, CA.

by the proposer, to the insurer.[16] Thus, a broker must not misrepresent his client's claims history to the insurer, and the failure to exercise reasonable care in presenting proposals to insurers is a breach of the broker's duty of care to his client.[17] Information regarding criminal convictions of employees or partners must likewise be disclosed to the insurer when required, otherwise the insurer will be entitled to repudiate the policy and the client may recover his loss from the broker who failed to correctly complete the proposal form on his behalf.[18]

Where a client instructs a broker to obtain a policy for him, and the broker has to himself instruct a Lloyd's broker in order to gain access to Lloyd's underwriters, the broker will be liable to his client (possibly together with the Lloyd's broker) should the Lloyd's broker fail to pass on material information to the Lloyd's underwriters, e.g. a material change in the circumstances of the insured client.[19]

Not long ago, the Court of Appeal held that a broker was not liable in negligence where the broker had incorrectly completed a proposal form on behalf of his client, and had then passed the completed form to his client to check the answers and sign the form. The client did not notice the incorrect answer to a question inserted by his broker and signed the form. In the event, when a loss was sustained by the insured client, the insurer avoided the policy because of the erroneous answer given in the proposal form. The client sued his broker for damages in the sum of the insurance moneys rendered irrecoverable, but was unsuccessful, the Court of Appeal holding, on previous authorities,[20] that it is the duty of the proposer for insurance to see and make sure that the information contained in the proposal form is accurate, it being no argument that he did not read it properly or was not fully appraised of its contents.[1]

In this regard, it should be noted that in the Code of Conduct issued by the Insurance Brokers Registration Council[2] for the guidance of insurance brokers, it is recommended that:[3]

16 *Woolcott v Excess Insurance Co Ltd and Miles, Smith, Anderson and Game Ltd* [1978] 1 Lloyd's Rep 633; see also *British Citizens Assurance Co v L Woolland & Co* (1921) 8 Ll L Rep 89; *Everett v Hogg, Robinson and Gardner Mountain (Insurance) Ltd* [1973] 2 Lloyd's Rep 217.
17 *Claude R Ogden & Co Pty Ltd v Reliance Fire Sprinkler Co Pty Ltd* [1975] 1 Lloyd's Rep 52, Aust Sup Ct.
18 *Roselodge Ltd v Bray, Gibb (Holdings) Ltd* [1967] 2 Lloyd's Rep 99.
19 *Coolee Ltd v Wing Heath & Co* (1930) 47 TLR 78.
20 *Biggar v Rock Life Assurance Co* [1902] 1 KB 516; *Newsholme Bros v Road Transport and General Insurance Co Ltd* [1929] 2 KB 356, CA.
 1 *O'Connor v B D B Kirby & Co* [1972] 1 QB 90, [1971] 2 All ER 1415, CA; distinguished in *Warren v Henry Sutton & Co* [1976] 2 Lloyd's Rep 276, CA.
 2 Pursuant to the Insurance Brokers (Registration) Act 1977, s. 10.
 3 Insurance Brokers Registration Council (Code of Conduct) Approval Order 1978 (SI 1978/1394), example 14.

In the completion of the proposal form, claim form, or any other material document, insurance brokers shall make it clear that all the answers or statements are the client's own responsibility. The client should always be asked to check the details and told that the inclusion of incorrect information may result in a claim being repudiated.

Clients may now be in a very difficult position if they seek to rely on their broker's advice about the completion of answers in a proposal form, the broker's liability in this direction now seems virtually non-existent.

Negligence of broker

As in the case of an allegation of negligence against any professional person, the question of negligence is a question of fact to be determined on the evidence before the court determining the issue. The evidence of persons in the same profession as the defendant may be called to give evidence of what they would have done on receipt of the instructions, for this may assist the court to consider the skill and care exercised by the defendant. This was determined long ago, in *Chapman v Walton*,[4] where it was alleged that an insurance broker had not procured the proper alterations to policies of insurance held by his client. Tindall CJ explained the court's approach:[5]

> The action is brought for want of reasonable and proper care, skill, and judgment shewn by the Defendant under certain circumstances in the exercise of his employment as a policy broker. The point, therefore, to be determined is, not whether the Defendant arrived at a correct conclusion upon reading the letter, but whether, upon the occasion in question, he did or did not exercise a reasonable and proper care, skill and judgment. This is a question of fact, the decision of which appears to us to rest upon this further enquiry, viz. whether other persons exercising the same profession or calling, and being men of experience and skill therein, would or would not have come to the same conclusion as the Defendant. For the Defendant did not contract that he would bring to the performance of his duty, on this occasion, an extraordinary degree of skill, but only a reasonable and ordinary proportion of it; and it appears to us, that it is not only an unobjectionable mode, but the most satisfactory mode of determining this question, to shew by evidence whether a majority of skilful and experienced brokers would have come to the same conclusion as the Defendant. If nine brokers of experience out of ten would have done the same as the Defendant under the same circumstances, or even if as many out of a given number would have been of his opinion as against it, he who only stipulates to bring a reasonable degree of skill to the performance of his duty, would be entitled to a verdict in his favour. And there is no hardship upon the Plaintiffs by this course of proceeding, for

4 (1833) 10 Bing 57.
5 Ibid at 63–64.

they might have called members of the same profession or trade to give opposite evidence, if the facts would have warranted it; and the jury would have then decided upon such conflicting testimony, according to the relative skill or experience of the witnesses on either side, or according to the strength of the reasons which were advanced by the witnesses in support of their respective opinions . . . If the letter, indeed, had contained an express or explicit order . . . there would have been no question at all: evidence as to the conduct of other men, on reading such a letter, would never have been received, because perfectly useless if received. But it is not a simple abstract question (in this case), as is supposed by the Plaintiffs, what the words of the letter mean: it is what others conversant with the business of a policy broker would have understood it to mean, and how they would have acted upon it under the same circumstances.

It is not open to a plaintiff, however, to bring allegations of negligence upon an appeal of a case where allegations of fraud and deceit have failed at the first hearing.[6]

It is not negligent for a broker to delay, for a matter of days, sending his client a copy of the insurance policy so that the client can verify that his instructions have been obeyed.[7] The non-compliance with the clear instructions of his client will always render the broker liable for any consequent loss of insurance benefit sustained by the client.[8] A broker must carry out his instructions within a reasonable time of their receipt,[9] but is not obliged, in the absence of contrary instructions, to carry them out immediately.[10]

The normal periods of limitation will apply for breach of professional duty by an insurance broker, and the special three year limitation period in respect of personal injury claims is not applicable where a claim is made against a broker for failing to effect a valid insurance covering a personal injuries risk.[11] Thus, if a broker fails to effect a valid professional indemnity policy for e.g. an architect, and a claim for personal injuries sustained through the professional negligence of that architect is made, the architect may pursue a claim for indemnity against the insurance broker within the six year time limits in contract and tort, even though the injured person is bound, in his claim against the architect, by the three year limitation period.

6 *Connecticut Fire Insurance Co v Kavanagh* [1892] AC 473, PC.
7 *United Mills Agencies Ltd v R E Harvey Bray & Co* [1952] 1 All ER 225n.
8 E.g. *Fraser v B N Furman (Productions) Ltd* [1967] 3 All ER 57, [1967] 1 WLR 898, CA; alternatively, the broker may be liable to indemnify the insurer, *Woolcott v Excess Insurance Co Ltd and Miles, Smith, Anderson and Game Ltd* [1978] 1 Lloyd's Rep 633.
9 *Turpin v Bilton* (1843) 5 Man & G 455; *Bromley London Borough v Ellis* [1971] 1 Lloyd's Rep 97, CA.
10 *Cock, Russell & Co v Bray, Gibb & Co Ltd* (1920) 3 Ll L Rep 71.
11 *Ackbar v C F Green & Co Ltd* [1975] QB 582, [1975] 2 All ER 65.

Dual agency of broker

It was long thought that an insurance broker, when acting on both marine and all non-marine insurances, was always the agent of the insured (his client), and not the agent of the insurer at any time.[12] This principle was based upon the basic principle of all agency contracts that—

> No agent who has accepted an employment from one principal can in law accept an engagement inconsistent with his duty to the first principal . . . unless he makes the fullest disclosure to each principal of his interest, and obtains the consent of each principal to the double employment.[13]

This principle was considered to apply both when the policy was placed by the broker, and thereafter, e.g. in the event of a claim under the policy.[14] The common practice of the insurance market, however, is to employ the insured's broker to obtain a confidential insurance assessor's report concerning the insured's claim. This report may not be disclosed to the insured by his broker,[15] even though the broker is acting in breach of his duty to the insured, for the communications with such claims assessor are made in a confidential capacity. The insured may recover damages from the broker, however, if and to the extent that the partial dislodgment of the single agency agreement causes him loss or damage.[16]

Furthermore, some insurance brokers will be empowered to issue insurance policies on behalf of insurers.[17] Such a position is common in the case of Master Policy professional indemnity insurance schemes, where it will be a broker who issues the certificates of insurance, as agent of the insurer, to his client – the insured. Sometimes, also, notice of claims will be specified to be served upon the same broker, and such notice is deemed good notice to the insurer – but all will depend upon the wording of the policy of insurance on this point. These acts, despite being inconsistent with the broker's duty to his client, will not, however, be a nullity in law, although the practice is wholly unreasonable and incapable of being a legal usage or custom to be upheld by the courts.[18]

12 *Rozanes v Bowen* (1928) 32 Ll L Rep 98 at 101, CA, per Scrutton LJ.
13 *Fullwood v Hurley* [1928] 1 KB 498 at 502, CA, per Scrutton LJ.
14 *Anglo-African Merchants Ltd v Bayley* [1970] 1 QB 311, [1969] 2 All ER 421.
15 *North and South Trust Co v Berkeley* [1971] 1 WLR 470.
16 Ibid at 486.
17 *Stockton v Mason and Vehicle and General Insurance Co Ltd and Arthur Edward (Insurance) Ltd* [1978] 2 Lloyd's Rep 430, CA.
18 *North and South Trust Co v Berkeley*, above.

Regulation of insurance brokers

The use of the description 'insurance broker' or 'assurance broker' is now limited to those persons or bodies corporate who are registered with the Insurance Brokers Registration Council established by the Insurance Brokers (Registration) Act 1977.[19] The Act does not prevent other persons or bodies corporate carrying on the business of an insurance broker, but merely prohibits the style or title 'broker'. Accordingly, non-registered individuals may act as insurance intermediaries, without incurring the control of the Act and the Council, under such descriptions as 'insurance consultant', 'insurance adviser', 'insurance specialist', and the like.

The qualifications necessary for registration as an insurance broker are as follows:[20]

(i) that the person is a Lloyd's broker accepted by the Committee of Lloyd's; or

(ii) (a) he satisfies the Council as to his character and suitability; and

(b) that he will comply with the Council rules regarding the financial control and management of his practice as an insurance broker;[1] and

(c) he satisfies the Council that he has adequate educational[2] qualifications and/or several years practical experience of insurance business gained with an insurance broker or an insurance company.

The Council was also required by the Act to set up two committees, the Investigating Committee and the Disciplinary Committee, to regulate the professional conduct of registered brokers, the sanction being removal from the Register.[3] Two other measures, apart from those mentioned, were introduced to protect the public and enhance the professional standing of insurance brokers. The first was the introduction of compulsory professional negligence insurance for registered practising insurance brokers and enrolled bodies corporate, with a minimum indemnity limit of £250,000.[4] The second measure was the power of the Council to draw up and issue a Code of Conduct.[5] A Code has been drawn up[6] to serve as a guide to insurance brokers and other persons (e.g. clients) concerned with

---

19 See ss. 1, 2, 4, 5, 8, 9, 22, 23 and 24.
20 Ibid, s. 3.
1 Ibid, s. 11.
2 Ibid, ss. 6 and 7.
3 Ibid, ss. 13–20.
4 Ibid, s. 12, and Insurance Brokers Registration Council (Indemnity Insurance and Grants Scheme) Rules Approval Order 1979 (SI 1979/408).
5 Ibid, s. 10.
6 Insurance Brokers Registration Council (Code of Conduct) Approval Order 1978 (SI 1978/1394).

their conduct, and acts or omissions that breach the three fundamental principles governing the conduct of practising insurance
brokers will be considered as amounting to unprofessional conduct.
The three fundamental principles are:

(1) Insurance brokers shall at all times conduct their business with utmost
good faith and integrity.
(2) Insurance brokers shall do everything possible to satisfy the insurance
requirements of their clients and shall place the interests of those
clients before all other considerations. Subject to these requirements
and interests, insurance brokers shall have proper regard for others.
(3) Statements made by or on behalf of insurance brokers when advertising shall not be misleading or extravagant.

The Code then lists some specific examples of the application of
these principles, e.g.:

(1) In the conduct of their business insurance brokers shall provide
advice objectively and independently.
(4) Insurance brokers shall on request from the client explain the differences in, and the relative costs of, the principal types of insurance
which in the opinion of the insurance broker might suit a client's
needs.
(6) Insurance brokers shall, upon request, disclose to any client who is an
individual and who is, or is contemplating becoming, the holder of a
United Kingdom policy of insurance the amount of commission paid
by the insurer under any relevant policy of insurance.
(9) Insurance brokers shall inform a client of the name of all insurers with
whom a contract of insurance is placed. This information shall be
given at the inception of the contract and any changes thereafter shall
be advised at the earliest opportunity to the client.
(13) Any information acquired by an insurance broker from his client
shall not be used or disclosed except in the normal course of negotiating, maintaining, or renewing a contract of insurance for that client
or unless the consent of the client has been obtained or the information is required by a court of competent jurisdiction.

The Insurance Brokers Registration Council is comprised of
seventeen persons.[7] Twelve (of whom one is Chairman of the
Council) represent registered insurance brokers; the remaining five
are appointed by the Secretary of State, of which one is a lawyer, one
an accountant, and one represents the interests of persons who are
policyholders of insurance companies.
The national organisation representing registered insurance
brokers is the British Insurance Brokers Association (BIBA), which
is an amalgamation of the four previous trade associations — the

---

7 Insurance Brokers (Registration) Act 1977, Sch 1.

228 Duties of the broker

Corporation of Insurance Brokers (CIB), Lloyd's Insurance Brokers Association (LIBA), the Association of Insurance Brokers (AIB), and the Federation of Insurance Brokers (FIB).

For those insurance intermediaries who are not registered insurance brokers, their trade association is the Institute of Insurance Consultants.

Professional insurance qualifications are conferred by the Chartered Insurance Institute (CII) upon completion of examinations and a specified minimum period of involvement in insurance business. The qualifications are Associate of the Chartered Insurance Institute (ACII), and the higher Fellow of the Chartered Insurance Institute (FCII).

Index